Food and Power

The relationship between development and democratization is one of the most compelling topics of research in political science, yet many aspects of authoritarian regime behavior remain unexplained. This book explores how different types of governments take action to shape the course of economic development, focusing on agriculture, a sector that is of crucial importance in the developing world. It explains variation in agricultural and food policy across regime type; who the winners and losers of these policies are; and whether policy influences the stability of authoritarian governments. The book pushes us to think differently about the process linking economic development to political change and to consider growth as an inherently politicized process rather than an exogenous driver of moves toward democracy.

Henry Thomson is an assistant professor in the School of Politics and Global Studies at Arizona State University. From 2014 to 2017 he was a Postdoctoral Prize Research Fellow at Nuffield College, Oxford. In 2015, his dissertation won the American Political Science Association's Juan Linz Prize for the Best Dissertation in the Comparative Study of Democracy.

Food and Power

Regime Type, Agricultural Policy, and Political Stability

HENRY THOMSON
Arizona State University

CAMBRIDGE
UNIVERSITY PRESS

CAMBRIDGE
UNIVERSITY PRESS

Shaftesbury Road, Cambridge CB2 8EA, United Kingdom

One Liberty Plaza, 20th Floor, New York, NY 10006, USA

477 Williamstown Road, Port Melbourne, VIC 3207, Australia

314–321, 3rd Floor, Plot 3, Splendor Forum, Jasola District Centre, New Delhi – 110025, India

103 Penang Road, #05–06/07, Visioncrest Commercial, Singapore 238467

Cambridge University Press is part of Cambridge University Press & Assessment, a department of the University of Cambridge.

We share the University's mission to contribute to society through the pursuit of education, learning and research at the highest international levels of excellence.

www.cambridge.org
Information on this title: www.cambridge.org/9781108701594

DOI: 10.1017/9781108568951

First published 2019
First paperback edition 2022

A catalogue record for this publication is available from the British Library

Library of Congress Cataloging-in-Publication data
NAMES: Thomson, Henry, 1984- author.
TITLE: Food and power : regime type, agricultural policy, and political stability / Henry Thomson.
DESCRIPTION: Cambridge, United Kingdom ; New York, NY : Cambridge University Press, 2019. | Includes bibliographical references and index.
IDENTIFIERS: LCCN 2018051440 | ISBN 9781108476812 (hardback) | ISBN 9781108701594 (paperback)
SUBJECTS: LCSH: Agriculture and state–Developing countries. | Agriculture–Economic aspects–Developing countries. | Authoritarianism–Developing countries. | Political stability–Developing countries. | Economic development–Political aspects–Developing countries. | BISAC: POLITICAL SCIENCE / General.
CLASSIFICATION: LCC HD1417 .T557 2019 | DDC 338.1/91724–dc23
LC record available at https://lccn.loc.gov/2018051440

ISBN   978-1-108-47681-2   Hardback
ISBN   978-1-108-70159-4   Paperback

Contents

Figures

Tables

Acknowledgments

I have incurred a great number of debts in the course of writing this book. The project began as a PhD dissertation in the Department of Political Science at the University of Minnesota from 2012 to 2014, and I must first thank my advisor, John Freeman, and the rest of my dissertation committee, Ben Ansell, Jane Gingrich, C. Ford Runge, and David Samuels, for steering me successfully through this enterprise. Of course, during my time as a graduate student I received help from a great number of others. I thank the Political Science and Applied Economics faculty at the University of Minnesota collectively for the training and support I received there. Dr. Christian Tuschhoff at the Free University of Berlin facilitated a visit in 2012–2013 and provided helpful advice and feedback, as always. Professor Dr. Asan Ali Golam Hassan at the Universiti Utara Malaysia invited me to his institution in 2013, gave very useful guidance, and introduced me to a range of researchers who generously taught me about their country. Participants at conferences in Mainz and Chicago in 2013 also commented on various parts of this project in preliminary stages, helping me to improve my work significantly. Marc Bellemare, Dan Berliner, James Hollyer, Mark Kayser, David Rueda, Christian von Soest, and Milan Svolik gave constructive feedback and advice during the latter stages of the dissertation. I thank all of these people for their input.

The first draft of this book manuscript was prepared during my time as a postdoctoral fellow at Nuffield College, Oxford, from 2014 to 2017. I would like to thank the staff, fellows, and other postdocs there for all the advice and support they provided during this period. Particularly deserving of my gratitude are the participants in a book workshop that I held in 2016: Ben Ansell, Jane Gingrich, Robin Harding, Jan Pierskalla, David Samuels, Luis Schiumieri, and Laurence Whitehead. However, others also provided valuable feedback during this period, including Catherine Boone, Halvard Buhaug, Martin Petrick, Bryn Rosenfeld, Nina von Uexkuell, and Henrik Urdal. I received helpful comments from audiences at the University of Oxford; the Risk Advisory Group, London; the Humboldt Universität, Berlin; the London School of Economics; the University of Navarra; the German Development Institute in Bonn; the Institute of Agricultural Development in Transition Economies (IAMO) in Halle; the University of Uppsala; and the University of Zurich.

I completed the final version of the manuscript while working as an assistant professor at Arizona State University. I could not have wished for a more welcoming and supportive group of colleagues, and I thank them all for providing the ideal environment for finishing this project. Four anonymous reviewers for both Cambridge University Press and Oxford University Press gave extremely thorough and helpful reviews, which served to significantly strengthen the manuscript. Robert Dreesen at Cambridge University Press has been a supportive and effective editor and a great help in guiding me through the publishing process.

This project could not have been completed without generous funding from a variety of sources, for which I am very grateful. The University of Minnesota supported my research through a series of grants, including the David and Janis Larson Research Fellowship in Political Economy, the Asher N. Christenson Memorial Fellowship, and the Doctoral Dissertation Fellowship. The German Academic Exchange Service (DAAD) funded a year of research in Berlin during 2012–2013. Nuffield College provided support for workshops in both 2015 and 2016.

I thank all of these individuals and organizations for their help. The usual disclaimer applies; all remaining errors or omissions remain my own.

I

Introduction

Erst kommt das Fressen, dann die Moral.
First food, then morality.
(Mackie Messer, in Bertolt Brecht, Die Dreigroschenoper, *Act II)*

The relationship between development and democratization remains one of the most compelling topics of research in political science. Democracy has come to be understood as the outcome of conflicts that play out in the course of economic growth: between rich and poor, or between property owners and a predatory state.[1] Scholars have also explored how autocrats mold the institutions of their regimes to manage and defuse these economic conflicts and coerce or co-opt threatening groups into supporting their rule.[2] However, a wide range of authoritarian regimes' behaviors remain unexplained. We know little about how they intervene in the economy to shape its development, although such interventions are pervasive and widespread. We know little about why their economic policies differ from democracies, although the divergence in policy outcomes is large. We know little about how policy affects political stability, although we have every reason to believe that its effects are profound. Put simply, we do not know much about the ways in which governments

---

[1] On the class cleavage and redistribution, see Boix (2003) and Acemoglu and Robinson (2006). On the property rights or elite-competition approach, see Ansell and Samuels (2014).

[2] On institutional regime typologies, see Geddes (1999) and Svolik (2012). On legislatures and parties, see, for example, Gandhi and Przeworski (2007), Brownlee (2007), and Magaloni (2006). On coercive institutions, see Davenport (2007b) and Chestnut-Greitens (2016).

manage fundamental social conflicts during the course of development and how their management of these conflicts affects political outcomes.

One of the most salient and contentious social cleavages to be managed in developing nations is not between the rich and the poor, or the middle class and the state. It is between cities and the countryside, and it plays itself out in markets for agricultural produce and food. This is vividly illustrated by the recent experience of Venezuela. In September 2016, the government of President Nicolás Maduro was trapped in an economic and political crisis. The country was suffering from a deep recession, and inflation ran at several hundred percent. Crime, looting, and murder made his country one of the most dangerous in the world. Opposition leaders mobilized hundreds of thousands of supporters to protest against his regime and demand a vote to remove him from office. At the core of the crisis, severe shortages of basic goods left citizens spending hours a day waiting to buy food. Maduro, a committed socialist revolutionary and loyal follower of his predecessor, Hugo Chávez, had been educated in Cuba and worked as a bus driver before entering politics. As the crisis deepened, he grasped at ever more desperate measures to address the food crisis in the country. In late August, he promised to implement a rationing system in supermarkets using mandatory fingerprinting to prevent fraud. He gave the army unprecedented powers to control food production and distribution, which some observers saw as a dangerous move toward a military dictatorship. Soldiers could be seen taking control of supermarkets and butchers' shops in the capital, enforcing state-dictated prices, and maintaining order over the increasingly unruly crowds waiting to buy basic necessities.[3]

The crisis facing President Maduro in 2016 was severe, but not unique. Food affordability and availability are critical issues in developing countries, where it is not uncommon for consumers to spend 30–40 percent of their income on food.[4] The large share of consumer income which is devoted to food purchases in poorer countries makes the price of food politically salient, and grievances around food security can quickly escalate to threaten political stability. To give one other recent example, in early 2008, as prices on world food markets hit record highs, President Hosni Mubarak of Egypt was forced to instruct the army to take control of the production and distribution of bread to meet consumer demand and stave off political strife. As in Venezuela in 2016, Egyptians were

---

[3] Rathbone (2016), Schipani (2016b,c,d), and Corrales and von Bergen (2016).
[4] Economic Research Service, USDA (2011) and Statistisches Bundesamt (2013).

waiting for hours outside bakeries to buy bread at low, subsidized prices. Violence and rioting broke out among frustrated, exhausted food consumers. This unrest destabilized the Mubarak regime and was seen by many as an important precursor to the uprising of the Arab Spring. During the 2011 unrest, which proved fatal for Mubarak's government, protesters on Tahrir Square wore loaves taped to their heads as "bread helmets" to symbolize their grievances against food shortages and defenselessness against state repression.[5]

Governments in the developing world must ensure that food markets meet the needs of consumers or face the threat of strife. Far from being a novel development, this has been true throughout the history. The rulers of ancient Rome provided free bread to citizens to stave off the danger of unrest, and food price increases played a significant role in provoking the 1848 revolutions in early modern Europe.[6] However, the agricultural policy problem facing these regimes is not as simple as providing stable, low prices for urban citizens. Around 2.5 billion people in the developing world depend on agriculture for their incomes, and they are predominantly poor (World Bank, 2008). Their interests must also be taken into account. Consider the experience of Prayuth Chan-o-cha, the infantry general who played a key role in the 2006 military coup in Thailand and led the junta that assumed power following another putsch in May 2014. The 2014 takeover followed months of protests, violence, and political crisis as his democratically elected predecessor, Yingluck Shinawatra, faced a storm of criticism for her agricultural policies. These guaranteed high prices to rice farmers but, when prices fell on world markets, proved economically disastrous for the government, angering Bangkok-based royalist and military interests. After seizing power, General Prayuth moved swiftly to reverse the controversial rice policy and appease the powerful urban groups that supported him. Price supports were eliminated, farmers were encouraged to plant alternative crops, and Shinawatra was forced to stand trial on negligence charges related to the rice price scheme.[7] However, Prayuth's policy shift proved short-lived. Despite his harsh criticism of his predecessor, and growing restrictions on political freedoms, by late 2015 protests and continued opposition by farmers loyal to Shinawatra forced him to implement significant price supports for rice farmers.[8] As the experience of General Prayuth shows,

---

[5] Knickmeyer (2008), Zurayk (2011), Economist (2012), and Cambanis (2015).
[6] Brunt (1966), Walton and Seddon (1994), and Berger and Spoerer (2001).
[7] Chomchuen and Steger (2014) and Peel (2014a,b, 2015).
[8] Kondalamahanty (2015) and Webb and Temphairojana (2015).

agricultural policy is not only politically salient in developing countries. It also creates clear winners and losers, with government interventions that benefit rural farmers generally running against the preferences of urban interests.

The turbulent political events in Venezuela, Egypt, and Thailand outlined above appear at first glance to be short-term crises, with governments resorting to drastic measures such as military provision of food to address them. However, they are all in fact the legacies of years of extensive government intervention in agricultural markets. As we will see, these interventions can take on myriad forms, from import and export tariffs through trade quotas and subsidies for farm inputs or foodstuffs. They all have the effect of distorting the prices facing farmers and consumers in markets for agricultural produce, having profound consequences for their welfare and behavior as producers and purchasers of food. These policies are not the only factors determining the economic welfare of the rural and urban sectors and are often complemented or offset by other actions that do not function through the price mechanism such as infrastructure and development projects. However, government policies affecting prices in agricultural markets are an important component of the politics of developing countries. They remain commonplace, despite the best efforts of international organizations such as the World Bank and the International Monetary Fund to eliminate them from the policy portfolios of developing countries. Their distortionary effects, though occurring within a broader palette of government economic initiatives, are very large and shape countries' long-term development trajectories. These effects extend beyond domestic markets to international trade in agricultural commodities, giving them global significance. As we will see, political stability in developing countries is also affected by agricultural policy. However, these agricultural market interventions are not included in contemporary models of authoritarian politics and democratization.

In Venezuela, Maduro's predecessor Chávez was a charismatic populist who used his country's growing oil revenues to finance social spending and embark on a path of state-led development. His strategy included an ambitious socialist reform program, which aimed to achieve national self-sufficiency in food production. From the early 2000s, the Chávez regime imposed a raft of policies in the agricultural sector including food price controls, state-run supermarkets, import restrictions, and expropriations of land and food processing plants. These all had the effect of depressing domestic agricultural production, making the country prone to shortages and dependent on imported food subsidized and distributed through state agencies.[9] They also led to anger among right-wing landed elites, who backed a short-lived military coup that removed Chávez from power for two days in 2002 (Lapper and Webb-Vidal, 2004). With falling oil revenues after 2013, the government lacked the resources to make up the shortfall between consumer needs and meager domestic food production, shortages worsened, and political instability grew (Schipani, 2016a).

The roots of Mubarak's bread subsidies in Egypt can be traced back over thirty years. The former Air Force officer and leader of the ruling National Democratic Party was Vice-President to Anwar el-Sadat in 1977, when violent rioting shook the country in response to cuts to government subsidies for bread, flour, and other staples. The scale and intensity of the 1977 unrest made Sadat and his successor commit to a subsidy and rationing system that made the government responsible for providing low-cost food to the entire population. This system was very costly, paid low prices to farmers, and depressed domestic food production. Despite market-oriented reforms from the mid-1980s, the country remained highly dependent on imports of wheat (Gutner, 2002; Cassing et al., 2009). This dependence became a political liability for Mubarak when soaring food prices in 2007 and 2008 led to surging demand for cheap subsidized bread, shortages, and civil strife.

Agricultural policy in Thailand has been the site of political conflict between rural and urban interests for decades, with more democratic regimes tending to follow policies that favor the rural sector. Viewed as a lucrative source of revenue by a series of urban-biased military governments, rice exports were taxed and farmers' incomes were depressed until the mid-1980s. Subsequently, policy was liberalized, but the agricultural sector was neglected until the former telecommunications magnate Thaksin Shinawatra was able to mobilize the rural poor to take victory in the 2001 elections. Before being ousted by a military coup in 2006, he implemented policies that significantly increased the price of rice, bolstered the incomes of farmers, and guaranteed him a loyal power base among the "red shirts" in the countryside. Shinawatra's policies were continued by his sister Yingluck after she harnessed her brother's rural constituency to win the 2011 election, until she was replaced by another urban-biased military regime in 2014 (Warr and Kohpaiboon, 2009; Economist, 2013).

---

[9] On expropriations, see Mander (2009b) and Albertus (2015b); on shortages, see Webb-Vidal (2006) and Mander (2009a, 2011).

1.1 QUESTIONS AND ANSWERS: AGRICULTURAL POLICY, REGIME TYPE, AND POLITICAL STABILITY

Agricultural markets are an arena for distributional conflicts between rural and urban interests, and the stakes of these conflicts are high for farmers and food consumers in developing countries. Unsurprisingly, then, political intervention in the sector is typical not just for Venezuela, Egypt, and Thailand, but also for most countries in the developing world. It also raises several important questions on the political economy of authoritarianism and democratization. There are questions of political influence and policymaking. What explains variation in agricultural market interventions, and would lead a government like Venezuela's or Egypt's to commit to measures that cause it to become dependent on fickle world food markets to feed its population? There are also questions of institutional variation and the effect of regime type on economic policy. Why do we observe so much policy volatility in Thailand, with military governments advocating drastically different strategies to those implemented by democratically elected politicians? Perhaps most important, the policies chosen by these governments appear to be linked closely with the stability of their regimes. Does agricultural policy make a significant contribution to the chances of political strife, unrest, and coups in the developing world, and can it be used as a tool by authoritarian leaders to prevent instability and transitions toward democracy? These questions form the core of this book.

I argue that interventions in agricultural markets generate rents – unearned income that can be used by governments to secure their position in power. Successive military governments in Thailand until the 1980s, for example, restricted exports of rice to extract rents from trade and fund infrastructure projects benefiting their urban supporters. However, agricultural policy also generates winners and losers: Behind the military regimes' infrastructure projects in Bangkok lay millions of farmers being paid less for their rice. Policy outcomes are the result of a trade-off between the interests of rural constituencies, who demand higher prices for agricultural commodities, and urban constituencies, who demand lower prices for farm produce and food. This trade-off is made by different rules depending on the institutional setting. Authoritarian leaders are self-interested actors who aim to maximize the rents that they can extract from the agricultural sector. They are subject to weak electoral constraints and possess the capacity to repress opposition to their rule. However, these leaders cannot act with complete autonomy in policymaking. They must address the threats posed to their position by rural and urban interests. When either group finds it easier to act collectively in opposition to the regime, leadership will adjust policy to address their demands and maintain political stability. Because the rural population struggles to organize in collective opposition to authoritarian governments, policy under autocracy tends to be urban-biased and decrease returns to agriculture, compared to democracies. However, when the rural sector is dominated by landed elites, policy is more likely to favor agricultural producers. By addressing the threat of collective action posed by rural and urban interests, the agricultural policies chosen by authoritarian leaders make significant contributions to the durability of their regimes. Intervening in agricultural markets to increase the price of farm produce, they can mitigate the risk of a challenge by powerful rural interests, while by intervening to decrease the price of food they can lower the likelihood of unrest among urban food consumers.

Policy and Stability under Authoritarianism

Variation between authoritarian and democratic regimes means that the rural and urban sectors pursue their interests under distinct sets of rules depending on their institutional context. Authoritarian governments respond to the threat of collective action, that is, of rural or urban interests acting together to remove them from power.[10] Because rural citizens struggle to organize to threaten authoritarian governments, authoritarian policy tends to be urban-biased, decreasing returns to farmers compared to democracies. The political expediency behind these policies is starkly illustrated by the experiences of Maduro in Venezuela and Mubarak in Egypt. Low food prices anger farmers, but they are powerless to translate this anger into a political threat comparable to that of a restive urban population faced with high food prices and shortages. As we saw, the threats to the Maduro and Mubarak regimes came from unrest in cities, not the countryside. When urban interests are powerful, an authoritarian leader will bow to their will, using trade restrictions, price controls, or other measures to keep food prices low and avoid the risk of urban strife.

However, this kind of urban bias cannot be attributed solely to authoritarian politics, and agricultural policy cannot be explained by simple

---

[10] My approach to political influence under authoritarianism draws on canonical studies of collective action, development, and democratization by Olson (1965) and Bates (1981).

TABLE I.I *Variation in Agricultural Policy under Authoritarianism*

Regime Type	Urban/Rural Bias	Effect of Policy	Example
Military	Urban-biased	Decrease prices	Thailand
	Rural-biased	Increase prices	Chile
Single-party	Urban-biased	Decrease prices	China
	Rural-biased	Increase prices	Malaysia
Personal	Urban-biased	Decrease prices	Venezuela
	Rural-biased	Increase prices	Russia

institutional categorizations of authoritarian regimes. Rural interests, when they include a powerful landed elite, possess the organizational resources and capabilities to be influential within the ruling coalition. They often dominate authoritarian legislatures and parties, as I will describe in detail for the German and Malaysian cases in this book. They can mount a coup either alone or in alliance with the military or powerful industrial interests. Powerful rural interests can also threaten a regime by withdrawing their financial support or reducing agricultural production and threatening food security. When landholding inequality is high, policy is more likely to favor farmers over food consumers and increase prices for farm produce. This trend holds regardless of the type of authoritarian regime in question. Policy outcomes will cut across the sorts of typologies used by previous scholars to classify authoritarian governments as the power of rural and urban interests varies.

I illustrate this point with examples in Table 1.1. The Thai military governments of the 1980s were urban-biased, but when backed by powerful landed elites military dictatorships implement policies that follow rural interests. We saw this during Chávez's brief removal from power in 2002, and it could also be observed in the policies of the Pinochet regime in Chile in the 1970s, which increased prices for agricultural producers (Silva, 1993). Similarly, single-party regimes' policies depend on the structural bases of their support. The Chinese Communist Party, like the former socialist dictatorships in the Soviet Union and Eastern Europe, has long followed urban-biased policies that decrease returns to agriculture in order to direct investment toward industrialization and provide cheap food for workers.[11] The Malaysian regime under the United Malays National Organization, on the other

---

[11] Wallace (2014). On the Soviet Union, see Ploss (1965); on Eastern Europe, see, for example, Schöne (2005).

TABLE 1.2 *Agricultural Policy and Political Stability*

| | Interests | | | Political Outcome | |
	Rural	Urban	Policy	Failure	Urban Unrest
Authoritarianism		↑	Urban-biased		↓
	↑		Rural-biased	↓	
	↑	↑			Instability
Democracy		↑	Urban-biased		
	↑		Rural-biased		Stability
	↑	↑	Moderate		

hand, has intervened in agricultural markets to bolster the incomes of farmers, one of their most powerful constituencies.[12] As we have seen, the personalist dictatorships of Chávez and Maduro in Venezuela were the paradigm of an urban-biased agricultural policy regime. On the other hand, as part of a broader project aiming at promoting domestic agriculture, Vladimir Putin's personalist regime in Russia responded to Western sanctions following the annexation of Crimea in 2014 by imposing import bans on Western farm produce. These bans have had the impact of significantly increasing domestic food prices in Russia, proving a boon to the local agricultural sector. In 2015, for the first time, Russia's agricultural exports were worth more than its international arms sales.[13]

The agricultural policies chosen by authoritarian governments have significant effects on political stability and the chances of regime failure, which I summarize in Table 1.2. For many authoritarian regimes, where urban interests are powerful, following urban-biased policies that keep domestic food prices lower than those on international markets does address economic grievances among food consumers, raise living standards, and reduce the risk of protests, strikes, and other unrest in cities. For those facing a significant threat from powerful rural interests, on the other hand, implementing policies that increase domestic farm produce prices can significantly reduce the risk of a coup or regime failure, by distributing rents to the agricultural sector. For some regimes, however, the trade-off between rural and urban interests is not clear, as they are faced by significant threats from both landed elites and urban areas. These governments face a very difficult problem in agricultural policymaking

---

[12] See Scott (1985), Shamsul (1986), and Faaland, Parkinson, and Saniman (1990).
[13] See Wengle (2017), Bidder (2016), and Economist (2016).

and, like Chávez in Venezuela in 2002, are confronted by political instability because a policy that benefits urban areas angers powerful rural
interests, and vice versa.[14]

Policy and Stability under Democracy

Unlike authoritarian regimes, which respond to the threat of collective
action and political instability, democratic governments seek reelection.
They therefore aim to maximize the support they will receive from both
voters and special interests who can contribute to their campaigns and
mobilize supporters. Policies are put forward with an eye to gaining support from both groups and winning an impending electoral contest.[15]
Elections solve the collective action problem for citizens because voting
does not imply the costs, including the risk of repression, that contentious
or violent collective action requires to influence authoritarian governments. This has important consequences for agricultural policy. The rural
population struggles to mobilize in defense of its economic interests under
authoritarianism, unless it is dominated by a small landed elite. Under
democracy, it is significantly better represented in policymaking. Although
rural smallholders like the "red shirt" supporters of Thaksin in Thailand
cannot mount a revolt to overthrow an authoritarian regime, they can
vote a government out of office when it does not implement policies that
follow their interests. Therefore, democratically elected governments are
more likely to support agriculture, implementing policies like those made
by the Thaksin governments in Thailand, which significantly increased
the price of rice above world market levels and improved rural incomes
compared to previous military regimes.[16]

The political equality implied by democracy means that large, unorga-
nized constituencies, like farmers in developing countries, are better represented and receive more support from government than under authoritarianism. However, special-interest groups are very adept at organizing

---

[14] Unforeseen international forces like spikes in global food prices or falling oil prices can
also disrupt a government's ability to follow their chosen strategy, forcing them away
from a stable policy equilibrium and toward repression, as we saw in the Venezuelan
and Egyptian cases earlier. However, here I focus on the domestic determinants of the
trade-off between rural and urban interests in agricultural policy. On exogenous influences, see Wallace (2014, 187–205), who shows that increases in oil prices are translated
into lower levels of support for farmers and greater support for food consumers.

[15] See, for example, Stigler (1971), Peltzman (1976), and Grossman and Helpman (1994).

[16] This has been confirmed in numerous empirical studies, for example, Bates and Block
(2013), Olper (2001), and Olper and Raimondi (2013).

and lobbying for favorable policy in democracies, meaning that in the course of development agriculture stands to receive still more favorable treatment. As the agricultural sector shrinks with economic growth, the number of farmers declines, and they find it easier to organize to pursue their interests.[17] Because agriculture makes up such a small share of output and employment in developed economies, supporting the sector also implies only a very small fiscal burden.[18] For these reasons, democracies tend to support agriculture compared to authoritarian governments, and rich democracies are more supportive still. Urban interests are not entirely neglected under democratic governments, however. Their preference for lower food prices remains the same as under authoritarian regimes, and though their political clout is mitigated by the electoral process on average, under some conditions governments will move closer to their preferred policy. Most important, when the average voter is relatively poor, democracies will use agricultural policy to lower food prices and increase living standards. Income inequality encourages democratic governments to use food policy as a tool of redistribution (Meltzer and Richard, 1981).

In contrast to its role under authoritarian regimes, agricultural policy is not critical to political stability under democracy. Democratic regimes are not likely to collapse in the face of distributional conflicts between the cities and the countryside, for two reasons. First, and most important, because although elected leaders rotate regularly, democratic institutions endure (Przeworski et al., 2000). The removal of an authoritarian leader from office often leads to a wholesale regime change. Democracies, on the other hand, are self-enforcing systems in which all relevant political actors voluntarily comply with the rules of the game and allow for the peaceful and orderly rotation of power.[19] In the case of agricultural policy, both rural and urban interests can use their votes to influence policy under democracy and are more likely to attempt to vote an unpopular government out office in defense of their economic interests than to engage in costly collective action in an attempt to undermine a democratic regime. The second reason why distributional conflicts between rural and urban interests are unlikely to fundamentally destabilize a democratic regime is development. The agricultural sector is much smaller, and food makes up a much lower share of consumer spending in democracies, because they tend to be richer than authoritarian regimes. This makes the distributional conflict between cities and the countryside much less politically salient

---

[17] This trend follows the classic logic of collective action put forward by Olson (1965).

[18] See, for example, Anderson and Hayami (1986), and De Gorter and Swinnen (2002).

[19] Fearon (2011), Przeworski (1991), Weingast (1997), and Gates et al. (2006).

and less likely to lead to regime instability. Indeed, the mitigation of the rural–urban cleavage could be a major contributing factor to the lack of democratic breakdowns observed above moderate levels of economic development (Przeworski et al., 2000).

1.2 WHAT DO WE LEARN? TOWARD A SOCIAL CONFLICT THEORY OF AUTHORITARIANISM

This book explores how regime type and agricultural policy interact to affect political stability in developing countries. Although this question is at the core of canonical works in political economy and democratization, my analytical focus on social conflict between rural and urban interests marks a departure from contemporary economic theories of authoritarian politics and regime change. These theories, represented most prominently by Boix (2003), Acemoglu and Robinson (2006), and Ansell and Samuels (2014), tell a story in which individuals' economic interests determine their preferences over regime type.[20] They do not emphasize how these individuals come together to mobilize in collective action in defense of their economic interests, or threaten the stability of authoritarian regimes and affect a change in the institutions of government. Here, I put forward a social conflict theory of authoritarian politics that builds upon previous work to focus on both economic interests and the collective mobilization of groups in defense of these interests.[21] In my account, the central economic conflict under authoritarianism is not between the rich and the poor, or a rising middle class and the state, but between the city and the countryside. Authoritarian politics revolves around the management of this distributive conflict through the use of agricultural policy and, where necessary, repression. The interests of the rural and urban sectors are clear, but the salience of the rural–urban cleavage and the policies chosen by authoritarian governments depend on the ability of these sectors to mobilize collectively and threaten the regime. Stable authoritarian rule is the result of the effective management of the rural–urban cleavage through agricultural policy.

Agriculture and distributive conflict between cities and the countryside played a central role in canonical theories of democratization. This is because the transformation of agriculture is central to economic development, and economic development is the fundamental structural process

---

[20] They are, in the words of Tilly (1978, 18–24), "Durkheimian"; in the words of Skocpol (1979, 9), "aggregate-psychological" theories.

[21] For the canonical statement, see Tilly (1978).

driving regime change.[22] The sector is destined to make up a smaller share of employment and output as an economy grows, but its characteristics and the sorts of policies shaping its evolution have a decisive impact on a country's broader trajectory of economic and political development.[23] This was as true for historical European cases as it was for the postcolonial world and is for contemporary developing nations. Drawing on the experience of nineteenth-century Europe to develop early economic models of democratization, Gerschenkron (1943) and Moore (1966) argued that the perpetuation of a landed elite supported by an interventionist agricultural policy was a major factor blocking democratic reform in Germany before the First World War. In Britain, development went hand in hand with democratization because capitalist agriculture enriched urban wool traders and promoted an emancipated, liberal middle class. Germany, on the other hand, developed without democratizing. There, the large estates of the east were run by a repressive class of elites who opposed democracy. Supported by an authoritarian regime that imposed tariffs on imports of cheap foreign grain, the Prussian aristocracy was able to perpetuate its economic position in the country and dominate German politics until the war.

Observing the newly independent nations of sub-Saharan Africa, Robert Bates (1981, 1983) famously argued that the political economy of the postcolonial world revolved around agriculture and agricultural policy. His research showed that markets for products like coffee and maize in Kenya and cocoa in Ghana were subject to pervasive government intervention. State control of agricultural exports provided a ready source of revenue for politicians seeking to divert resources to themselves, the state, and powerful urban industrialists and manufacturers. These revenues were used to buy support for incumbent regimes. Governments set domestic prices for agricultural commodities lower than those on international markets and made a profit as middlemen in external trade. Food prices were kept low, decreasing farmers' incomes, while markets for consumer and industrial goods were protected, increasing household expenses and the cost of production for smallholders. This combination of policies became known as urban bias, was widespread across the

---

[22] Although the exact causal path by which economic growth drives democratization is contested, there is a broad consensus that there is a significant relationship between the two. See, for example, Lipset ([1959] 1963), Przeworski et al. (2000), and Boix and Stokes (2003).

[23] Timmer (1988, 2009), Easterly (1993), World Bank (2008), and IFAD (2016).

developing world, and had severe negative effects on economic and political development (Lipton, 1975, 1977).

The contemporary importance of urban bias in authoritarian politics is explored in recent work by Wallace (2013, 2014). In this account, population concentration in large cities poses the risk of collective opposition and authoritarian regime instability. However, paradoxically, these same governments tend to induce urbanization by taxing the countryside in order to spur industrialization and keep food prices low for urban consumers. By following urban-biased policies they are, therefore, sowing the seeds of their own destruction. The worst examples of this combination of urban bias, population concentration, and political instability are seen in North Africa and the Middle East. The Chinese government, by contrast, was able to avoid the difficult trade-off between industrialization and urban instability by imposing controls on internal migration and pursuing aggressive slum-clearance programs that slowed urbanization and mitigated the worst of its social consequences. These repressive policies have made a major contribution to the stability of the Chinese regime.

Wallace's analysis provides great insights into one element of agricultural policymaking under authoritarianism: the need to address threats from urban food consumers. It also rightly points out the important role that repression plays in the policy calculations of undemocratic governments. He has little to say, however, about farmers' role in the strategies of authoritarian regimes and the threats that they can pose to political stability. This is also a shortcoming of the broader literature on the political economy of agricultural market distortions. Since Bates' seminal contributions, economists and political scientists have devoted a considerable amount of research to exploring how some countries, beginning with South Korea, Taiwan, and Japan in the 1960s, escaped the postcolonial urban bias trap, supported farmers, and moved to a more sustainable model of agricultural development (Anderson and Hayami, 1986). They found that, ironically, development must come before favorable policy: Governments tend to support agriculture more as their economies grow and the number of farmers dwindles. This is because the cost of supporting farmers is relatively low in a large developed economy, and farmers find it easier to organize and lobby for favorable policies when there are fewer of them.[24] Subsequent studies also identified an important role for political institutions in policymaking. Democracies support agricul-

---

[24] See the reviews by De Gorter and Swinnen (2002) and Swinnen (2010b).

ture more than authoritarian regimes on average, a finding that has been confirmed in various settings from nineteenth-century Europe through contemporary developing and developed countries.[25] However, because democracy tends to go hand in hand with development, the existing literature on agricultural policy leaves us with a series of reinforcing positive trends: democratizing, growing polities adopt policies that support farmers and promote further growth and democratization. We know little about variation in policy among authoritarian governments and the circumstances under which regimes might support farmers without democratizing.

The recent literature on democratization and authoritarian politics provides us with insufficient analytical tools to understand agricultural policymaking and its consequences for regime stability. In most accounts, rural interests are reduced to an authoritarian landed elite, which can occupy a central position within the regime, opposing transitions to democracy.[26] We learn little about rural elites' preferences in agricultural policy or how they might exert influence on undemocratic governments to pursue their interests. Models of economic policymaking under authoritarianism remain underdeveloped, and only recently a prominent account described authoritarian regimes as "too much of a mixed bag" to attempt any systematic explanation of this aspect of authoritarian politics (Chang et al., 2011, 50).[27] Influential approaches to authoritarian politics, as summarized in Table 1.3, provide even fewer tools for understanding economic conflict and economic policy under authoritarianism. Geddes (1999) categorized authoritarian regimes as personalist, military, single-party, or amalgams. She sees the roots of their durability in the interests and incentive structures of these different types of governments: military regimes, for example, are more likely to collapse because officers – in contrast to party functionaries – always have the option of returning to the barracks with their careers intact. Subsequent authors have taken issue with Geddes's typology of authoritarian regimes, but their contributions have still focused on institutional characteristics of these governments. Svolik (2012, 26–39) argues for a four-dimension scale of classifying regimes; Slater (2003) argues for a distinction between

---

[25] Beghin and Kherallah (1994), Varshney (1995), Olper (2001), Swinnen (2009), and Bates and Block (2013).

[26] Boix (2003), Acemoglu and Robinson (2006), Ansell and Samuels (2014), Ziblatt (2008a, 2009), Baland and Robinson (2012), Thomson (2015), and Mares (2015).

[27] Some research has examined how authoritarian governments behave in the areas of trade and exchange rates. See, for example, Steinberg and Shih (2012), Steinberg and Malhotra (2014), and Hankla and Kuthy (2013).

TABLE 1.3 *Urban-Biased and Rural-Biased Regimes in Comparative Perspective*

Author	Type of Regime	Example	Dimensions of Variation
Thomson (2016)	Rural-biased Urban-biased	Malaysia Thailand, Egypt	Economic cleavages, agricultural policy
Geddes (1999)	Personalist Military Single-party	Uganda (Idi Amin) Thailand Malaysia	Institutional organization of power
Slater (2003)	Machine Bossism Junta Strongman	Malaysia pre-1998 Malaysia 1998–2003 Thailand pre-1988 Pakistan (Musharraf)	Personalization, institutionalization
Schedler (2006)	Electoral Authoritarian	Malaysia, Mexico	Degree of electoral competition
Svolik (2012)			Militarization, political parties, leg. selection, exec. selection

personal and institutional power under authoritarianism; and Schedler (2006) focuses on the role of electoral institutions in maintaining authoritarian regime stability.[28] These predominantly institutional accounts do little to advance our understanding of how economic cleavages shape the behavior and stability of authoritarian governments.

Nonetheless, previous generations of research into the link between development and democratization has taught us that the rural–urban cleavage is the dominant economic conflict in developing dictatorships. This cleavage, and how it is addressed using agricultural policy, has a significant effect on political stability and the type of regime that emerges in the course of development. Therefore, to fully understand authoritarian politics and the chances for democratization, the types

---

[28] This brief discussion only scratches the surface of the voluminous literature on political institutions under authoritarianism. See also, for example, Levitsky and Way (2010), Gandhi and Przeworski (2007), Magaloni (2006), Blaydes (2011), and Slater (2010).

of threats and policies that define these regimes must be considered alongside institutional features highlighted by other authors, as depicted in Table 1.3. Agriculture and agricultural policy affect how regimes maintain political stability, but they also alter the potential payoffs to democratization. Urban residents are less likely to revolt when food prices are lower, but they are also less likely to see redistribution under a potential democratic regime as a valuable goal. Similarly, rural elites will be still more opposed to democratization when they are afforded a large say in agricultural policymaking under an authoritarian government, despite having a basic preference for a repressive regime that provides them with control over rural labor. Agricultural policies also affect the broader trajectory of development and structural transformation in a country. Gains in productivity in agriculture lead to stronger growth in other parts of the economy, reductions in poverty, and the development of larger industry and service sectors (World Bank, 2008, 6–8). The sorts of measures that authoritarian governments put in place to address short-term political threats affect agricultural productivity growth and therefore have long-term consequences for development, urbanization, and inequality.[29] These are economic structures that significantly affect the chances of democratization. Therefore, the politics of agricultural policy under authoritarianism have effects on the probability of regime change. There is no simple causal path from economic development to democratization, the process is instead inherently political, contested, and shaped by government intervention.

1.3 THE PLAN OF THE BOOK

I put forward a more detailed account of the relationship between agricultural policy, regime type, and political stability in Chapter 2 before presenting several chapters of empirical analysis that provide support for this theory. My logic of agricultural policymaking has implications for both policy outcomes and political stability, which I illustrate in three cross-national statistical analyses. However, it also rests on a theory of the political influence of rural interests under authoritarianism, which is difficult to test by looking cross-nationally at policy outcomes or the stability of authoritarian governments. For this reason, I include two case studies in which I trace the causal mechanisms linking landholding inequality to rural influence, policy, and political stability under authoritarian regimes.

---

[29] Timmer (1988, 2009) and Easterly (1993).

The first prediction of my account of agricultural policymaking is that variation in regime type and the strength of rural and urban interests will be associated with variation in policy outcomes. In Chapter 3, I provide empirical evidence that confirms this prediction. I engage previous literature on the political economy of agricultural policy, which has found that authoritarian governments provide significantly lower levels of support to farmers than democratic governments. Informed by the arguments in Chapter 2, I show that significant policy variation exists among authoritarian regimes, which correlates with that in socioeconomic structures facilitating collective action among rural and urban interests. Using a new cross-national dataset on landholding inequality and World Bank data on agricultural market distortions, I show that higher levels of support to the rural sector occur under autocracy when landholding inequality creates a smaller, richer, and better-organized group of farmers. When food consumers are concentrated in urban areas, they pose a greater threat of unrest. This leads autocracies to provide lower levels of agricultural support and lower food prices.

If authoritarian governments use agricultural policy to manage the threat of urban collective action by lowering food prices, governments that implement policies increasing food prices should face a greater threat of urban unrest. In Chapter 4, I test this proposition. I show how global food prices are not fully passed on to domestic consumers, but are distorted by government market interventions, which determine the final cost of food. I assess these policies' effects on urban unrest, testing the hypothesis that governments whose interventions decrease prices less vis-à-vis world market prices are more prone to unrest. I extend an existing city-level dataset on urban social disturbances to match cross-national data on consumer food taxes. This allows me to analyze the relationship between food policy and urban unrest in fifty-four cities across the entire developing world from 1965 to 2009. I find that higher food taxes are significantly correlated with greater unrest, but only under regimes that combine a lack of democratic accountability with a relatively permissive political opportunity structure. Neither democracies nor repressive autocracies are faced with greater unrest when food taxes are higher.

My account of agricultural policymaking suggests not only that higher levels of landholding inequality indicating a powerful landed elite will be associated with significantly greater support for agriculture under authoritarianism. It also suggests that policies that distribute rents to landed elites will mitigate their threat to the stability of authoritarian governments. In Chapter 5, I examine the effects of agricultural market interventions on the likelihood of authoritarian regime collapse. I construct new measures of agricultural rents constructed from product-level market distortions data and examine their effects on regime durability. I find that the magnitude of rents created by government policy has no effect on the likelihood of regime collapse by itself. Instead, it is the interaction between landholding inequality and rents that leads to significant changes in regime stability. Authoritarian governments are more likely to collapse when landholding inequality is high, indicating a powerful rural sector, and policy disadvantages farmers by extracting rents from the countryside.

In two case studies, I probe the causal mechanisms behind the association between landholding inequality, agricultural policy, and regime stability, which I find cross-nationally in Chapters 3 and 5. I draw out in detail how the structural ability of the rural and urban sectors to engage in collective action translated into influence over agricultural policy and how this related to political stability in nineteenth-century Germany and 1960s to 1970s Malaysia. I selected cases that are both typical and deviant for my theory, and lie within and beyond the temporal scope of my cross-national statistical analysis. These cases therefore establish the broad relevance of my approach to agricultural policymaking and its relationship to political stability across a range of contexts in the developing world. I have deliberately selected cases that illustrate the logic of rural collective action and policy influence under authoritarian regimes, which is what distinguishes this book from previous work on urban bias and political stability. Because this is the major theoretical contribution of my approach, it demands more detailed empirical evidence to demonstrate its causal mechanisms at work.

The first of these case studies, presented in Chapter 6, is a detailed case study examining the political causes and consequences of a shift in agricultural policy that took place in the late 1870s in Imperial Germany, significantly increasing domestic food and agricultural produce prices. The Imperial German case lies outside the temporal scope of my cross-national statistical analysis, showing that my arguments have traction outside the post-1945 world. It is typical for, and confirmatory of, the theory laid out in Chapter 2, showing how landholding inequality translates into policy influence and regime stability under almost-ideal circumstances. Germany also occupies a theoretically prominent place in the literature on development and democratization, meaning that my findings in this chapter build on and inform a large, established body of research. I analyze an original district-level dataset to show that landowners formed a large group in the Imperial legislature because of high levels of landholding inequality and low urbanization across electoral districts. These structural factors led to a large number of mandates being won by conservative landowners and relatively few being won by representatives of urban food consumers such as industrialists, left Liberals, or Social Democrats. Models of Reichstag delegates' votes on the 1879 tariff bill show that representatives of districts with strong preferences for lower food prices were opposed to the protectionist policy shift, but were not numerous enough to block the tariff bill. Subsequent gains from the protectionist trade policy fell disproportionately on areas dominated by the Prussian aristocracy and characterized by higher levels of landholding inequality. Agricultural policy thus played a key role in ensuring the aristocracy's political support for Chancellor Bismarck for the duration of his tenure.

The second case study is presented in Chapter 7, where I examine the role of agricultural policy in the perpetuation of the authoritarian regime in Malaysia. I look at a critical juncture in the country's political development: the 1969 election, which resulted in surprise losses for the government, an extended period of political instability, and a consolidation of the regime, including a move to an interventionist, rural-biased development policy. The Malaysian case lies within the temporal scope of my cross-national empirical analysis. It is deviant, but confirmatory of the theory laid out in Chapter 2, establishing that a focus on patterns of structural influence and agricultural policy can explain variation in regime outcomes across a broad range of cases. Rural collective action in Malaysia was not based exclusively on structures of landholding inequality, which was higher in Malaysia than in neighboring countries at this time, but not high by global comparison or relative to Imperial Germany. Malaysian politics is dominated by ethnic, rather than economic, cleavages. Nonetheless, because of the powerful position occupied by rural Malay elites in the ruling party, they were able to act collectively to threaten the government as rural landed elites were in the German case. I analyze an original dataset to show that the government's electoral support in 1969 was significantly weaker in Malay, rice-growing areas, which traditionally had been strong bastions of the Alliance. I link this important shift in mass politics to subsequent contentious developments within the elite which significantly strengthened rural interests in the ruling coalition. I explain how a pro-rural agricultural policy reform, which increased the incomes of Malay rice farmers at the expense of urban food consumers, played a vital role in placating restive rural Malay interests within the elite and heading off their demands for a complete reorganization of the political system as a single-party dictatorship. Thus, the power shift within the ruling coalition led to a more producer-friendly policy, which in turn ensured regime stability. In this way, agricultural policy was an important tool promoting regime stability in 1970s Malaysia, which has been overlooked by previous scholars of authoritarianism in the country.

2

Agricultural Policy, Regime Type, and Political Stability

In this chapter, I will lay out a theory of agricultural policymaking and political stability under authoritarian and democratic governments. From this theory, I derive a series of empirical hypotheses on policy outcomes and the consequences of agricultural policy for regime stability, which I will go on to test in the remainder of the book. I argue that government market interventions in agriculture are the result of a trade-off between the interests of rural constituencies, who demand higher prices for agricultural commodities, and urban constituencies, who demand lower prices for farm produce and food. This trade-off is made by different rules depending on the institutional setting. Authoritarian leaders are self-interested actors who aim to maximize the rents that they can extract from the agricultural sector. They are not subject to electoral constraints and possess the capacity to repress opposition to their rule. However, these leaders cannot act with complete autonomy in policymaking. They must address the threats posed to their position by rural and urban interests. When either group finds it easier to act collectively in opposition to the regime, leadership will adjust policy to address their demands and maintain political stability. Because the rural population struggles to organize in collective opposition to authoritarian governments, policy under autocracy tends to be urban biased and decrease returns to agriculture, compared to democracies. However, when the rural sector is dominated by landed elites, policy is more likely to favor agricultural producers. By addressing the threat of collective action posed by rural and urban interests, the agricultural policies chosen by authoritarian leaders make significant contributions to the durability of their regimes. Intervening in agricultural markets to increase the price of farm produce, they can mitigate the risk of a challenge by powerful rural interests, while by intervening to decrease the price of food they can lower the likelihood of unrest among urban food consumers.

Democratic governments do not respond to the threat of collective action, but aim to win elections and remain in office. They make policy by weighing the support of large constituencies of voters and that of smaller but better-organized special-interest groups. Because elections solve the collective action problem for rural farmers, they hold more political sway under democracy than under undemocratic regimes. However, because democracies tend to be more developed than dictatorships, the agricultural sector is also smaller and finds it easier to organize and lobby government for favorable policy. For both of these reasons, democracies tend to support agriculture more than authoritarian governments. This tendency is moderated when income inequality among food consumers drives elected governments to use agricultural policy to decrease food prices as a form of redistribution to the median voter. Democracies are inherently more stable political institutions than authoritarian regimes, and because they tend to be richer, the rural–urban cleavage is not as salient as under dictatorship. Agricultural policy therefore does not have the significant influence on regime stability under democracy that it does under autocracy.

2.1 AGRICULTURAL POLICY AND AGRICULTURAL RENTS

The definition of agricultural policy as used in this project is broad. Here, agricultural policy includes any government intervention in markets for farm produce and food that affects prices facing farmers and consumers.[1] This definition of policy as market distortions takes free markets as a benchmark, but does not presume that agricultural markets are, or

---

[1] I therefore follow the definition of agricultural market distortions used by the World Bank's Agricultural Distortions Project (Anderson et al., 2008). I do not consider broader development policies, which could be directed at alleviating rural poverty and improving health outcomes and food security, or entail large-scale capital projects such as irrigation or electrification schemes. Although these undoubtedly have important effects on the welfare of rural populations and could conceivably play a role in determining political outcomes in developing countries, they are distinct from agricultural market interventions and lie outside the scope of my analysis here.

should be, free of government interventions at any time.[2] Some analysts advocate minimal intervention in agricultural markets, as this allows for the optimal efficient allocation of resources in the sector. However, others point out the importance of these commodities for the broader economy and the welfare of the rural and urban poor, argue that efficiency losses of policy interventions are small, and contend that distributive concerns or price stability should be paramount in agricultural policymaking.[3] While many developed economies have heavily supported their farmers for decades, powerful international institutions such as the International Monetary Fund and World Bank have strongly advocated a noninterventionist approach to agricultural policy for developing countries. Goals of reducing government intervention and "getting the prices right" were often tied to structural adjustment loans made in the developing world by these institutions in the 1980s and 1990s (Easterly, 2005). Furthermore, agriculture was incorporated into the global trade regime under the World Trade Organization in 1994, leading to hopes for a global retreat from interventionist policies (Anderson, 1998).

Despite this consensus against state intrusions into agricultural markets, governments both democratic and autocratic still intervene heavily in the sector through myriad measures.[4] These include tariffs, subsidies, and quantitative restrictions which affect trade in agricultural products. Trade distortions are most common in developing and relatively weak states: import tariffs were the main form of agricultural policy intervention in Europe in the nineteenth century, for example, and taxes on exports were imposed by agricultural marketing agencies in Africa during the period following decolonization.[5] More developed states intervene in agricultural markets using diverse policy instruments, including subsidies for farm inputs and direct consumer subsidies. In Malaysia, India, and Indonesia, for example, trade, procurement, and marketing of rice is controlled by state agencies that set prices and in some

---

[2] Government market interventions are deviations from an equilibrium at which the marginal social cost to consumers and the marginal social return to producers are equal. The economic costs of these market distortions can be measured using the tools of welfare economics (Anderson et al., 2001). However, this study is concerned with the political, not economic, effects of agricultural market distortions.

[3] See Timmer (1989) for a summary of these arguments. Rashid and Cummings (2007) argue that justifications for greater market intervention by governments that were valid in the 1970s and 1980s no longer hold in contemporary market conditions.

[4] See, for example, Anderson et al. (2001), Anderson (2009), and Thies (2015).

[5] On Europe, see the case study of German grain tariffs in Chapter 6 and also Swinnen (2010a). On Africa, see Bates (1981).

cases also provide access to credit and subsidized fertilizer for farmers.[6] Since the establishment of the Common Agricultural Policy in the early 1960s, Western European countries have provided significant support to the sector by imposing higher prices than those on world markets, restricting trade in agricultural commodities, and increasingly, making direct payments to farmers based on farm size and environmental goals (Josling, 2009).

Agricultural policies are particularly economically and politically salient in developing countries, where a relatively large share of the population works on farms and food makes up a significant share of consumer spending. Furthermore, because these countries have much more modest social welfare programs than developed nations, their agricultural policies make up a much larger component of governments' total effects on citizens' welfare. Agricultural policy has an important redistributive function and creates clear winners and losers. Policies that favor producers by increasing prices for their produce typically pass on these costs to consumers in the form of higher prices for food. They therefore serve as an important mechanism for the transfer of resources from the city to the countryside and vice versa (Wallace, 2013). Interventions in the sector are also an important source of government revenue in the developing world. Even where the agricultural sector is not predominant, the taxation of export cash crops such as rubber, coffee, or cocoa can still make significant contributions to the state's coffers (Bates, 1981, 1983). In the context of weak states, because agricultural output is often exportable, trade restrictions at the border can be one of the most reliable sources of revenue for governments that lack the capacity to impose more technically onerous kinds of taxes such as those on individuals or firms (Herbst, 1990).

As such an important contributor to the treasury, agricultural policy is critical for the fiscal health of the state. However, it can also be used to generate rents that accrue to political and bureaucratic elites. Rents are profits that result from government regulation, and rent-seeking is the pursuit of revenues that result from government interventions in markets.[7] The allocation of import licenses, the imposition of protectionist tariffs for select industries, and the creation of government-sanctioned monopolies all generate rents that are pursued by firms, bureaucrats, and

---

[6] See Fane and Warr (2009), McCorriston and MacLaren (2016), and Athukorala and Loke (2009). Control of food grain markets by state-owned agencies remains common across Asia. See Rashid and Cummings (2007).

[7] Tullock (1967) and Krueger (1974).

politicians. Because the rents resulting from regulation are smaller than the total social costs they impose on the economy, rent-seeking does not create wealth but instead redistributes it from one actor to another while generating waste. Rent-seeking is economically inefficient and commonly associated with poor governance, corruption, even general economic decline.[8] However, it can be politically efficient because the creation of rents gives leaders the ability to distribute economic resources, a powerful and fungible guarantor of political support. This is particularly important under authoritarian governments where the distribution of patronage and rents makes a key contribution to political stability, alongside the repression of dissent.[9] State intervention in markets allows resources to flow to critical constituencies to buy their support and stave off possible political instability (Herbst, 1990; Oi, 1993).

Rents generated by agricultural market distortions can accrue both to broader constituencies and to the state. The major effects of agricultural market distortions are diffuse: Government policy has the potential to have dramatic consequences for farmer welfare, through its effect on produce prices, and for consumer living standards, through its effect on food prices. Relatively small interventions in markets have large aggregate effects that are spread over all participants in the sector. Although some accounts of authoritarian agricultural policy focus on these consequences for consumer food prices and farmer welfare (Olper and Raimondi, 2013), it is not only such diffuse groups that are affected by these market distortions. Indeed, authors such as Bates (1981, 1983) and Herbst (1990) argued that the major factor driving policy toward agriculture in Africa was the imperative for governments to raise revenue, for which there were scarce other opportunities. Rents from taxing trade in agricultural products were used to distribute patronage and fund industrial development projects and were frequently embezzled by corrupt government bureaucrats. Agricultural rents accruing to the state can therefore be seen as having similar effects to natural resource rents, which have long been associated with durable authoritarian rule (Ross, 2012). Although they do create clear winners and losers among food consumers and farmers, these rents can be used to buy off potential challengers, and they give authoritarian leaders an incentive to cling to power to maintain access to resource flows.

---

[8] See, for example, Olson (1982), Rama (1993), and Keefer and Knack (2007).
[9] Wintrobe (1990, 1998) and Acemoglu and Robinson (2006).

2.2 RURAL AND URBAN INTERESTS

Agricultural policy is an important tool at the disposal of governments that intervene in the sector. The rents that are generated through interventions in the sector can be used to buy the support of agricultural producers and food consumers, who have divergent interests in policy outcomes. My theory of agricultural policy and authoritarian politics is based on the interaction of three actors, or groups: a ruling elite, rural interests, and urban interests. I assume that elites aim to remain in power, but by different means: Authoritarian elites aim to secure their position by mitigating collective threats to their rule and simultaneously maximize the rents that they extract from the economy. Democratic elites aim to remain in power by winning elections and maximize their support from both broad constituencies and narrow special-interest groups. Rural interests aim to maximize their profits and have an interest in higher prices for agricultural produce, while urban interests aim to maximize their profits and living standards and have an interest in lower prices for agricultural produce and food.

I use the terms *rural* and *urban interests* in order to encompass different types of actors who reside in the countryside and cities, respectively, but who have shared interests in agricultural policy. It is, of course, a simplification to assume that all rural and urban residents have identical interests in agricultural policy. Important cleavages exist, particularly within the rural sector, for example, between smallholders and large-scale agricultural producers; farmers and commodity traders or marketing boards; and net food consumers versus net food producers. Indeed, I will question the assumption of unitary rural and urban sectors in several important respects as my analysis proceeds, and many of these finer distinctions will be discussed in detail in my case studies. However, for theoretical purposes, assuming a divergence of interests between the rural and urban sectors is a useful simplification, as it allows me to clearly formulate and test hypotheses on the determinants and effects of agricultural policies. It also follows the precedent of prominent previous accounts and therefore allows the material in this book to clearly build on important findings in related areas. Differentiating between rural and urban constituencies in this way follows Lipton (1977, 56–63), for example, who makes the case for a stark geographic and economic division between the town and countryside. Varshney (1995, 2) also bases his analysis on an identical distinction between the rural and urban sectors. Similarly, Wallace (2014, 19–34) views large cities as fundamentally different from rural areas, because their populations have distinct economic interests, are easier to mobilize politically, and are more difficult to repress.

Rural interests seek market interventions from the state that increase the price of agricultural produce and their profits. Farmers are typically among the most impoverished groups in a society, especially as development leads to growth in high-output manufacturing and services sectors. At the same time, they are subject to significant economic uncertainty. International agricultural commodity markets are volatile, with price fluctuations of over 20 percent within a single calendar year commonplace. For example, from April 2015 to April 2016, the international price of dairy products declined by around 25 percent, while prices for sugar increased by around 16 percent. Acute economic uncertainty, such as that during the oil shocks of the 1970s or the recent economic crisis, can cause annual fluctuations in prices of 50 percent or more.[10] In the face of relative economic deprivation and uncertainty, farmers have strong interests in government market interventions that increase their incomes, particularly in times of low world market prices. However, the broader rural sector shares these interests in higher agricultural prices. In particular, suppliers of inputs and services to farmers are reliant on their financial health for their livelihoods and profit from government interventions, which benefit the sector.

Urban interests, on the other hand, seek government market interventions that lower the price of agricultural produce and food. Such policies raise consumers' living standards, cheapen inputs for manufacturers, provide opportunities for arbitrage and profits to traders and marketing boards, and generate resources to fund development projects. In developing countries, consumers spend a significant share of their income on food. In contemporary African and Asian countries, it is not uncommon for food to make up more than one-third of total consumer expenditure. It made up around 40 percent of consumption expenditure in Egypt and Cameroon in 2009, while in South Africa the figure was 15 percent and in Vietnam and China it was 40 percent and 33 percent, respectively (Economic Research Service, USDA, 2011). Urban residents are more dependent on purchased and processed foods to meet their consumption needs, and they can rely less on social networks for assistance. They therefore have a very strong interest in government policies that

---

[10] These data are from the Food and Agriculture Organization of the United Nations monthly food price index.

decrease the price of food (Ruel, Haddad, and Garratt, 1999). These sorts of policies have large effects on the welfare of urban food consumers and rural–urban inequality in developing countries (Oi, 1993). However, urban actors aside from food consumers also profit from government policies which lower the price of agricultural produce because they often entail a more general transfer of investment and economic resources from the countryside to cities.[11] Manufacturers benefit from lower prices for primary agricultural inputs. For example, a policy that decreases the price of palm oil can increase the profits of soap-makers, as a policy decreasing the price of cotton increases the profits of textile manufacturers. Policies that impose domestic prices below those on world markets provide opportunities for private or state-sanctioned actors such as traders and agricultural marketing boards to benefit by acquiring farm output at low domestic prices and selling it at higher world market prices. The resources gained thus can be used to fund industrialization and development projects in infrastructure that predominantly benefit urban elites.[12]

2.3 REGIME TYPE

The theoretical account put forward here draws important distinctions between types of political institutions, or regimes. The key aspect over which regimes vary here is to what degree they are democratic: whether they provide citizens the opportunity to formulate and signal their preferences to government through elections and have these preferences weighed equally in policy. What dictates the type of regime in my analysis is the extent to which these rights are granted, so members of the political system can contest the government, and what proportion of the population can participate in this process of contestation (Dahl, 1971).

This definition of regime type as degree of accountability is minimalist and focuses on the procedures of electoral democracy, but it captures the key aspects of institutional variation that affect agricultural policymaking.[13] The degree of political contestation and participation in electoral

---

[11] The resultant allocation of resources is inefficient due to lower returns in the urban sector, having pernicious effects on broader development which I do not discuss here. See Timmer (1988).

[12] More examples could be given here; see Lipton (1977, 287–307), Bates (1981), and Bates (1983, 107–133) for the classic treatments.

[13] On minimalist conceptions of democracy as a system in which rulers are selected by competitive elections, see Schumpeter (1942) and Przeworski et al. (2000, 33–36).

politics are the crucial axes of institutional variation in my account because I predict that reductions in the extent of these freedoms generate political inequalities across the rural–urban cleavage. To the extent that the conduct of the government is not contestable, its policies are likely to favor the urban sector over rural interests. As I will discuss in more detail later, influencing policy outcomes under any regime type involves a collective action problem for large groups such as urban food consumers or rural food producers. Elections make a significant contribution to solving this problem, but particularly for rural residents who face greater barriers to collective action than the urban population. Under less democratic regimes, therefore, the rural sector faces a structural disadvantage in acting collectively to influence agricultural policy. In addition to electoral procedures, the definition of regime type here also captures restrictions to civil liberties and patterns of repression that are relevant to collective action and policymaking. Regimes that do not guarantee citizens' rights to form and join political organizations, to express their preferences freely, or to access alternative sources of information also reduce their ability to act collectively and influence policy. This aspect of democracy is particularly pertinent to the urban population, whose collective influence is more likely to run through mass mobilization than the rural sector's. My definition of regime type therefore captures the institutions of electoral democracy, which have unequal effects on the representation of the rural and urban sectors in agricultural policymaking.

The definition of regime type used here has further advantages. Crucially, it does not include any economic outcomes such as growth, investment, or distributional equality (Schmitter and Karl, 1991). Variation in economic policy – in this case, agricultural policy – is predicted to be a function of institutional variation in my model, not a constituent element of regime type. This avoids tautological, circular reasoning in which democracies implement certain types of agricultural policies, which in turn mark them as democracies, and so on. Empirically, regime type as defined here can be measured as a continuous or categorical variable following the long-established and widely recognized criteria of the Polity dataset (Marshall and Cole, 2011). Finally, conceiving of regime type as the degree of electoral accountability in a political system follows the established approach of other scholars of agricultural policy such as Bates (1981), Bates and Block (2011), and Olper and Raimondi (2011, 2013). This allows my theoretical and empirical contribution to be assessed against, and clearly build upon, previous literature.

Alternative classifications of political regimes have proliferated in the field of comparative politics over the last two decades.[14] Some authors, most notably Cheibub, Gandhi, and Vreeland (2010) and Boix, Miller, and Rosato (2012), adopt a similar minimalist definition of democracy to that outlined above, but are purely procedural, omitting civil liberties, and measure regime type only as a dichotomous variable. The limitation of these measures lies in their omission of civil liberties, which can affect the likelihood of collective action, making a broader definition of regime type, which includes these elements of democratic practice preferable in the context of this study. By contrast, the Freedom House classification of regime type (Freedom House, 2017) errs on the side of focusing too much on phenomena such as lack of conflict or socioeconomic inequality, which in my analysis are outcomes of political institutions rather than constitutive components. The Varieties of Democracy project (Coppedge et al., 2011; Lindberg et al., 2014) defines democracy as a multidimensional concept that can be measured through five distinct components. However, only one of these, the electoral component of democracy, neatly captures one of the major axes of institutional variation that are salient for collective action and economic policymaking in my account. Two further components, participatory and deliberative, contain information on some institutional factors relevant for collective action, such as civil liberties and freedom of expression. However, this useful information is confounded by the inclusion in the same measures of mechanisms of direct democracy and standards regarding the type of political expression predominant in a state, factors, which have no obvious relevance for collective action or influence on policymaking.

Increasingly, scholars of comparative democratization are interested institutional variation *among* authoritarian regimes and its effects on regime durability and other outcomes. In this literature the "type" of regime in question is the variety of undemocratic government rather than a democracy or autocracy. Most notably, Geddes, Wright, and Frantz (2014) and Svolik (2012) have developed measures of the involvement of the military in politics under authoritarianism, the personalization of authoritarian rule, and the presence of parties and legislatures in autocracies. These are undoubtedly important distinctions among authoritarian regimes that have significant effects on some political outcomes, but they do not clearly capture differences in the politics of collective action

---

[14] This short review does not attempt to assess this literature exhaustively. For more exhaustive reviews, see Munck and Verkuilen (2002), Cheibub, Gandhi, and Vreeland (2010), and Boix, Miller, and Rosato (2012).

and agricultural policymaking. I do not expect these factors to have an impact on agricultural policy, and I make use of these measures primarily as control variables in some of my empirical models of political stability.

2.4 POLICY UNDER AUTHORITARIANISM: GRIEVANCES, COLLECTIVE ACTION, AND THREATS TO POLITICAL STABILITY

A small but growing body of research in comparative politics investigates economic policymaking under authoritarianism. Existing accounts contrast the interests of narrow groups of elites versus those of the mass population, making predictions for policy outcomes based on the relative power of the elite. Steinberg and Malhotra (2014), for example, argue that authoritarian regimes with smaller selectorates are more responsive to narrow interests and more likely to follow a fixed exchange rate. Relatedly, Hankla and Kuthy (2013) find that more institutionalized regimes follow open trade policies because they are less likely to favor selective interests and more likely to favor policies promoting long-term growth. These models of authoritarian policymaking, though instructive, are not directly applicable to the agricultural sector because rural and urban interests both consist of relatively large, diffuse groups. Theories that focus on the interests and power of the ruling elite versus the entire population have difficulty predicting how policy will respond when mass interests diverge as they do between the rural and urban sectors. For this reason, I base my account of agricultural policymaking under authoritarianism on the threat of collective action by rural and urban interests, not the power of the ruling elite versus the mass population.[15]

Authoritarian elites, in my account, do not have any a priori preferences over agricultural policy outcomes. Instead, they aim to maximize the rents that they can extract from the economy and therefore to secure their position in power. Authoritarian governments are, in essence, revenue maximizers. They seek to increase the flows of resources directed to the state, which they can then use to pursue their own personal objectives.[16] However, they do so under constraints. Authoritarian elites must

---

[15] My theoretical approach is therefore much closer to that of canonical authors such as Olson (1965) and Bates (1981) and more recent work by Wallace (2014).

[16] My conception of the state hews closely to that of Levi's (1981, 1989) theory of "predatory rule" and Olson's (1993) notion of "stationary bandits." Evans's (1989) argument for "developmental states" disputes the a priori assumption of predatory state behavior and argues that states can have significant positive effects on economic development. However, his preconditions for developmental state behavior such as uncorrupt and

minimize the transaction costs to their rent-seeking, that is, encourage economic development to generate revenue. They do this with an eye to their prospects for remaining in power, or their time horizon. Therefore, although authoritarian governments are by nature predatory, or raise revenue as a form of banditry, they do not steal indiscriminately from the population in a way that would massively deter investment and impede growth (North and Weingast, 1989).

Most important, however, to maintain access to the revenue streams that control over the government can grant them, and to avoid the real possibility of posttenure exile, imprisonment, or death, authoritarian elites must first remain in power.[17] To do so, they must address political threats from both rival elites and the mass of the population (Svolik, 2012). By definition, authoritarian governments maintain their position in power partly by repressing rivals' abilities to challenge them through coercive means (Davenport, 2007b). However, coercion is costly and therefore an inefficient means of maintaining power and revenue flows to the elite. Large-scale redistribution, of land for example, usually involves coercion and is also very costly. It is therefore relatively rare compared to the sorts of soft interventions in agricultural pricing policy which I study here (Albertus, 2015a). Regimes prefer to use noncoercive measures, such as economic patronage and redistribution, to buy off rivals and mitigate threats to their rule.[18] Assuming that the transaction costs of interventions in the economy that maintain the regime's position are lower than the costs of repression, authoritarian leaders will choose economic policy as a tool to maintain political stability over coercion.

Agricultural market interventions are therefore an important policy instrument for authoritarian leaders. They serve both to generate rents accruing to the state and to redistribute resources from cities to the countryside or vice versa, with both effects helping leaders distribute patronage and buy off threatening rivals. In the extreme case, political elites and agricultural interests overlap, and policies divert resources to the sector

---

meritocratic bureaucracies are unlikely to hold under authoritarian governments, despite important exceptions, particularly in East Asia.

[17] The benefits accruing to rulers do need to be contrasted with the dramatic negative consequences of losing power. Around half of outgoing dictators are jailed, exiled or killed (Escribá-Folch, 2013).

[18] See Levi (1989, 50), who argues that coercion is costly as a means of rule. Wintrobe (1998, 33–39) argues that dictatorships have a "power production function," which determines their trade-off between repression and redistribution, or what he calls "loyalty." Acemoglu and Robinson (2006, 186–189) also discuss the dictator's trade-off between (costly) repression, redistribution and democratization in the face of revolutionary threats.

to enrich rulers. This occurred in Ivory Coast during the 1960s to the 1980s, where the president's family had substantial interests in export agriculture, and policy therefore provided high prices for producers (Widner, 1993). However, in most cases rents extracted from agriculture are directed to a broader set of actors. For example, Konings (1986, 4, 16) describes how taxes on cocoa production in postcolonial Ghana were used to finance government expenditure on wages for bureaucratic, military, and party personnel who were members of the ruling elite. Relatedly, O'Donnell (1978) argues that an alliance between the ruling elite and urban constituents in Argentina was cemented by their shared interest in taxing beef exports, a policy that generated rents for the government while keeping prices low for urban food consumers.[19] In postreform China, taxation of peasants is a major source of revenue for meeting targets in infrastructure development but also for corruption and patronage by local authorities (Bernstein and Lü, 2003, 48–83).

Agricultural policy helps authoritarian governments redistribute resources to the state or powerful allies. However, regimes use agricultural policies not only to extract rents from the sector but also to maintain broader political stability. Stability, in the authoritarian context, implies remaining in power, such that challengers both at the elite and mass level prefer to acquiesce to the status quo regime rather than attempt a revolt to impose an alternative government. Agricultural policy affects the likelihood of political instability by altering the cost-benefit calculation of rural and urban interests considering removing the ruling elite from power.[20] If the regime were led by rural interests, they could set their ideal agricultural policy, which would implement higher farm produce prices, just as urban interests could implement a policy leading to lower agricultural market prices if they led the government. The ruling elite can reduce the incentives to mount a revolt by moving policy closer to the ideal point of either group. However, as I made clear in my

[19] As pampean production patterns shifted away from foodstuffs toward soybeans, Argentine governments have been able to raise revenue by promoting agricultural exports, as this does not imply increased consumer food prices (Richardson, 2009).

[20] This conception of authoritarian stability follows that of Ansell and Samuels (2014) and Acemoglu and Robinson (2006). Other theories of authoritarian rule and economic policymaking conceive of power in different ways. Levi's (1989, 17–23) notion of bargaining power, for example, refers to the control of essential resources. Svolik (2012, 69–71) conceives of power as the likelihood that a dictator will renege against power-sharing agreements and acquire more influence within the ruling coalition. For Wintrobe (1998, 46–53), power and remaining in office are not necessarily the same thing; tinpot dictatorships seek to remain in office at the minimum cost, while totalitarian dictatorships aim to maximize their power over the population.

discussion earlier, agricultural policy creates clear winners and losers and cannot move closer to the ideal points of both rural and consumer interests simultaneously. Regimes must choose whether to buy off rural or urban interests when making policy. Therefore, policymaking under authoritarianism involves the assessment of the threat that rural and urban interests pose to political stability, that is, the probability that a challenge mounted by either group would be successful. If rural interests are more threatening than urban interests, agricultural policy will increase returns to the sector; policy will decrease prices for agricultural produce if the threat of urban interests is more acute than those emanating from the countryside.

In my account, authoritarian stability requires the ruling elite to assess the political threats posed to the regime by these groups before distributing economic resources to mitigate them.[21] This is a significant divergence from some previous theories of authoritarian rule, which see the problem of economic redistribution as determining political stability and do not foresee groups facing significant challenges in acting collectively to threaten a regime.[22] However, collective political action is notoriously difficult because actions that are beneficial to a group as a whole are often a costly proposition for any given individual. Acting together to provide public goods creates incentives to free-ride and avoid the costs of collective action, which generates nonexcludable benefits (Olson, 1965). For this reason, among others, economic grievances alone have seldom been found to be sufficient in provoking political instability such as civil wars and revolutions.[23]

Agricultural market distortions that affect consumer and producer prices are a clear example of the type of nonexcludable common good

---

[21] In order to avoid a tautology in which interests are threatening because they possess economic resources, and thus receive further resources, I must specify structural bases for the calculation of political threats, which can be observed and allow us to analytically reproduce the sorts of threat assessments carried out by elites. I do so later by conceiving of threats as the likelihood of collective action by rural and urban interests and develop arguments about structural conditions that facilitate such collective action. See Levi (1989, 17–23) for a discussion of the pitfalls of arguments based on threats or "bargaining power" and possible solutions.

[22] See in particular Boix (2003) and Acemoglu and Robinson (2006, 118–128), who discuss collective action problems at length but still assume that they are always solved by the masses in their models of autocracy and democratization. Ansell and Samuels (2014, 78–79, 85–88) see the probability of a successful revolt depending primarily on the wealth of the bourgeoisie and the masses. Problems of collective action have featured prominently in more recent theories of revolution and authoritarian rule (Bueno de Mesquita, 2010; Hollyer, Rosendorff, and Vreeland, 2015).

[23] See, for example, Tilly (1978), Collier and Hoeffler (2004), and Thomson (2016).

that is notoriously difficult for groups to act collectively to provide.[24] Contributing to the production of a favorable agricultural policy – that is, mobilization in opposition to high food prices on the part of urban interests, or mobilization in opposition to low prices on the part of rural interests – implies costs to these actors. However, the benefits of the policy may not match the costs of mobilization for all individuals. In addition, all actors benefit from the price policy whether they contribute to mobilization or not, giving incentives to free ride. For this reason, both rural and urban interests face significant collective action problems in the provision of policies that favor their interests. My account of authoritarian agricultural policy requires the regime to assess the capacity of rural and urban interests for collective opposition to their policies and to respond by shifting policy in their favor.

Strategic action on the part of the regime and both the rural and urban sectors will result in authoritarian governments assessing the trade-off between the threats posed by the rural and urban sectors and making policy to address these threats. In equilibrium, therefore, policy should mitigate threats, and misjudged agricultural policies will only rarely cause political instability. However, the possibility of policy diverging from the equilibrium path and causing political instability remains, for several reasons. First, regimes may possess incomplete information on the likelihood of collective action by the rural or urban sector. Although some forms of influence, such as lobbying by agricultural interest groups, are relatively transparent, the probability of profoundly destabilizing events such as coups or mass uprisings is very difficult for a regime to assess, and actors have an interest in obscuring their intentions, making a perfect policy response to threats challenging to achieve (Kuran, 1989). Second, regimes may face a commitment problem in making and implementing policy, even when correctly assessing the threats that are massed against them (Acemoglu and Robinson, 2006). If a regime is faced with significant threats from both the rural and urban sectors, a situation that I will take up in more detail in Chapter 8, policy will be more difficult to calibrate, and when calibrated, it will be difficult for regimes to convince opponents that it will not be changed. As I will discuss in more detail in Chapter 4, economic and bureaucratic structures can cause some regimes to have an intrinsic bias against the rural sector, which deviates from equilib-

---

[24] This is one reason why the market distortions examined here are quite distinct from more targeted development projects. Because some agricultural commodities are only produced in certain areas or by some groups, pricing policy can in fact be targetable to some extent, but to a much lower extent than other types of development policy or rents.

rium policy. Large agricultural export sectors are ready targets for rent extraction by state actors such as marketing boards and customs agencies, which can affect prices while being difficult for a government to control. These problems of incomplete information and commitment to equilibrium policy mean that even rational autocrats making optimal policy face the possibility of political instability in response to interventions in agricultural markets.

Despite these information and commitment problems, authoritarian regimes weigh the threat of collective opposition posed to their regime by rural and urban interests, and use agricultural policy to address the threat that is most pressing. The generic outcome of this process is an urban-biased policy that decreases returns to the rural sector. This is the well-established pattern observed in developing countries by Lipton (1977) and Bates (1981, 1983) but also in more recent literature such as the empirical studies by Olper and Raimondi (2011, 2013), who show that democratic transitions reduce bias against the rural sector.[25] Where governments are not constrained by elections, urban interests find it easier to organize and are more educated, wealthy, and politically salient than rural populations. Under authoritarianism, they therefore often receive policies that follow their interests and decrease agricultural produce prices. This effect of regime type on policy outcomes is the first hypothesis that I test empirically in Chapter 3,

$H_{1.1}$, *Regime Type:* Democratic regimes are more responsive to rural interests than authoritarian governments and are associated with greater levels of support to agriculture, holding all else equal.

Urban Collective Action

Urban collective action plays a central role in the political economy of authoritarian rule and democratization. Influential political elites, business interests and mass populations that can mobilize in opposition to a regime are all located in cities. Urban collective action also plays a central role in my theory of agricultural policy and political stability under authoritarianism. Authoritarian policies are more likely to favor urban interests by lowering the price of agricultural commodities vis-à-vis world markets when urban interests are powerful. These policies

---

[25] The original urban bias contributions were the subject of considerable debate, and the authors subsequently defended and amended their arguments, for example, in Lipton (1984, 1993) and Bates (1993).

have consequences for political stability. The urban masses have an interest in mobilizing in collective opposition to higher food prices under authoritarianism, as they cannot effectively influence policy through the ballot box. However, mobilization depends not only on their economic interests but also on political opportunity structures, which facilitate grievance attribution and lower the costs of protest. I expect that urban unrest in response to food taxes will be most likely under more open and less repressive authoritarian governments.

The collective threat of urban interests plays out at both the mass and elite levels. At the mass level, urban food consumers are a powerful constituency under authoritarianism (Bates, 1983, 121–122). Food makes up a large proportion of many urban residents' budgets in low-income dictatorships. This cost is difficult for city dwellers to avoid as they cannot produce any food themselves. High food prices therefore have negative effects on consumer welfare, and when this segment of the population airs its grievances over standards of living, they often center on food affordability. Urban food consumers pose a direct risk to the stability of authoritarian governments due to their capacity for opposition to high food prices. Because they are concentrated in a relatively small space, they find it easier to solve collective action problems and quickly mobilize in defense of their economic interests. Population density facilitates protests, strikes, and riots because cities contain social networks that allow individuals to share their preferences and intentions to mobilize, solving coordination problems.[26] For this reason, increases in the cost of food have been associated with urban unrest in empirical studies.[27] Such mobilization in urban areas can be especially damaging due to its potential to escalate and the fact that it often implies direct confrontation between the opposition and symbols or agents of the state (Wallace, 2014, 20–25).

However, aside from food consumers, elites in cities have an interest in lower food prices and can mount powerful collective opposition to adverse government policy. Many urban manufacturers prefer lower prices for agricultural produce as they lower their input costs and can ease pressure for higher wages for workers. These firms tend to be large, are located in close proximity to governing elites, and possess the administrative capacity to lobby and apply for privileged treatment from the

---

[26] There is a rich literature on these effects, for example, Kuran (1989) and Lohmann (1994).

[27] For example, Bellemare (2015) and Hendrix and Haggard (2015) found a link between global food prices and civil unrest, while Smith (2014) found that domestic food prices cause civil strife.

state (Bates, 1981, 67–68). Urban elites within the state also have an interest in government intervention in agricultural markets because it implies control over resources by bureaucrats and provides them opportunities for rent-seeking and self-enrichment. Parastatal agricultural marketing agencies, which control procurement, distribution, and trade in agricultural commodities and farm inputs, are common in developing countries and have proven stubbornly resistant to reform.[28] They often impose trade restrictions and costs on farmers, which decrease rural incomes. They also provide bureaucrats and politicians access to rents, which are derived from the agricultural sector. These actors use this access for self-enrichment and to distribute resources to allies. For example, government agricultural agencies grant high salaries and extensive benefit packages to their employees. This remuneration is often grossly disproportionate to the incomes of the farmers who are subject to agencies' control of commodity markets (Buccola and McCandlish, 1999). In addition, the rents funneled through agricultural parastatals are prime targets for corruption, embezzlement, and graft by their employees and politicians (Cooksey, 2011). Apart from economic self-interest, urban bureaucrats often hold developmental ideas that are distinctly antirural. In the more extreme socialist examples like the former communist block or China these are partly due to a commitment to the interests of the working class and state-owned urban enterprises.[29] However, in many cases they rest on a view that the rural sector is backward, stagnant, and unresponsive to economic incentives.[30] Such antirural views result in a tendency for policymakers to give the interests of the rural sector less weight when making decisions on the shape of government interventions in the agricultural sector.

Urban areas pose significant threats to authoritarian governments because they can erupt in mass protest against food taxes and are home to powerful elites with an interest in lower food prices. For these reasons, the second hypothesis that I test in Chapter 3 relates to response of these governments to the threat posed by urban areas,

$H_{1.2}$, *Urban Interests:* Urbanization increases the capacity of urban interests to mobilize and threaten authoritarian governments. It

---

[28] See, for example, the canonical accounts by Bates (1981) and Krueger (1990) but also more recent studies such as Rashid and Cummings (2007), Kherallah et al. (2000), and Birner and Resnick (2010).

[29] On Socialism and the Soviet Union, see Lipton (1977, 107–130). On China, see Bernstein and Lü (2003, 48–83) and Oi (1993).

[30] For example, see Lipton (1977, 63–66) and Varshney (1993).

is correlated with lower levels of support to agriculture under authoritarian regimes versus democracies, holding all else equal.

Urban collective action at the mass level plays an important role in the political economy of agricultural policy under authoritarianism. Unlike in democracies, food consumers in cities cannot affect policy through the ballot box. However, they have the ability to mobilize collectively in protests and demonstrations to oppose policies that increase the price of food. This threat drives authoritarian governments to implement policies that lower food prices, particularly where a larger proportion of the population lives in cities. However, collective opposition to unfavorable policy does not occur automatically as a direct function of consumer welfare. It depends, first, on consumers' ability to attribute blame for high food prices to government policies and, second, on their ability to solve collective action problems blocking mobilization. Both grievance attribution and mobilization are more likely to occur under more open authoritarian regimes, making urban unrest in response to higher food prices most likely in those countries with middling levels of democratization.

Increases in food prices caused by policy affect consumer welfare to the same extent as those caused by impersonal market forces. However, the relationship between government interventions in food markets and the potential for urban unrest is complex because these interventions, their consequences for consumer welfare, and how they are perceived by consumers are all opaque. As in democracies, there is not necessarily a direct link between political attitudes and real economic outcomes (Kayser and Peress, 2012). Economic grievances among consumers that could drive unrest are determined by the prices that they pay for food, and what defines consumer prices is not only the magnitude of government food subsidies or taxes, but also the combination of market prices and policy. Disentangling the effects of government interventions from exogenous market forces is difficult for consumers. In addition, as we have seen, a wide range of policies have effects on domestic food production and consumption. Their total effects must be taken into consideration when assessing the consequences of government interventions for the welfare of urban residents. This is also a very challenging task for food consumers. The question of how government policy provokes contentious opposition therefore revolves around consumers' propensity to attribute responsibility and blame for economic grievances around food prices to government policy. Where governments are held accountable for changes in food prices, a response in the form of collective opposition is more likely (Javeline, 2002). I remain agnostic on the exact mechanisms through which food consumers attribute their grievances around food prices to government market interventions. Consumers can respond to food price fluctuations in markets (Smith, 2014; Bellemare, 2015), or media reports and statements by the political opposition on prices and policy (Kayser and Peress, 2012). However, attributing blame for higher prices to government policy is easier in more transparent regimes that allow for a free press and actors such as political parties and nongovernmental organizations that can draw attention to, and oppose, the consequences of existing policy.

Urban collective action in response to food taxes is also contingent on broader political opportunity structures, and these are likewise more conducive to mobilization in more open autocracies. Assuming that rational individuals protest when the net gains from collective action are positive, factors that decrease the cost of mobilization increase the likelihood of mass opposition to food taxes. Free access to information from media and social networks allows opponents of the regime to share their discontent with others. This increases the likelihood of protest, as preference revelation bolsters the prospects of successful collective action while lowering the chances of punishment (Kuran, 1989; Lohmann, 1994). There is significant variation in media freedom among authoritarian regimes, with the least open and most repressive also clamping down the most on the press, on average (Egorov, Guriev, and Sonin, 2009). In addition, a lack of protection of civil liberties and prevalence of surveillance and repression under autocracies increase the costs of collective action and risk of severe punishment for opposition to the state (Davenport, 2007a,b). Therefore, because they significantly increase the costs of mobilization, the most closed authoritarian regimes experience a lower likelihood of collective opposition to food taxes.

This account of the effects of agricultural policy, specifically food taxes affecting urban consumers, revolves around the interaction of economic grievances and political opportunity structures. I predict that urban unrest will result from situations where policy produces grievances, while regime structures promote grievance attribution and mobilization, leading me to test the following hypotheses in Chapter 4:

$H_{2.1}$, *Urban Collective Action:* Policies that increase the consumer price of food will be associated with greater levels of urban unrest, holding all else equal.

$H_{2.2}$, *Urban Collective Action:* The effects of food taxes on urban unrest will be greatest among undemocratic regimes with relatively permissive opportunity structures, holding all else equal.

Rural Collective Action

Autocracies are less developed than democracies and have larger agricultural sectors, making rural areas economically and politically salient for these regimes. However, rural collective action under authoritarianism is difficult. Farmers do not find it as easy as urban food consumers and elites to mobilize and threaten authoritarian governments. Therefore, their interests are not as heavily weighted in the agricultural policy-making process, on average. Nonetheless, when the rural sector is characterized by a landed elite that can act collectively to threaten the regime, policy is more likely to follow the interests of farmers and increase agricultural produce prices. Addressing the threat of the rural sector in this way significantly reduces the likelihood of regime instability.

The importance of the rural sector under authoritarian governments, and its role in the twin processes of development and democratization, have been central themes in the political science literature on authoritarianism and regime change. Farmers have been portrayed, variously, as reactionary landed elites, independent businessmen or smallholders vigorously resisting the predation of the state, and peasant revolutionaries against capitalist imperialism. Two major themes emerge from this voluminous literature that form the centerpiece of my account of rural collective action and agricultural policy under authoritarianism. First, the structure of land ownership is critical not only for the composition of rural interests, but also for their mobilization. An agricultural sector characterized by large numbers of smallholders is prone to peasant unrest and, rarely, revolution, but is not able to make its policy preferences heard under an authoritarian regime. An unequal distribution of land, on the other hand, implies a small landed elite that can organize and threaten an autocratic government. Second, the economic conditions of the rural sector and the potential threat that it poses are dependent on international market conditions and policies imposed by the state. Violent swings in commodity prices, government market interventions, and encroaching capitalist imperialism, all phenomena that previous authors argue drive the politics of the rural sector, amount to varying configurations of the nexus between international market forces and government policy on which I focus in this study.

The structure of land ownership in the countryside has long been seen as an important determinant of the path that countries take to modernity. Large landowners have been posited to have an interest in continued authoritarian rule for a number of reasons. They occupy powerful political positions that would be jeopardized by democratizing reform;[31] they fear taxes or expropriation under democracy;[32] they rely on repression to secure cheap rural labor;[33] and they have no interest in the broad provision of public goods under a more egalitarian political regime (Galor, Moav, and Vollrath, 2009). Democratization is thus likely to be resisted by landowners (Ziblatt, 2008a, 2009). However, these existing accounts focus predominantly on the interests of landed elites and their aversion to democratic institutions, not their political power. They do not explore how landowners are able to organize and influence authoritarian governments. By contrast, explaining the ability of landed elites to act collectively and threaten autocratic rulers is a central element in my account of agricultural policymaking and authoritarian regime stability.

The rural sector on the mass level is typically depicted as relatively powerless against predation by an authoritarian state, and thus unlikely to have a say in agricultural policymaking. On the one hand, civil war and insurgency are rural phenomena, and almost all developing countries are at risk of some level of unrest in the countryside.[34] More dramatically, the explosive potential of the peasantry was vividly demonstrated by the crucial role it played in revolutionary France, China, Vietnam, and Angola, for example.[35] This threat of the rural sector could therefore be seen as giving it weight in agricultural policymaking under authoritarianism (Pierskalla, 2016). On the other hand, mass collective opposition to ruling elites has been found to be very difficult to achieve and sustain in the countryside. As Scott (1985, 27) famously argues, peasant insurgency and revolutions are rare: They are not reflective of "the normal context in which class conflict has historically occurred." In fact, rural populations find it very difficult to resist predatory states or powerful economic elites and to protest against unequal development or exploitation, let alone

---

[31] Gerschenkron (1943), Baland and Robinson (2012), and Thomson (2015).

[32] Boix (2003) and Acemoglu and Robinson (2006).

[33] Moore (1966), Rueschmeyer, Stephens, and Stephens (1992), Ansell and Samuels (2014), and Mares (2015).

[34] See, for example, Fearon and Laitin (2003), Kalyvas (2004), Albertus, Brambor, and Ceneviva (2016), and Thomson (2016).

[35] Moore (1966, 453–483), Paige (1975), and Skocpol (1979, 112–157).

mount a revolutionary uprising. Instead, the peasants who Scott studied in 1970s Malaysia engaged in everyday resistance such as foot-dragging, pilfering, or sabotage, which avoided direct confrontation with authority or elites.[36] Bates (1981) also argues that the rural sector is relatively powerless in the face of the authority of central government. The regimes of postcolonial Africa possessed the capacity to suppress open opposition to their rule through violence or repression of political organizations. For this reason, smallholders did not generally seek to organize against them or their policies, but instead resorted to alternative measures of resistance: shifting production patterns to avoid taxation or expropriation of their crops, moving into off-farm employment where possible, and trading on the black market or smuggling. Reviewing research on peasant revolutions in the wake of the Vietnam war, Skocpol (1982) similarly concluded that although the rural masses can be a crucial element of a successful revolution, peasants engage in autonomous collective action only when the state is fundamentally weakened by exogenous forces or the countryside is mobilized by urban revolutionary movements. More recently, Kalyvas (2004, 166) argued that bureaucrats and politicians in developing countries dismiss rural collective action and insurgencies as "mere criminal affairs solely intent on looting and homicidal destruction and completely devoid of politics." When collective opposition to the state does occur it does not effectively communicate the demands of the rural sector to an unresponsive authoritarian government. Echoing the findings of previous generations of scholars, contemporary research on the link between climate change and civil conflict has found that rural populations find it very difficult to mobilize in violent insurgencies, even in the face of drought and significant deprivation, and when mobilization occurs it tends to result in communal conflict rather than challenges to the state.[37]

I agree that obstacles to collective action hinder mass opposition to authoritarian governments in the rural sector. Smallholders or landless peasants can only very rarely threaten the stability of a regime in the face of discriminatory agricultural policies. By contrast, structural factors facilitating collective action provide landed elites with a stable source of power with which to threaten and influence authoritarian regimes.[38]

---

[36] I explore the role of rural Malay elites in agricultural policymaking in Chapter 7. See also Shamsul (1986).

[37] See, for example, Fjelde and von Uexkuell (2012) and von Uexkuell et al. (2016).

[38] The influence of agricultural elites runs through lobbying and the threat of intra-elite instability. Landowners only rarely resort to protest or other forms of contentious collective action. When they do so, it is due to weakness and a failure to influence policy through lobbying. See Fairfield (2011).

Where landowners pose a greater threat to the stability of these governments, policy is more likely to increase returns to agriculture in order
to meet their demands and mitigate the likelihood of regime instability.
The structure of landholding in the countryside influences the ability of
rural interests to threaten authoritarian regimes for several reasons. First,
due to the logic of collective action (Olson, 1965). As the concentration
of landholdings increases, a smaller number of farmers holds a greater
proportion of total productive resources in the sector. This smaller group
of well-endowed producers finds it easier to organize politically to lobby
government for policies that increase returns to farming. Furthermore,
concentration of land ownership facilitates collective action by farmers
because inequality in asset endowments affects the distribution of the ex-
post benefits from favorable policies. Larger landowners stand to make
greater profits from higher produce prices than owners of smaller farms.
For this reason, they are more likely to contribute to the mobilization
effort, rather than make no contribution and free-ride (Baland and Platteau, 1997, 2007). The ability to organize collectively makes it likely that
agricultural elites will play a pivotal role within authoritarian regimes
and have a large influence on agricultural policymaking, whether alone
or in coalition with other interest groups. Second, because of the indirect
threat that a small group of well-organized farmers can pose to political
stability by withholding production. Only a cohesive group of agricultural
producers can overcome incentives to free-ride and refuse to deliver food
to market. However, when they can this is a formidable threat to wield
when demanding agricultural policies that deliver greater profits to the
rural sector (Herbst, 1988; Fairfield, 2015). Finally, because of the local
political power of landed elites and the dependence of central government
on these elites for maintaining political stability. Large landowners have
traditionally held privileged positions in local political and religious organizations. They often possess repressive resources to enforce contracts and
prevent land invasions and can use their position to control the political activities of their tenants and workers.[39] For these reasons, national
governments have incentives to use agricultural policy to buy off rural
elites, enlist them in maintaining political order in the countryside and
prevent regime instability. In Chapter 3, I therefore test the hypothesis that
landholding inequality is correlated with greater support to agriculture
under authoritarianism:

---

[39] See, for example, Scott (1976), Anderson (2000), Wood (2003), Baland and Robinson
(2012), Thomson (2015, 2016), and Albertus, Brambor, and Ceneviva (2016).

$H_{1.4}$, *Rural Interests:* Landholding inequality increases the capacity of rural interests to organize and threaten authoritarian governments. It is correlated with higher levels of support to agriculture under authoritarian regimes versus democracies, holding all else equal.

Because concentrations of landholdings increase the ability of landed elites to mobilize in opposition to a regime, they reduce the costs to such mobilization and therefore the likelihood of a challenge to an established regime by rural interests. The ability of landed interests to act collectively to threaten authoritarian governments is the first empirical hypothesis I test in Chapter 5,

$H_{3.1}$, *Rural Collective Action:* Landholding inequality will be associated with an increased probability of authoritarian regime failure, holding all else equal.

Landed elites have the *ability* to threaten authoritarian governments, but when is it in their *interest?* In my account, regime instability results from the intersection of both. The ability of landowners to threaten authoritarian regimes is due to the concentration of land ownership, but the interests of landed elites over regime type depend on economic policy. Landowners can act collectively to be threatening to, and influential over, authoritarian governments in a way not possible for rural masses. They use their influence not only to resist democratizing reform, as explored in previous research, but also to steer state intervention in the agricultural sector and control the effects of international market forces on their economic and political fortunes. This ability to organize and effect a favorable agricultural policy is a crucial but recently overlooked element of landed elites' preference for authoritarian government over democracy, which needs to be reinserted at the center of our understanding of the link between landholding inequality, development, and democratization. Contemporary theories, which highlight landed elites' fear of land reform and expropriation under democracy, are challenged by the finding that both are rare under democratic regimes, and in fact more likely under autocracy (Albertus, 2015a). Similarly, landed elites are not subject to significantly greater taxation for social spending under democracy than authoritarianism (Ansell and Samuels, 2014, 141–170) and can avoid such tax burdens using modern financial instruments (Freeman and Quinn, 2012). Landowners' much-referenced reliance on repression to secure labor inputs is dramatically diminished by mechanization in agriculture (Eberhardt and Vollrath, 2017) and is thus unlikely to completely explain their preference for authoritarian government, especially in the contemporary era (Albertus, 2017). In short, our fundamental assumptions about the reasons for landed elites' opposition to democratic reform rest on shaky foundations or hold only under specific historical circumstances.

Government market interventions and rent-seeking in the agricultural sector, on the other hand, have large and enduring effects on the welfare of landed elites. They do so because farmers produce for volatile international commodity markets. Government policy determines their incomes by steering the transmission of international market prices to the rural sector. These policies have, however, been largely overlooked in contemporary theories of authoritarian politics.[40] This is remarkable, because canonical economic theories of development and democratization highlight not only the power of landed elites but also their ability to influence government policy as determinants of regime outcomes. In particular, aristocratic German landlords were able to secure protection from sinking international grain prices in order to perpetuate their economic and political position before the first World War.[41] Relatedly, work on the political economy of development in the postcolonial era argued that imperialism subjected peasants around the world to violent dislocations as it forced them to adapt to production for export to international markets (Scott, 1976; Skocpol, 1982). In the postindependence third world, colonial-era institutions that gave governments control over domestic agricultural markets and international trade had decisive effects in determining the welfare of farmers (Bates, 1981, 1983). Whether they were used to tax the agricultural sector, as in the canonical urban-biased cases (Lipton, 1975; Bezemer and Headey, 2008); to support farmers, as in the East Asian developmental states (Anderson and Hayami, 1986); or to stabilize domestic prices, as in Southeast Asia (Timmer, 1989, 1993), agricultural market distortions had large, ubiquitous effects on farmers' incomes and welfare.

Referring to my conception of authoritarian regime stability earlier, I argue that flows of rents generated by agricultural policies have significant effects on the likelihood of the collapse of a regime. Agricultural

---

[40] As an exception, Ansell and Samuels (2014, 12) note that "High land inequality signifies that a relatively small and cohesive groups controls agricultural policy ... low land inequality signifies ... the relatively weaker position of large land owners vis-à-vis control over agricultural policy." However, a systematic study of these policies and regime type is beyond the scope of their study and remains unexplored, until now.

[41] See, for example, the classic accounts of Gerschenkron (1943), Moore (1966), and Gourevitch (1978).

rents, which are most easily captured by the state, do not necessarily accrue to the rural sector. They are in fact more commonly extracted at the expense of farmers' incomes and distributed to the leadership, its allies, or bureaucratic elites. This can help the regime to maintain elite cohesion through the distribution of patronage. However, it simultaneously raises the stakes of political conflict as access to rent streams are an attractive target for challengers. In particular, such rent-seeking in the agricultural sector encourages challenges from rural interests whose profits are squeezed by policies that direct resources toward the state. For this reason, in Chapter 5 I test the hypothesis that the volume of rents directed toward the state is positively associated with regime instability:

> $H_{3.2}$, *State Rent-Seeking:* Policies that provide greater state access to agricultural rents will be associated with a greater risk of regime collapse, holding all else equal.

When rents created by authoritarian market interventions are not captured by the state but instead distributed to the rural sector through higher prices, they will have different effects on regime stability. Landed elites that have the ability to threaten the regime are much less likely to attempt to mount a challenge in favor of an alternative if agricultural policy follows their interests and distributes rents to the rural sector. Therefore, in Chapter 5 I test the hypothesis that landholding inequality and rents have an interactive effect on regime stability:

> $H_{3.3}$, *Rural Collective Action:* Policies that increase returns to agriculture will be associated with a lower likelihood of authoritarian regime collapse when landholding inequality is high, holding all else equal.

2.5 POLICY UNDER DEMOCRACY: POLITICAL SUPPORT AND POLITICAL STABILITY

In the previous section, I laid out a theory of authoritarian agricultural policy that is based on the capacity of the rural and urban sectors to act collectively to threaten an autocratic government. This approach has important precedents in canonical accounts of development and democratization, but is a novel addition to contemporary theories of economic policymaking under authoritarianism. My explanation of agricultural policy outcomes under democracy, on the other hand, builds on a large, established literature on the political economy of regulation, redistribution, and trade policy. It is also closely related to a body of more recent studies of agricultural policy. Although I derive and test a novel hypothesis on the link between income inequality and agricultural policy, I make my main theoretical contribution by contrasting policymaking under democracy with analogous processes under authoritarian regimes. I begin this section by outlining how development accounts for the main dynamics of agricultural policymaking under democracy. I then explain why urbanization and landholding inequality, which I predict to have significant effects on policy under autocracy, do not determine outcomes under democratic governments. I go on to argue that income inequality leads to pressure for redistribution to the median voter and decreases in support for farmers under democratic governments. Finally, I argue that democracies are inherently more stable than authoritarian regimes, and agricultural policy does not have a significant effect on urban unrest in these polities.

Like authoritarian regimes, elected governments do not have any natural preferences in agricultural policy and intervene in markets for farm produce with an eye to remaining in power. However, unlike authoritarian regimes, democratically elected governments do not seek to maximize the rents they can extract from the sector, and they are not primarily responsive to the threat of collective opposition when making policy. Instead, they adopt a stance toward agriculture while seeking to maximize their political support at the polls. They therefore respond to electoral incentives, although this does not necessarily mean that policy follows the interests of the majority of the population, because democratic governments' support is comprised of both contributions by special interests and votes at the next election.[42] The weight put on special interests versus votes by governments, and the position of the rural and urban sectors in this trade-off, explain agricultural policy outcomes under democracy.

The most important dynamic in agricultural policymaking under democracy is driven by the structural shift of the rural sector from comprising the majority of the population at low levels of development to comprising a small special-interest group at high levels of development. This structural transformation is necessarily accompanied by a shift of the urban sector from a small special-interest group at low levels of development to the majority of the population at high levels of development. These structural changes associated with economic growth have important consequences for agricultural policymaking, leading

---

[42] See, for example, the canonical models of Stigler (1971), Peltzman (1976), and Grossman and Helpman (1994).

democratic governments to support the rural sector more as their economies develop. Relatively little weight is placed on the interests of the urban sector under poorer democratic regimes, compared to under authoritarian governments. The costs of an urban-biased policy are high in developing democracies, because elected governments must appeal to a broad constituency of rural voters. They therefore support the rural sector more than autocracies, on average.[43] However, farmers' demands for intervention in the agricultural sector become still more pressing in the course of development, as incomes in the rural sector decline compared to those in the urban sector. The cost of supporting rural areas also declines as the size of the agricultural sector shrinks to make up only a small share total output, and agricultural producers go from being a broad constituency to the small special-interest group that they make up in industrial societies. These trends, which I do not emphasize here but control for in my empirical analyses, lead democratic governments to significantly increase their support for agriculture as economic output increases.[44]

Institutional features of democracy that lead politicians to favor narrow versus broader constituencies also shape the trade-off between rural and urban interests in agricultural policymaking. Although my main interest in this book is in policy differences across regime type, and I do not explore more fine-grained institutional differences among democratic states, empirical evidence from advanced industrial democracies supports this proposition. Park and Jensen (2007), for example, find that majoritarian electoral systems are associated with significantly greater levels of support to agriculture than proportional electoral systems, and Thies and Porche (2007) find that federal states and more fragmented party systems are correlated with support for the rural sector. More recently, and for a larger sample of countries, Weinberg (2012) found that proportional electoral systems are associated with significantly greater consumer food taxes than majoritarian systems. As important as these institutional differences *among* democratic regimes are, it appears unlikely that they can significantly inform my analysis of policy *across* regime type. The shape of political institutions and their effects on policymaking under authoritarianism are likely to differ systematically from those under

---

[43] See, for example, Varshney (1995), Olper and Raimondi (2011, 2013), Bates and Block (2013), and Shifa (2013).

[44] This the result of a large literature in applied economics. See Anderson and Hayami (1986), De Gorter and Swinnen (2002), and Swinnen (2010b).

democracy, making institutional distinctions of little use for analyzing policy across democracy and dictatorship.

Because they are responsive to the interests of voters, developing democracies support agriculture more than dictatorships, and because they respond to demanding special-interest groups, richer democracies are still more generous to the rural sector. We see, therefore, that differences in agricultural policy are not determined only by institutions but there is also variation among democracies, which is associated with broader structures such as levels of development. However, the structures that affect electoral incentives, and matter for agricultural policymaking under democracy, are different from those that affect the ability of the rural and urban sectors to oppose an authoritarian government and matter for policymaking under autocracy.

Unlike under dictatorship, higher levels of urbanization do not translate into greater influence for the urban sector and lower levels of support to agriculture under democracy. Under dictatorship, urbanization implies increased capacity of urban interests to mobilize and threaten the government. Under democracy, the political salience of contentious collective action is greatly reduced, as governments maximize contributions from special interests and votes at elections, responding less to both the danger of protests and the demands of well-connected elites. The geographic concentration of economic activity and population in cities also does not increase the urban sector's influence through electoral mechanisms. Although industries that are concentrated in specific regions are more adept at lobbying for favorable policies from democratic governments, the barriers to collective action among urban food consumers are far greater than those among producers within the same sector (Busch and Reinhardt, 2005). Urban voters are also not more likely to turn out to vote in developing democracies,[45] and where urban residents do vote, electoral systems tend to give them less weight than rural voters due to malapportionment.[46] These institutional factors make it unlikely that democratic governments will weigh urban interests more heavily as the population is concentrated in cities. Similarly, the concentration of landholdings has less effect on agricultural policymaking under democratic governments than under autocracy. Landholding inequality should be expected to lead to a more cohesive rural sector under democracy, as under authoritarianism, and to foster its ability to lobby for favorable policy. However, democratic

[45] Foros, Power, and Garand (2004) and Kostadinova and Power (2007).
[46] See Samuels and Snyder (2001), Snyder and Samuels (2004), and Boone and Wahman (2015).

governments are unlikely to depend heavily on landed elites' local political power and repressive capacity to maintain regime stability, making land inequality less likely to be a factor in policymaking. In addition, because they are more responsive to broader constituencies, democratic governments are more likely to come under pressure to use agricultural policy to provide lower food prices to poor voters (Meltzer and Richard, 1981). For this reason, one study of developed democracies found that they tax agriculture at higher rates when landholding inequality is high (Olper, 2007).

I predict that pressure for redistribution to poor voters will drive democratic governments to intervene in agricultural markets to lower food prices as income inequality increases. Following the familiar logic of the Meltzer and Richard (1981) model, and the prominent theory of redistribution and regime type by Boix (2003) and Acemoglu and Robinson (2006), democratic governments seek to secure the support of the median voter. As inequality increases mean income relative to that of the pivotal voter, these governments have an incentive to redistribute from those with relatively high incomes to those who are relatively poor. In agricultural policy, because support for farmers implies higher prices for consumers, income inequality will be associated with greater demands by the median voter for lower levels of agricultural support and cheap food. Democratic governments will be more responsive to these demands than authoritarian regimes because they need to appeal to the pivotal voter to win elections. For this reason, in Chapter 3 I test the hypothesis that greater levels of income inequality lead to lower levels of support to agriculture under democracies:

$H_{1.3}$, *Urban Interests:* Income inequality drives pressure for democratic governments to use food policy to redistribute income to poorer urban voters. It is correlated with higher levels of support to agriculture under authoritarian regimes versus democracies, holding all else equal.

Development and income inequality have significant effects on agricultural policy outcomes under democratic governments. However, unlike under authoritarian regimes, agricultural policy does not significantly affect political stability under democracy. In democracies, political conflict is channeled through regular electoral contests. Citizens can therefore make their preferences in agricultural policy heard through the ballot box, rather than through collective threats, as under an authoritarian regime. Food consumers, for example, are less likely to mobilize in protests or political unrest when confronted with a government tax on staples that runs against their interests. In addition, the repeated nature of competition under democracy gives actors, most importantly political parties and voters, incentives to comply with the democratic system and compete in the next election rather than seek to subvert it, even if they lose in a given electoral cycle. Democracies are therefore generally more stable than authoritarian regimes, and conflict over agricultural policy is likely to run through electoral mechanisms even when one party loses control at a single election.[47] This is particularly true at higher levels of development, when distributional conflicts between the winners and losers of elections become less pronounced, promoting democratic stability.[48] The proportion of food in total consumer expenditure declines sharply with increasing incomes, for example, making the conflict between the rural and urban sectors less acute in more developed polities. Because they give citizens an alternative to collective mobilization in opposition to policy, and because they are inherently more stable than authoritarian regimes, I anticipate finding no relationship between consumer food taxes and urban unrest in Chapter 4:

$H_{2.2}$, *Urban Collective Action:* Food taxes will have no effect on urban unrest under democracy, holding all else equal.

2.6 CONCLUSION

In this chapter I argued that government interventions in agricultural markets follow a distinct political–economic logic. Policies that increase prices for farm produce are in the interest of the rural sector but impose costs on urban constituencies; policies that lower the cost of agricultural commodities are in the interest of the urban sector but lower the incomes of rural constituencies. Governments making the trade-off between the competing interests of the rural and urban sectors do so under very different rules depending on whether they are democratically elected or not. Authoritarian governments respond to the threat of collective action by each sector, setting policy closer to the ideal point of the more powerful constituency to prevent regime instability. When policy imposes a tax on food consumers, these governments risk urban unrest; when it lowers agricultural commodity prices in the presence of a powerful landed elite,

---

[47] See, most notably, Przeworski (1991), Weingast (1997), Gates et al. (2006), and Fearon (2011).

[48] Przeworski (1991) and Przeworski et al. (2000).

authoritarian regimes run the risk of collapse. Democratic governments, on the other hand, respond to electoral incentives when making policy, most notably demands among poorer voters for lower food prices in the face of economic inequality. Because of their inherent stability and higher levels of development, democracies do not risk political instability by taking ill-considered stances in agricultural policy.

The logic of agricultural policy and authoritarian politics put forward in this chapter generates a series of hypotheses that I put to the test in the rest of the book. In Chapter 3, I examine cross-national variation in agricultural policy outcomes. I show, first, that democracies support agriculture more than dictatorships, on average. However, I also show that there is significant variation in agricultural policy across regime type, which correlates with that in socioeconomic structures facilitating collective action among farmers and urban interests. In Chapter 4, I examine the frequency of political unrest events in cities across the developing world. I find that food consumers pose a threat in the form of higher rates of urban unrest when confronted with policies that increase the price of food. This threat is conditional on regime type, with the risk of urban collective action highest under less-repressive authoritarian regimes. Democracies and the most repressive autocracies are relatively immune to the risk of unrest in response to food taxes. In Chapter 5, I explore the effects of landholding inequality and agricultural rents on authoritarian regime durability cross-nationally. I show that where landholding inequality is high, landed elites pose a threat to regime stability. These regimes maximize their chances of survival by intervening in agricultural markets to distribute rents to the rural sector when landholding inequality is high. Finally, in Chapters 6 and 7 I use case studies of Germany in the 1870s and 1880s, and Malaysia in the 1960s and 1970s, to illustrate in more detail how authoritarian governments respond to shifting threats of rural and urban interests through agricultural policy, and how these policies have effects on political stability.

3

Political Regime Type and Agricultural Policy Outcomes

In Chapter 2, I laid out a theory of agricultural policy under democracy and authoritarianism. I argued that policy outcomes are the result of a trade-off between rural and urban interests, which is made under different rules in democracies versus dictatorships. Authoritarian governments respond through economic policy to the ability of a sector to organize and threaten the regime through collective action such as an urban uprising or the formation of a hostile elite coalition, while democratic governments seek to maximize the support of voters at the ballot box. These different institutional incentive structures lead to the first significant difference in policymaking, which I predict to occur across regime type. Because rural interests struggle to mobilize and threaten undemocratic regimes, authoritarian governments tend to support agriculture less than democracies, on average. This is one important component of the widely observed and long-established trend toward urban bias in public policy in developing countries.

However, aside from these institutional factors, I argue that variation in broader socioeconomic structures leads to a second set of differences in policy outcomes. These structures affect the ability of the rural and urban sectors to influence the policymaking process, depending on the institutional context. First, urbanization strengthens urban interests under authoritarianism, but electoral rules tend to tilt the playing field against urban populations under democracy. I therefore predict that greater levels of urbanization will be associated with lower levels of support to agriculture under dictatorships vis-à-vis democracies, on average. Second, income inequality drives pressure for democratic governments to lower food prices as a form of economic redistribution to poorer voters. I therefore predict that greater levels of inequality will be associated with significantly lower levels of support to agriculture under democracies versus dictatorships, on the whole. Finally, landholding inequality is an indicator of the power of rural interests to organize and threaten authoritarian governments. I predict that it will be associated with greater levels of support to agriculture in dictatorships versus democracies, on average. This second set of policy differences is an important amendment to established findings on urban bias because it specifies the conditions under which we can expect the rural sector to be taxed, and the urban sector to be subsidized, under different types of political system. I argue that urban bias is a product of the *interaction* of regime type with socioeconomic structures that weaken the rural sector and strengthen urban interests.

The purpose of this chapter is to put these arguments to the test. I do so by using cross-national data on agricultural market distortions, regime type, and the structures outlined earlier, which are indicators of the strength of rural and urban interests. Because the analysis in this chapter is quantitative, it involves some discussion of modeling choices and results that is technical in nature. However, in order to make the results as accessible and easy to interpret as possible, I have gone to lengths to present my key findings graphically. The most important model results on regime type, and levels of agricultural support are presented in Figures 3.3 and 3.4, urbanization in Figure 3.5, inequality in Figure 3.6, and landholding inequality in Figure 3.7. Readers who are interested in the empirical findings, but less interested in the details of model specification, can proceed directly to these plots to gain an overview of the chapter's contribution.

I proceed as follows. In a preliminary step, I review existing literature on the determinants of agricultural policy and on economic policymaking under authoritarian regimes. I show that although scholars have explored differences between democracies and dictatorships in various policy areas, previous findings do not account for policy variation among dictatorships as I do here. I then go on to present several sets of important empirical results that confirm the theoretical predictions on the sociopolitical determinants of agricultural policy outlined earlier. First, I use different indicators of regime type to show that democracies support agriculture more than authoritarian regimes, on average. Political systems that are the least open and allow for the least competition for the highest offices are associated with policies that support rural interests the least. I look at different world regions separately and show that the association between democracy and agricultural support is strongest in Africa and holds more weakly in Asia and Latin America. Importantly, I find that influential distinctions between party, military, and personalist dictatorships are not associated with significant differences in agricultural policy outcomes. Second, I look at the effects of urbanization, inequality, and unequal distributions of landholdings on agricultural support. I find that urbanization is associated with less support for agriculture under dictatorship, particularly in Asia. Inequality is associated with declining support for agriculture in democracies, particularly in Latin America and high-income countries, but not in Africa. Landholding inequality is correlated with greater support for agriculture under dictatorship, particularly in Latin America and Asia.

3.1 PREVIOUS LITERATURE: AGRICULTURAL AND ECONOMIC POLICYMAKING UNDER DEMOCRACY AND AUTHORITARIANISM

This chapter addresses an important gap in existing research on the political economy of agricultural policy and the political economy of authoritarian regimes. Although previous studies have shown that governments tend to support farmers more as their economies develop and as they become more democratic, very little research has examined variation in the agricultural policy environment among authoritarian regimes. Similarly, although a number of political economists are interested in a range of differences across regime type, from education policy through child mortality and calorie intake, relatively little work explores variation in economic policy among authoritarian regimes.

Since the 1980s, successive national and cross-national studies have measured the effects of the various policies that governments put in place to distort domestic agricultural markets, which range from trade measures such as export tariffs through subsidies for inputs like seed, water and fertilizer to food price ceilings and transfer payments for farmers and consumers. These studies have consistently revealed the ironic trend for government support for farmers to increase as countries develop and the importance of agriculture in their economies declines.[1] This regularity has

---

[1] The seminal works are Anderson and Hayami (1986) and Krueger (1992). For a recent review, see Swinnen (2010b). Cross-national empirical estimates of agricultural price distortions were published by Krueger, Schiff, and Valdes (1988) and, more recently, Anderson (2009).

been explained by the incentives and abilities of farmers and consumers to organize politically and influence the government. Under the "development pattern," countries shift from taxation to support of agricultural producers as average income increases. When an economy grows, agriculture makes up a declining share of output compared to industry, and food consumption decreases as a share of consumers' incomes. Thus opposition to supporting the agricultural sector declines because of its relatively small size and the low real cost to consumers of increasing food prices. Under the "anti-comparative advantage pattern," support increases when farm incomes fall relative to those in the rest of the economy. Returns to the sector decline while the number of farmers also decreases, increasing both farmers' demand for higher prices and their ability, as a smaller group, to lobby government. The central story in economists' explanations of agricultural policy outcomes is therefore one in which development leads to increasing support for farmers, through two related but distinct mechanisms. There is, however, also a story relating to political institutions, and because of data constraints many scholars first found differences in agricultural policy outcomes among the developed democracies. Democratic electoral systems that encourage politicians to appeal to narrow interest groups rather than the broader electorate have been associated with higher levels of producer support in a number of studies.[2]

Arguments relating political institutions to agricultural policy outcomes become more compelling when we consider a broader range of countries and political regimes. States lacking democratic political institutions have been found to be less responsive to the interests of rural agricultural producers and have lower levels of producer support and lower consumer food prices than democracies, on average. Authoritarian governments follow urban-biased agricultural policies, as they discriminate against the rural population in order to cheapen food and nonfarm inputs, promote industrialization, and enrich urban and commercial interests.[3] Wallace (2013, 636) argues that urban-biased policies are "overdetermined and endemic in poor nondemocracies" as authoritarian governments implement policies that decrease food prices to prevent urban unrest in the short term. Democratic governments, holding all else equal, are significantly less likely to discriminate against the agricultural sector because they need the support of rural voters in order to win elections. Olper and Raimondi (2011), for example, show

---

[2] See Park and Jensen (2007), Thies and Porche (2007), Olper and Raimondi (2011, 2013), and Weinberg (2012).

[3] See Lipton (1975, 1977) and Bates (1981, 1983).

that democratic transitions are associated with increases in support for farmers. Similarly, Bates and Block (2013) find that improvements in executive accountability in Africa since the 1960s have been associated with increased price supports in the region.

This relatively large body of literature on policy differences *between* democracies and dictatorships does not account for significant differences in agricultural policymaking and policy outcomes *among* dictatorships. Although Bates (1981, 87–95) identifies several groups that are able to extract relatively favorable policies from authoritarian governments – such as the rice industry in Ghana and the large-scale farmers of Kenya – these are rare exceptions to the general rule of urban-biased policies under authoritarianism outlined earlier. Little work has attempted a systematic theory that seeks to explain agricultural policy variation under authoritarian regimes and lay out the conditions under which policy outcomes do and do not differ from democracy to dictatorship.

This gap in the literature is surprising when one considers the importance of the agricultural sector in the average economy ruled by authoritarian regimes and the significant role played by these countries in global agricultural trade. It is, however, not surprising when one considers the relative paucity of scholarship examining variation in economic policy among authoritarian governments. Research has found that nondemocracies spend less on primary education and health than democracies and are less effective in translating economic growth into positive social outcomes such as increased caloric intake and lower child mortality rates.[4] However, we know far less about differences in economic policy outcomes among nondemocracies, and according to one prominent account, dictatorships are "too much of a mixed bag" to attempt any general theory of their policies (Chang et al., 2011, 50). Theories of authoritarian rule and democratization generate only general predictions on the balance between repressive and redistributive policies and are not applicable to conflicts within a single sector like agriculture.[5]

In this chapter, I contribute to a growing literature that theorizes and empirically assesses the determinants of economic policy under authoritarian regimes. Previous research here has focused on the size of the "selectorate" (Bueno de Mesquita et al., 2003) rather than its composition as an explanation of policy variation. Along these lines, and making assumptions about the openness of different types of authoritarian regimes, Stein-

---

[4] Ansell (2008), Blaydes and Kayser (2011), Gerring, Thacker, and Alfaro (2012), and Ross (2006).
[5] Acemoglu and Robinson (2006, 287–320) and Wintrobe (1990, 1998).

berg and Malhotra (2014) find that regimes with smaller selectorates are more responsive to selective interests and more likely to follow a fixed exchange rate. Relatedly, Hankla and Kuthy (2013) find that more institutionalized regimes follow open trade policies because they are less likely to favor selective interests and more likely to favor policies promoting long-term growth, and Wright (2008) argues that binding legislatures constrain authoritarian regimes' confiscatory behavior and foster economic growth.

Here, I push this research agenda forward in two ways. First, I extend it to explain agricultural market distortions, a policy area of great importance for development and international trade. Second, I do not base my analysis on selectorate theory and the institutional characteristics of authoritarian regimes. Rather than examining the *size* of the selectorate, my approach looks to socioeconomic factors to derive testable hypotheses on the relative political and economic *power* of competing groups – producers and consumers – within the agricultural sector. I predict that authoritarian governments respond to the interests of groups who can plausibly engage in collective action to threaten their position in power. My power-based approach to economic policymaking under authoritarianism is therefore an important theoretical addition to existing institutional approaches.

3.2 HYPOTHESES, MODEL, AND DATA

My account of agricultural policy formulation under democracy and dictatorship laid out in Chapter 2 generates several hypotheses on the relationship between regime type, socioeconomic structures, and policy outcomes:

$H_{1.1}$, *Regime Type:* Democratic regimes are more responsive to rural interests than authoritarian governments and are associated with greater levels of support to agriculture, holding all else equal;

$H_{1.2}$, *Urban Interests:* Urbanization increases the capacity of urban interests to mobilize and threaten authoritarian governments. It is correlated with lower levels of support to agriculture under authoritarian regimes versus democracies, holding all else equal;

$H_{1.3}$, *Urban Interests:* Income inequality drives pressure for democratic governments to use food policy to redistribute income to poorer voters. It is correlated with higher levels of support to agriculture under authoritarian regimes versus democracies, holding all else equal;

$H_{1.4}$, *Rural Interests:* Landholding inequality increases the capacity of rural interests to organize and threaten authoritarian governments. It is correlated with higher levels of support to agriculture under authoritarian regimes versus democracies, holding all else equal.

In the remainder of this chapter, I test these hypotheses using linear panel regressions of the form,

$$y_{i,t} = \beta_1 + \beta_2 D_{i,t} + \beta_3 P_{i,t} + \beta_4 D_{i,t} \times P_{i,t} + \beta_5 X_{i,t} + v_i + \varepsilon_{i,t} \quad (3.1)$$

where $y_{i,t}$ is a measure of agricultural support in a given country i and year t; $D_{i,t}$ is an indicator of political regime type in a given country-year; $P_{i,t}$ are country-year measures of political threats, that is, of urbanization, income inequality and landholding inequality; $X_{i,t}$ is vector of country-year control variables; v_i is a country fixed effect; and $\varepsilon_{i,t}$ is an error term that, in most models, I specify to be clustered by country. The key parameters in my models are β_2, which estimates the effect of regime type on policy outcomes; β_3, which estimates the effect of political threats on policy under democracy; and β_4, which estimates the difference between these variables' effects on policy under democracy and those under dictatorship.

The inclusion of fixed effects in these models controls for unobserved heterogeneity among countries, which could affect agricultural policy outcomes. In my models, it also implies that I am in effect only analyzing cases in which we observe variation on the regime type variable. This means that the choice to include fixed effects should be taken with some care.[6] Therefore, I first run a random-effects model including all of my relevant covariates and use a Hausman test to decide whether it is appropriate to use the fixed-effects models. Because this test rejects the null hypothesis that the random-effects model produces consistent coefficient estimates, I opt to include fixed effects in my main models. However, in the models run separately for each region, I do not use country fixed effects or clustered standard errors, as the number of observations in the models is very low, and there are relatively few cases where regime type varies over time. I also estimate my main models reported in Table 3.4 both with and without country fixed effects for the same reasons, and happily my main results are stable in both specifications.

Like all cross-national observational studies, the empirical analysis in this chapter only approaches the identification of a causal relationship between my measures of consumer and producer power and policy out-

---

[6] I am grateful to an anonymous reviewer for emphasizing the importance of this point in these analyses.

comes. Levels of democracy, landholding inequality, income inequality, or urbanization are not randomly assigned to a given country in a given year, as these socioeconomic factors are codetermined by long-term development processes. Analysis of subnational variation in agricultural policy could conceivably offer a better strategy for identification of the causes of policy changes. However, it would be relatively uninformative and lose external validity because the policies that have the greatest effect on farmer and consumer welfare and that are comparable across countries – such as export restrictions, input or consumption subsidies – are almost always implemented at the national level. For these reasons, I believe that my empirical strategy offers the best compromise between methodological rigor and results that correspond to meaningful policy outcomes. I also go to some lengths to address problems of endogeneity in my models. To mitigate possible measurement error, I use the newest data available on global agricultural market distortions. I collected a new dataset on landholding inequality that maximizes the coverage and consistency of my data and use different model specifications to address concerns about its quality. To mitigate concerns about omitted variable bias, I follow previous research and include a full set of variables to control for relevant confounding factors in my models, as well as the country fixed effects discussed earlier. Concerns about autoregression and autocorrelated errors have mitigated by testing for autocorrelation using a Hausman test and specifying fixed-effects panel regressions with standard errors clustered by country. Problems of simultaneity, or a causal loop between policy and structural measures of consumer and producer power, are also mitigated by the fixed-effects regressions that look only at changes in variables within countries across time, but also by the fact that my measures of each group's power are unlikely to be affected by agricultural policy outcomes except in the very long run.

Dependent Variable

The dependent variable in my models is agricultural policy data collected in an international World Bank research project on agricultural market distortions between 1955 and 2010.[7] Building on the results and methodology of previous studies such as those by Krueger, Schiff, and Valdes (1988), these data cover all large agricultural producing states over the period 1955 to 2010. However, the coverage of the data is not even across space and time. Developed democracies are conspicuously overrepresented due to their importance to global agricultural trade. The

---

[7] Anderson and Valenzuela (2008) and Anderson and Nelgen (2012).

former Soviet Union, socialist Eastern Europe, and the Middle East are notably underrepresented due to their lack of integration into world markets and low food exports. Only the larger countries in Africa and Latin America are included, while even the smallest developed countries are in the dataset. This said, the data are a very rich source of information on agricultural policy outcomes and great improvement over previous sources. They cover all regions, including countries that account for 92 percent of global population and a wide variety of political systems.

The agricultural market distortions data estimate the direct and indirect effects of domestic government policy on the price incentives faced by farmers and food consumers. These policies include tariffs and trade measures, producer and consumer price distorting measures, exchange rate policy, distortions to intermediate input prices, and post-farmgate costs such as those imposed by state marketing monopolies.[8] The variables in the dataset measure policy by relating domestic prices to world market prices, summarizing aggregate national policy for all products for each country-year in measures which are production- and consumption-weighted to capture the total effects of agricultural policy within a given economy.

The key dependent variable **Ag Support** is a country's *Nominal Rate of Assistance* (NRA) to total agriculture. A country's total NRA is the production-weighted percentage by which domestic producer prices are above (or below if negative) the border price of like products. It should be noted that increases in agricultural support, as analyzed in my models, generally imply a corresponding increase in consumer prices. Governments almost invariably pass the benefits of support to farmers on to consumers in the form of consumer taxes, and the variables in the dataset measuring agricultural support and consumer taxes are correlated at 0.94. However, for completeness I also estimate two further models taking the Consumer Tax Equivalent (CTE or **Cons Tax**) and Relative Rate of Assistance (RRA or **Relative Ag Supp**) to agriculture as dependent variables. The results of these models are reported as Models 2.4 and 2.5 in Table 3.4 and are broadly in line with Models 2.1–2.3, which take the NRA as the dependent variable.

The NRA can logically vary between negative one (prices are reduced to zero) and any positive value (by which percentage prices are increased). For example, if a country's NRA value in a given year is 0.5, government

---

[8] See Chapter 2 for a more detailed description of what agricultural policy means in the context of this study.

policy increases producer prices by 50 percent compared to world market prices. If a country's NRA value in the same year is −0.5, it decreases producer prices by 50 percent. The extent of government intervention in the agricultural sector varies widely across and within regions. Figure 3.1 illustrates this variation on the producer side by showing the average absolute RRA from 1990 to 1999 for all countries included in the World Bank dataset. Darker shades of gray indicate greater distortions to prices in the agricultural sector, compared to those in the non-agricultural sector. Among developed countries, East Asian governments such as those in South Korea, Japan, and Taiwan intervene very heavily in their agricultural sectors to increase prices for producers, as do Scandinavian governments, Switzerland, and members of the European Union under the Common Agricultural Policy. Australia, New Zealand, South Africa, Canada (the "Cairns Group" of free-trading agricultural exporters at the WTO), and the United States have relatively low levels of distortions to agricultural prices. Governments in developing regions such as South Asia and Africa tend to decrease farmers' produce prices. In a naive comparison, democracies also subsidize farmers more than authoritarian regimes; in the 1990s the average democracy increased farm produce prices slightly compared to world market prices, while the average autocracy or anocracy decreased them by around 20 percent. Summary statistics of all variables used in my analysis are presented in Table 3.2.

FIGURE 3.1 Global Distortions to Agricultural Incentives, 1990 to 1999

Darker shades of gray indicate greater absolute deviations from world market prices. Data is the absolute value of the total NRA.
Source: Anderson and Valenzuela (2008) and Anderson and Nelgen (2012) data matched by the author to GIS shapefile.

Independent Variables

To test my hypotheses on the policy differences between democracies and authoritarian regimes, I use three regime type indicators. These are derived from the Polity IV dataset by Marshall and Cole (2011). This is because, more than any other dataset, Polity matches my definition of regime type: whether political systems provide citizens the opportunity to formulate and signal their preferences to government through elections, and have these preferences weighed equally in policy. The Polity score measures freedoms to formulate and express policy preferences that are binding on the government, most importantly by capturing the competitiveness and openness of recruitment of the executive, regulation of political participation, and constraints on the executive. It therefore captures the ability of citizens to influence agricultural policy through the ballot box. Alongside purely procedural aspects of democracy that facilitate collective action for the rural population in particular, the Polity score measures the ability of opposition groups to organize and for individuals to access information critical of the regime, factors that are necessary for collective action by urban food consumers.

I operationalize regime type in three ways using the Polity dataset in this chapter. A country's Polity score can range from −10, a fully institutionalized autocracy, to 10, a fully institutionalized democracy. It therefore contains a lot of information on variation in democratic contestation and participation. In most of my analyses, I use a dummy variable, **Dict**, which indicates a country's Polity score is below 6, and it is not a democracy. Any definition of regime type necessitates establishing a point at which political systems are no longer considered democratic. The threshold for defining a regime as a nondemocracy in this coding captures where political institutions lose full democratic coherence, for example where rules for the selection of leaders are not clearly centered on elections or constraints on executive authority are limited. I choose to create an indicator of regime type from the underlying continuous Polity variable rather than use a different, binary measure of regime type like that by Cheibub, Gandhi, and Vreeland (2010) because the Polity score contains information on civil liberties, which is excluded from these data.[9] In Table 3.1, I list all the autocracies and democracies included in my analysis according to this classification. The reader will note that due

---

[9] However, the main results in this chapter, from Table 3.4, are also robust to using the Cheibub, Gandhi, and Vreeland (2010) indicator of dictatorship instead of the binary measure created from the Polity data.

TABLE 3.1 *List of Autocracies and Democracies Included in Analysis,*
Chapter 3

Autocracy	Years	Autocracy	Years
Bangladesh	1980–1990	Burkina Faso	1974–1983
Cameroon	1970–1999	Chile	1963–1988
China	1981–1986	Ivory Coast	1966–1983, 1994–1997
Dominican Republic	1966–1977	Egypt	1965–1998, 2002
Ethiopia	1990	Ghana	1963–1987, 1993–1995
Indonesia	1970–1998	Kenya	1963–2001
Korea	1965–1986	Madagascar	1967–1988
Malaysia	1969–2001	Mexico	1979–1996
Mozambique	1990–1996, 2000	Pakistan	1977–1987
Philippines	1963–1985	Portugal	1970–1973
South Africa	1963–1968, 1970–1991	Senegal	1980–1999
Spain	1970–1974	Sudan	1972
Tanzania	1990–1999	Thailand	1970–1991
Togo	1970–1984	Turkey	1971–1972, 1980–1982
Uganda	1984–2001	Zambia	1965–1982, 1990
TOTAL	490		

Democracy	Years	Democracy	Years
Argentina	1984–1999	Australia	1972–2001
Austria	1970–2000	Bangladesh	1991–1992, 1995, 1997
Brazil	1990, 1992–1995	Canada	1965–2001
Chile	1964–1972, 1989–2000	Colombia	1965–2000
Czech Republic	1993–1995	Denmark	1966–1998
Dominican Republic	1978–1985	Finland	1965–2000
France	1977–2000	Germany	1971–2000
Ghana	1979–1980	Hungary	1992–2000
India	1965–2001	Indonesia	1999–2002
Ireland	1970–2000	Italy	1970–2000
Japan	1970–1993	Kenya	2002
Korea	1988–2001	Mexico	1997–2000
Netherlands	1970–2000	New Zealand	1971–1998
Pakistan	1973–1976, 1988–1991, 1996	Philippines	1987–1997
Poland	1992–2000	Portugal	1976–2000
South Africa	1994–2002	Senegal	2000–2002
Spain	1978–2002	Sweden	1970–2000
Thailand	1993–1994	Turkey	1963–1979, 1983–2000
UK	1970–2000	USA	1970–2001
Zambia	1994		
TOTAL	739		

to missing data, particularly on agricultural policy and land inequality, coverage of some countries is patchy. However, around 40 percent of observations are dictatorships in my analysis, meaning that although data coverage is a problem for these regimes, in the case of agricultural policy and the covariates I am interested in, I am still able to draw conclusions on differences in policy across regime type.

In some models, I also use a country's **Polity** score as a continuous indicator. Using the variable in this way utilizes all information on the ability of voters to constrain the government and influence policy, and also to mobilize collectively to oppose the government. Finally, in some models I use the threefold Polity categorization of regimes as **Autocracies**, with a Polity score of −6 or lower; **Anocracies**, with a Polity score between −5 and 5; and **Democracies**, with a Polity score of 6 and above. This coding captures the distinction between coherent democratic and authoritarian regimes and hybrid political systems, which include significant aspects of both democratic and autocratic authority. This distinction is widely used in theoretical (Diamond, 2002, 2015) and empirical (Gates et al., 2006) work on democratization, in which hybrid regimes have been associated with political instability and civil conflict but, in some cases, stubborn resistance to democratization. With respect to my theory, this threefold classification is particularly useful because it captures regimes where influence on policy runs primarily through electoral institutions (democracies), those where it runs through elections and contentious mobilization (anocracies), and those where diffuse interests can influence policy only through contentious mobilization, which is very costly (autocracies). In one further analysis, I examine the effects of institutional differences among authoritarian regimes on agricultural policy outcomes. To do so I use the typology of **Personalist, Party,** and **Military** dictatorships by Geddes, Wright, and Frantz (2014). None of these variables cleanly capture the ability of the rural and urban sectors to act collectively to influence agricultural policymaking as spelled out in my theory. However, I include this model to allay fears that such widely used institutional distinctions among authoritarian regimes could better account for variation in agricultural policy than the variables I focus on in my account.

To measure the power of urban interests to threaten an authoritarian regime, I use the variable **Urban**: the proportion of a country's population living in cities, data that is available annually for many countries from the World Development Indicators (World Bank, 2012b). This variable ranged from 6 percent in Burkina Faso in 1968 to 91 percent in Australia in 2001. The mean level of urbanization in an authoritarian regime was 35 percent in my dataset, while in democracies the average was 66 percent. To measure income inequality, I use the variable **Inequality**, taken from the 2008 version of the Estimated Household Income Inequality dataset (Galbraith and Kum, 2005). This dataset includes 3,419 Gini coefficients for 153 countries between 1963 and 2002, with a mean Gini of 0.39, a minimum of 0.20, and a maximum of 0.64. Gini coefficients used in my analysis ranged from 0.26 in Sweden in 1980 to 0.58 in Mozambique in 1995. The mean level of inequality in an authoritarian regime was 0.44, while in democracies the average was 0.37.

To capture the power of rural interests to threaten authoritarian governments, I use a Gini coefficient (**Land Gini**) measuring the inequality of land ownership in a country. Data measuring land inequality are scarce and not evenly distributed across space and time. The Food and Agriculture Organization of the United Nations (FAO) has published national summary statistics on the distribution of land holdings since the 1950s, but the inclusion of each country's results was dependent on the successful completion and publication of national agricultural censuses, and coverage is sporadic in many developing countries. No single dataset has calculated all the landholding Gini coefficients available from the FAO data; therefore, I make use of three datasets that utilize the same underlying data and maximize the number of observations I can include in my analysis: Erickson and Vollrath's study, plus additional observations from Frankema and those published by the FAO.[10]

Data for land inequality are not available for every country included in the agricultural distortions dataset. Notably, Russia, Central Asia, and Eastern Europe are not included in the landholding inequality dataset, but these areas are not well represented in the agricultural policy dataset either because they enter only after 1989. In addition, some countries have as many as seven land Gini observations between 1945 and 2000 (Pakistan and India; OECD countries have five or six), while eleven others have only one data point (eight African nations, China, Mexico, and Slovenia).

Relatively rare agricultural censuses are sufficient for capturing a state's level of landholding inequality, which does not change much over time, but the patchy nature of this data is still problematic (Erickson and Voll-

---

[10] Erickson and Vollrath (2004), Frankema (2010), and Food and Agriculture Organization of the United Nations (1997). I am grateful to Dietrich Vollrath for kindly providing me access to his data. Results from the 2010 round of agricultural censuses are not yet available.

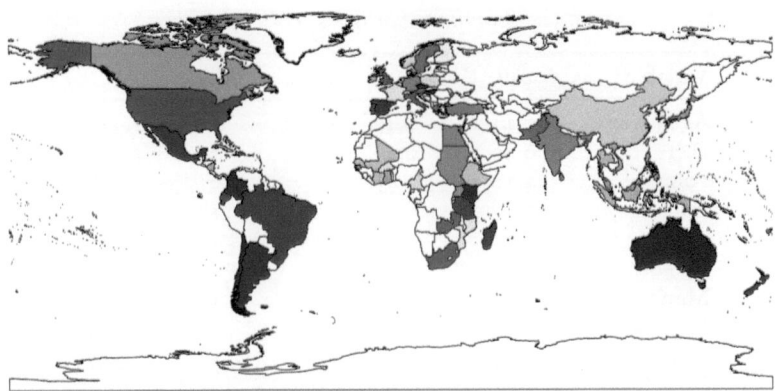

FIGURE 3.2 Landholding Inequality, 1960 to 2000

Darker shades of gray indicate greater land Gini coefficients.
Source: Agricultural census data matched by the author to GIS shapefile.

rath, 2004). I deal with the missing data problem in two ways. First, for countries with more than one observation between 1945 and 2000, I linearly interpolate them and perform an extrapolation them to fill out the missing country-years, censoring any resulting values that exceed the maximum found in the original data (0.98).[11] For countries with only one observation, I use that value for all country-years. I use the resulting data in a first set of analyses. Second, I take only data that are linearly interpolated between two values, excluding countries from my analysis that have only one land Gini datapoint. I use this data, **IP Land Gini,** in a further analysis, reported in Table 3.4.

Taking the first set of landholding Gini data, with the greatest coverage, the mean landholding Gini coefficient was 0.60. The highest average levels of land inequality were to be found in Australia and New Zealand and South America, where the average coefficients are 0.84 and 0.83, respectively. The lowest levels of land inequality in the dataset are in East Asia, with an average coefficient of 0.43. The lowest overall value was in Sweden in 1971, with a coefficient of 0.29. On average, the dictatorships included in subsequent analysis have slightly lower landholding Gini coefficients than democracies (0.57 compared to 0.62). I show the distribution of the land Gini data in Figure 3.2.

---

[11] The extrapolation is the fitted value of a regression of the interpolated values on country dummies interacted with a linear time trend. I prefer this to a simple extrapolation because the resulting values do not simply continue a linear trend in the data, but model the tendency of each country's land Gini to change over time. Values are thus less likely to tend toward very high or very low values.

TABLE 3.2 *Summary Statistics, Policy Analysis*

Variable	Mean	Std. Dev.	Min.	Max.	N
Ag Support	0.24	0.47	−0.66	3.19	1,326
Dict	0.39	0.49	0	1	1,326
Polity	4.22	6.89	−9	10	1,308
Autocracy	0.2	0.4	0	1	1,326
Anocracy	0.2	0.4	0	1	1,326
Democracy	0.61	0.49	0	1	1,326
Military	0.06	0.25	0	1	1,325
Personalist	0.09	0.29	0	1	1,325
Party	0.24	0.42	0	1	1,325
Land Gini	0.6	0.16	0.23	0.98	1,326
Urban	0.53	0.23	0.06	0.91	1,326
Inequality	0.4	0.06	0.26	0.58	1,326
Log GDP	7.97	1.67	4.67	10.55	1,326
Ag in GDP	0.16	0.14	0.01	0.65	1,326
Food Index	133.57	44.13	85.66	281.46	1,326

Control Variables

The following models also control for all major existing results in the literature on the political economy of agricultural policy. I include the natural log of per capita GDP (**Log GDP**), agriculture's share of GDP (**Ag in GDP**), arable land per capita, and agricultural land as a percentage of total land mass, to account for the development and anti-comparative advantage patterns outlined earlier, with data from the World Bank World Development Indicators. I include a yearly international **Food Index** variable, which takes 2005 as a reference level (100) and is published by the World Bank (2012a) in its regular commodity reports also known as "Pink Sheets." Finally, I include binary decade indicators for the 1970s, 1980s, 1990s, and 2000s, leaving the 1960s as a base category, to control for any global trends in agricultural policy across time. Summary statistics of all variables included in the models are shown in Table 3.2.

3.3 RESULTS

I test each of the hypotheses $H_{1.1}$–$H_{1.4}$ outlined earlier sequentially, examining first the relationship between political regime type and policy outcomes in models presented in Table 3.3, then moving on to examine the effects of urbanization, inequality, and landholding inequality under

TABLE 3.3 *Regime Type and Agricultural Support*

	(1.1) Dict	(1.2) Polity	(1.3) Type	(1.4) Type	(1.5) Africa	(1.6) Asia	(1.7) LA	(1.8) HIC
Dict	−0.07 (0.04)							
Polity		0.01*** (0.00)			0.00** (0.00)	0.00 (0.00)	0.00 (0.00)	0.01* (0.01)
Democracy			0.12** (0.04)					
Anocracy			0.07** (0.02)					
Party				0.00 (0.03)				
Military				−0.03 (0.03)				
Log GDP	0.13 (0.07)	0.10*** (0.02)	0.14 (0.07)	0.14* (0.06)	0.11*** (0.03)	0.34*** (0.03)	−0.00 (0.02)	0.08 (0.10)
Food Index	−0.00*** (0.00)	−0.00*** (0.00)	−0.00*** (0.00)	−0.00* (0.00)	−0.00* (0.00)	−0.00*** (0.00)	−0.00*** (0.00)	−0.00*** (0.00)
Ag in GDP	−0.92*** (0.23)	−1.00*** (0.11)	−0.89*** (0.23)	−0.38* (0.18)	−0.22* (0.11)	1.12** (0.39)	−1.34*** (0.28)	0.45 (0.53)
Observations	2,492	2,430	2,492	987	741	433	282	718
Countries	73	71	73	40	21	11	8	18

Standard errors in parentheses.
Models 1–5 with country fixed effects.
All models include Arable land, Ag land, Decade dummies.
* $p < 0.05$, ** $p < 0.01$, *** $p < 0.001$.

71

democracy and dictatorship. I depict all the main results of these analyses in graphs to give the reader a clear picture of their statistical and substantive significance. For $H_{1.2}$–$H_{1.4}$, I present the main results in Table 3.4. The fully specified model including urbanization, income inequality, and landholding inequality, as well as their interactions with regime type, is presented as Model 2.1 in Table 3.4, and I will refer back to this model as I look at results for urbanization, income, and landholding inequality. However, I also estimate separate models for each key independent variable and look at their effects on policy independently before interacting it with a regime type indicator. After examining several global models for each key independent variable, I look at their effects in separate models for African, Asian, Latin American, and high-income countries. These help give the reader a more complete picture of which countries are really driving the global results, where my theoretical story holds most strongly, and where it does not have as much explanatory power. These models are presented in Tables 3.5–3.7.

Regime Type

I begin by estimating a range of models that explore the effect of political institutions on agricultural policy outcomes. I present the results of these models in Table 3.3 and in Figures 3.3 and 3.4.[12] The analysis begins by looking at the effects of democracy on policy outcomes, before examining the correlation between different types of authoritarian regime on support for agriculture, and the effects of democracy by region.

Model 1.1 uses the binary indicator of dictatorship **Dict** to test whether these regimes support agriculture significantly less than democracies, on average. In this model, there is only a weakly significant difference in policy between democracies and dictatorships. As I show in the upper-left panel of Figure 3.3, the average dictatorship follows a policy that increases agricultural prices by 13 percent versus world markets, while average support levels in democracies are 18 percent. This is a relatively small difference, of around one-tenth of one standard deviation on the **Ag Support** variable, and it is only statistically significant at the $p <$ 0.07 level in this model. The main control variables are all signed as predicted, as countries with larger agricultural sectors support agriculture less and policy tends to move inversely to world agricultural prices. The

---

[12] All graphs are point estimates surrounded by 95 percent confidence intervals, generated using the predictive margins package in Stata.

TABLE 3.4 *Regime Type, Threat Structures, and Agricultural Support*

	(2.1)	(2.2)	(2.3)	(2.4) RRA	(2.5) CTE	(2.6) Dict
Dict	−1·01***	−1·20***	−1·25***	−0·91***	−1·18***	
	(0·22)	(0·17)	(0·27)	(0·24)	(0·33)	
Urban	0·87	0·59***	0·68	1·24*	0·83	1·28
	(0·45)	(0·17)	(0·73)	(0·54)	(0·54)	(0·64)
Urban*Dict	−0·62**	−0·60***	−0·57*	−0·80***	−0·62*	
	(0·18)	(0·11)	(0·27)	(0·20)	(0·24)	
Land Gini	−0·15	−0·79***		0·08	−0·25	1·16*
	(0·57)	(0·17)		(0·63)	(0·74)	(0·52)
Land G*Dict	0·93***	1·03***		1·13***	1·16***	
	(0·19)	(0·13)		(0·21)	(0·23)	
IP Land G			−0·95*			
			(0·46)			
IP Land G*Dict			1·17***			
			(0·31)			
Inequality	−1·25***	−1·42***	−1·24**	−0·96*	−1·03	0·07
	(0·33)	(0·27)	(0·43)	(0·37)	(0·56)	(0·23)
Ineq*Dict	1·54***	1·74***	1·69**	1·28**	1·59*	
	(0·39)	(0·35)	(0·49)	(0·48)	(0·61)	
Military						0·06
						(0·05)
Party						0·08
						(0·07)
Log GDP	0·09	0·06*	0·13	0·15	0·21	0·03
	(0·08)	(0·03)	(0·12)	(0·09)	(0·11)	(0·13)
Observations	1,326	1,326	954	1,291	1,327	520
AIC	−774.73	.	−431.55	−545.12	−159.30	−531.70
Countries	56	56	47	53	56	31

Standard errors in parentheses.
All models except 2.2 with country fixed effects, 2.2 includes five region dummies.
All models include Arable land, Ag land, Food Index, Ag/GDP, and Decade dummies.
* $p < 0.05$, ** $p < 0.01$, *** $p < 0.001$.

association of output per capita with agricultural support is insignificant in this model, however. From Model 1.1, I can conclude only that democracy is weakly associated with support for agriculture, noting that the binary distinction between democracy and dictatorship is a relatively crude measure of regime type which is further disaggregated in subsequent models.

In Model 1.2, the binary dictatorship indicator is replaced with the continuous **Polity** variable, which ranges from −10, a fully institutionalized autocracy, to 10, a fully institutionalized democracy. This regime type indicator therefore contains a lot more information on the openness

TABLE 3.5 *Urbanization and Agricultural Support*

	(3.1)	(3.2)	(3.3) Africa	(3.4) Asia	(3.5) LA	(3.6) HIC
Urban	0·24	0·29	−0·84*	1·84***	0·72	0·20
	(0·43)	(0·44)	(0·37)	(0·27)	(0·43)	(0·37)
Dict	−0·06	−0·01	−0·13	0·10	0·19	0·13
	(0·03)	(0·06)	(0·14)	(0·08)	(0·15)	(0·22)
Urban*Dict		−0·11	0·38	−1·10***	−0·20	−0·38
		(0·10)	(0·30)	(0·18)	(0·21)	(0·37)
Land Gini			0·06	−1·61***	0·46	−1·08***
			(0·22)	(0·24)	(0·41)	(0·27)
Inequality			0·31	−0·10	−1·59***	−1·31*
			(0·26)	(0·30)	(0·48)	(0·63)
Log GDP	0·12	0·12	0·09	0·07	−0·09	0·16
	(0·07)	(0·07)	(0·05)	(0·05)	(0·06)	(0·11)
Ag in GDP	−0·87***	−0·89***	−0·56*	0·44	−1·09**	0·58
	(0·23)	(0·23)	(0·23)	(0·50)	(0·35)	(0·79)
Food Index	−0·00***	−0·00***	−0·00***	−0·00***	−0·00*	−0·00***
	(0·00)	(0·00)	(0·00)	(0·00)	(0·00)	(0·00)
Observations	2,487	2,487	313	264	136	537
Countries	73	73	16	10	6	18

Standard errors in parentheses.
Models 3.1, 3.2 with country fixed effects.
All models include Arable land, Ag land, Food Index, Ag/GDP, and Decade dummies.
* $p < 0.05$, ** $p < 0.01$, *** $p < 0.001$.

and competitiveness of a political system than that included in Model 1.1. Here, I find a strong positive association between more democratic regimes and support for agriculture. The coefficient on the **Polity** variable is positive and significant at the $p < 0.001$ level. As I show in the upper-right panel of Figure 3.3, increases in a country's Polity score are associated with relatively large increases in support for agriculture, holding all else constant. Moving two standard deviations, from −3 to 10 on the Polity indicator, increases the predicted level of support from 10 percent to 19.5 percent, a shift around double the magnitude seen in Model 1.1, and one-quarter of a standard deviation of the **Ag Support** variable. In this model, the coefficients on all control variables are signed as in Model 1.1, but the positive association between GDP per capita and support for agriculture is highly significant. Using a more fine-grained measure of democracy, Model 1.2 finds a statistically and substantively significant relationship between regime type and support for agriculture.

The third measure of regime type examined here is the Polity typology, which distinguishes between **Autocracy**, **Anocracy**, and **Democracy**.

TABLE 3.6 *Inequality and Agricultural Support*

	(4.1)	(4.2)	(4.3) Africa	(4.4) Asia	(4.5) LA	(4.6) HIC
Inequality	−0·19	−0·97	0·50	−2·69***	−3·08***	−1·32*
	(0·20)	(0·58)	(1·16)	(0·42)	(0·79)	(0·63)
Dict	−0·09***	−0·72*	0·14	−2·35***	−0·94*	0·93
	(0·02)	(0·30)	(0·54)	(0·24)	(0·43)	(1·86)
Ineq*Dict		1·47*	−0·24	4·81***	2·26*	−2·48
		(0·64)	(1·17)	(0·56)	(0·97)	(4·57)
Urban			−0·36	1·57***	0·32	0·21
			(0·26)	(0·24)	(0·31)	(0·37)
Land Gini			0·26	−1·97***	0·16	−1·08***
			(0·26)	(0·22)	(0·40)	(0·27)
Log GDP	0·14***	0·15	0·10*	−0·06	−0·04	0·17
	(0·04)	(0·10)	(0·05)	(0·05)	(0·05)	(0·11)
Ag in GDP	−0·95***	−0·92**	−0·53*	−0·02	−1·30***	0·88
	(0·18)	(0·31)	(0·24)	(0·47)	(0·36)	(0·73)
Food Index	−0·00***	−0·00***	−0·00***	−0·00***	−0·00*	−0·00***
	(0·00)	(0·00)	(0·00)	(0·00)	(0·00)	(0·00)
Observations	1,428	1,428	313	264	136	537
Countries	65	65	16	10	6	18

Standard errors in parentheses.
Models 4.1, 4.2 with country fixed effects.
All models include Arable land, Ag land, Food Index, Ag/GDP, and Decade dummies.
* $p < 0.05$, ** $p < 0.01$, *** $p < 0.001$.

I present the effects of these types of regime in Model 1.3, which takes **Autocracy** as a base category. This model suggests that the main differences in policy outcomes are seen when we distinguish between autocracies and democracies. Both anocracies and democracies support agriculture more than autocracies, on average. As I illustrate in the lower-left panel of Figure 3.3, the average level of support under autocracy is 8 percent, under anocracy and democracy it is 16 percent and 20 percent, respectively. The differences between the support levels in anocracies and other regimes are not statistically significant, even at the $p < 0.10$ level, however. Those between autocracies and democracies are significant at the $p < 0.05$ level. The results of this model suggest that the reason why the binary **Dict** variable used in Model 1.1 was only weakly significant is because it includes a number of regimes with a relatively open and competitive political system. Overall, the results of these three models lend strong support to the hypothesis that democracies support agriculture more than authoritarian regimes, on average.

TABLE 3.7 *Landholding Inequality and Agricultural Support*

	(5.1)	(5.2)	(5.3) Africa	(5.4) Asia	(5.5) LA	(5.6) HIC
Land Gini	0·39**	0·34	−0·18	−3·26***	0·56	−1·08***
	(0·13)	(0·39)	(0·44)	(0·34)	(0·48)	(0·27)
Dict	−0·06***	−0·12	0·00	−1·29***	0·51	1·49
	(0·02)	(0·18)	(0·25)	(0·19)	(0·58)	(1·52)
Land G*Dict		0·10	0·03	1·94***	−0·54	−1·94
		(0·25)	(0·44)	(0·37)	(0·69)	(1·88)
Urban			−0·49***	1·24***	0·64	0·20
			(0·14)	(0·26)	(0·41)	(0·37)
Inequality			0·37	0·19	−1·61***	−1·31*
			(0·25)	(0·31)	(0·48)	(0·63)
Log GDP	0·15***	0·14	0·07*	0·02	−0·11	0·16
	(0·03)	(0·08)	(0·03)	(0·05)	(0·07)	(0·11)
Ag in GDP	−0·88***	−0·86***	−0·39**	0·28	−1·11**	0·58
	(0·12)	(0·23)	(0·15)	(0·51)	(0·36)	(0·79)
Food Index	−0·00***	−0·00***	−0·00***	−0·00***	−0·00*	−0·00***
	(0·00)	(0·00)	(0·00)	(0·00)	(0·00)	(0·00)
Observations	2,240	2,240	313	264	136	537
Countries	61	61	16	10	6	18

Standard errors in parentheses.
Models 5.1, 5.2 with country fixed effects.
All models include Arable land, Ag land, Food Index, Ag/GDP, and Decade dummies.
* $p < 0.05$, ** $p < 0.01$, *** $p < 0.001$.

I also estimate one model, Model 1.4, which includes only indicators of institutional variation among authoritarian regimes. Including only undemocratic country-years, I include indicators of **Party** and **Military** regimes, leaving **Personal** dictatorships as the reference category. Interestingly, these models show lower average levels of support under authoritarianism than Models 1.1–1.3, and only very small and statistically insignificant differences in policy outcomes across the three types of regime. The lower average support levels generated from this model can be explained by low average levels of development in dictatorships, compared to the country-years included in Models 1.1–1.3, as development is strongly associated with greater support for agriculture. Predicting **Ag Support** based on Model 1.4, personal dictatorships have a support level of −5.6 percent, on average, while party dictatorships are barely more supportive with an average value of −5.1 percent on the **Ag Support** variable. Military dictatorships support agriculture the least, with average levels of −8.5 percent, but these differences are not statistically significant from other types of regime. This model lends robust support to my argument that it is the balance of structural threats between rural and urban inter-

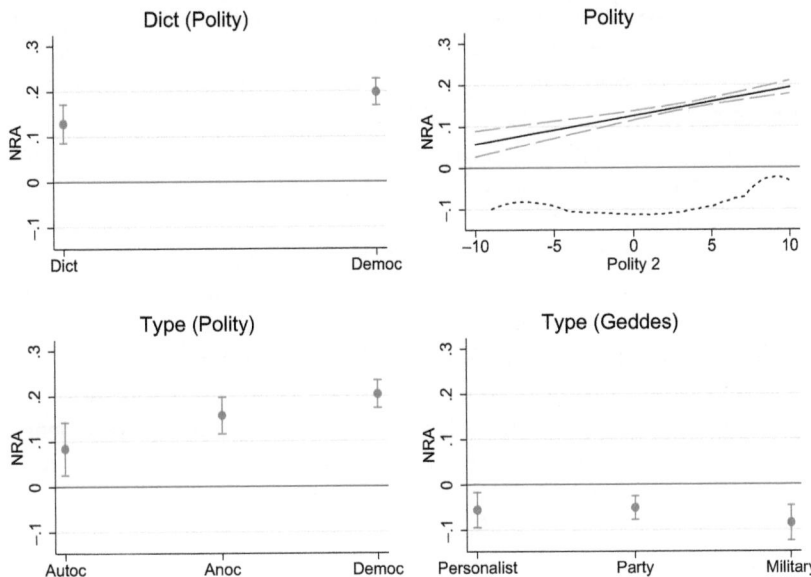

FIGURE 3.3 Regime Type and Agricultural Support

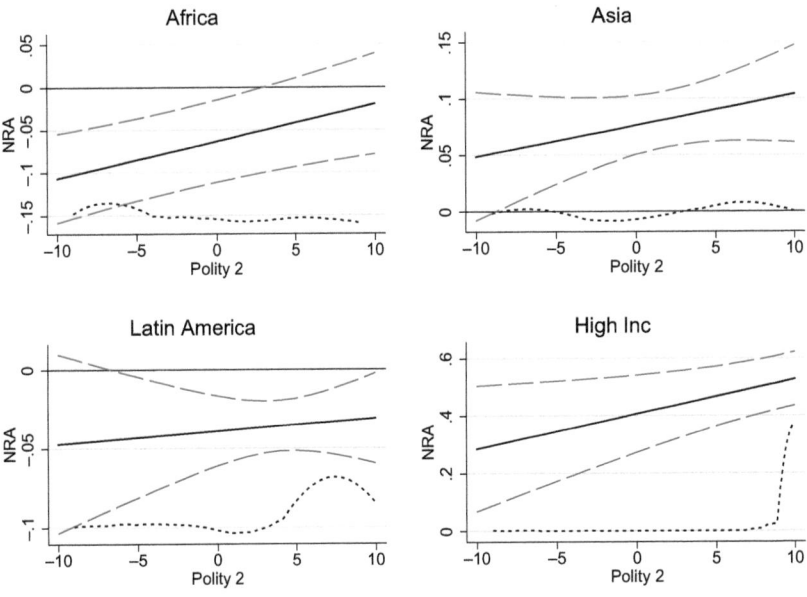

FIGURE 3.4 Democracy and Agricultural Support, by Region

Note: Asia does not include Japan, which is included as a high-income country.

ests, which has the decisive impact on policy under authoritarianism, rather than the institutional composition of the regime. I will test the effects of structural threat variables against these institutional categorizations in Model 2.6 presented in Table 3.4.

I conclude my exploration of the simple relationship between regime type and policy outcomes in four models, which include observations from African (Model 1.5), Asian (Model 1.6), Latin American (Model 1.7), and high-income countries (Model 1.8). Many regional specialists have studied developments in agricultural policy in one geographic context alone, making it important to take this step and see where my global results hold up robustly, and where they do not. I graph the results of these models in Figure 3.4. They show that in Africa democratic regimes have supported agriculture significantly more than authoritarian governments. In Africa, the average Polity score for countries in my analysis was stable at around −4.6 from the 1960s to the 1980s. This average increased to −1.6 in the 1990s and 1.9 in the 2000s. These increases in Polity score are associated with a four percentage point increase in agricultural support from −9 percent to −5 percent in Model 1.5. Dramatic regime change resulting in an increase across the entire range of the **Polity** variable from −10 to 10, which are broadly representative of the democratization process in Kenya between 1990 and 2010, for example, are associated with increases in support from −11 percent to −2 percent. In Asia excluding Japan, regime change is not significantly associated with greater levels of support for agriculture. Polity scores increased from an average of −1.7 in the 1970s and 1980s to 3.5 in the 2000s. This smaller political shift in the region was associated with a smaller increase in agricultural support levels from 7 percent to 9.4 percent in Model 1.6. A sixteen-point increase in the Polity score as seen in Korea between 1980 and 2000 is associated with an increase in support levels from 5 percent to 10 percent, holding all else equal. This is a change of a similar magnitude to that seen in the model for Africa. In Latin American countries we see a much weaker positive relationship between democracy and agricultural support in Model 1.7. Although the coefficient on the **Polity** variable is positive, it is small and statistically insignificant. In high-income countries, there is a positive, significant association between democracy and agricultural support in Model 1.8. However, there is very little variation in the Polity score among this set of cases, as they are predominantly democratic for the entire period of the study. A shift from 7 to 10 on the Polity score, which is almost a two-standard-deviation shift on the variable in this context, results in a five percentage point increase in support to agriculture, on average, from 48 percent to 53 percent.

A major empirical prediction in my theory of regime type and agricultural policy is that less-democratic governments are less responsive to the interests of the rural sector and support agriculture less, on average. The models presented in this section, with some minor exceptions, confirm this proposition. Although the binary indicator of regime type is not an ideal measure of democracy and is only weakly associated with differences in policy outcomes, using more fine-grained measures of political institutions shows that more democratic systems do support agriculture significantly more, on average. This relationship is borne out in most regions, particularly in Africa, where we observe significant variation in regime type, with Asia and Latin America being weak exceptions where we see a positive, but statistically insignificant correlation between democracy and policy. Readers should also note that previous institutional categorizations of authoritarian regimes do not have a significant association with agricultural policy outcomes in the model presented here. This supports my emphasis on socioeconomic structures that facilitate collective action as the determinants of economic policymaking under undemocratic regimes, which I will now proceed to explore for both urban and rural interests.

Urban Interests

I now turn to $H_{1.2}$ and $H_{1.3}$, which relate to the ability of urban interests to influence agricultural policy. First, I explore whether urbanization is associated with declining support to agriculture under dictatorship, compared to democracy, as in more urbanized polities food consumers and other elites based in cities can better organize and threaten an authoritarian government. I present the full models of policy as Model 2.1 in Table 3.4 and graph key results in Figure 3.5, but present six further models of urbanization and agricultural support in a separate Table 3.5.

In Model 3.1, Table 3.5, I estimate the simple effect of the variable **Urban** on agricultural support. Without distinguishing urbanization's effects on policy under democracy from those under dictatorship, Model 3.1 finds no statistically significant relationship with agricultural policy outcomes. The coefficient on the **Urban** variable is positive but insignificant. In Model 3.2, I interact **Urban** with the binary regime type indicator **Dict**, but I do not include the full set of interactions as in Table 3.4. Here,

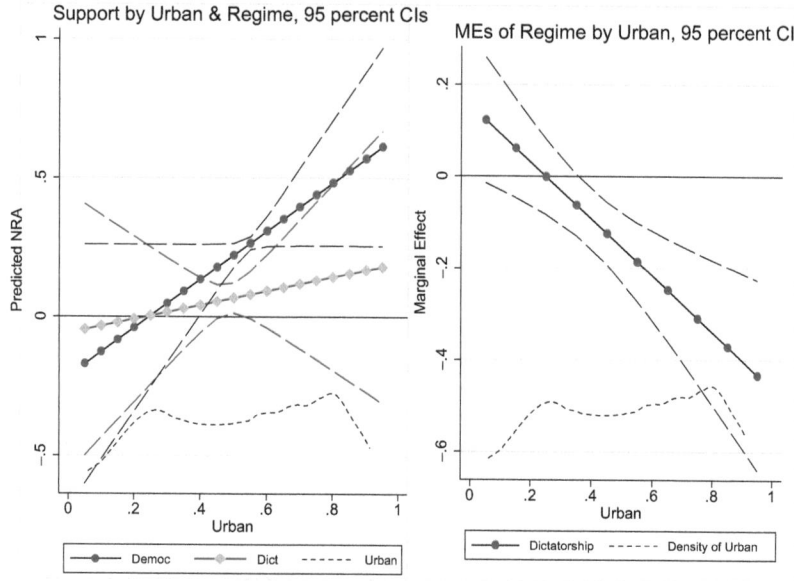

FIGURE 3.5 Effects of Urbanization on Agricultural Support by Regime Type
Results are from Model 2.1, Table 3.4.

the relationship between urbanization and agricultural support is negative
under dictatorship, but does not approach statistical significance. Under
democracy, increases across the range of the **Urban** variable are associated
with an increase in agricultural support of 26 percentage points from 6
percent to 32 percent; these are much larger shifts than those associated
with shifts in the institutional **Polity** score in Table 3.3, which were under
ten percentage points. Under dictatorship, support is still increasing in
Urban but at a much lesser rate: by 16 percentage points from 4 percent
to 20 percent under dictatorship. Although urbanization seems to be
associated with much greater variation in policy than democracy, there
are not statistically significant differences associated with urbanization
across regime type in this model.

It is when controlling for other measures of political threats, inequality, and landholding inequality that significant policy differences across
regime type are associated with increases in urbanization. Model 2.1 in
Table 3.4 includes **Inequality** and **Land Gini** alongside their interactions
with **Dict**. This is the fully specified model according to my theory of
agricultural policy and regime type. It predicts dictatorships to have significantly lower levels of support to agriculture than democracies when

urbanization is high. The coefficient on the **Urban** variable is positive and insignificant, while the coefficient on its interaction with the binary dictatorship indicator is negative, and statistically significant at the $p < 0.01$ level. The substantive effects of this model are graphed in Figure 3.5. As in Model 3.2, support for agriculture is still increasing in **Urban** under dictatorship, but it is increasing at a significantly lower rate than under democracy. At very low levels of urbanization, dictatorships are predicted to support agriculture 12 percentage points *more* than democracies vis-à-vis world markets; at an urbanization level of 0.5, which is the mean of all observations in the model, this relationship is reversed, and democracies support agriculture significantly more than dictatorships; 15 percentage points more at 22 percent versus 7 percent above world markets.

I also estimate a Model 2.6 in Table 3.4 including only undemocratic country-years, as in Model 1.4 in Table 3.3 but including indicators of structural threats according to my theory of regime type and agricultural policy. As in Model 1.4, the indicators of **Military** and **Party** regimes have only very small coefficients, estimated with very large uncertainty. Previous institutional characterizations of authoritarian regimes have no relationship with their agricultural policies. As in Models 3.3 and 3.4, support for agriculture is increasing in **Urban**, but this coefficient is only weakly significant at the $p < 0.06$ level.

Breaking up the analysis by region in Models 3.3–3.6, Table 3.5, I find more support for my hypothesis that urbanization is associated with lower levels of support to agriculture under dictatorship than in democracies. On the whole, these results show the strongest support for $H_{1.2}$ in Asia and high-income countries. In Africa, the correlation between urbanization and agricultural support is negative under both types of political regime, though the declines in the NRA across the range of urbanization are slightly greater under democracy than under dictatorship. In Model 3.4 including only observations from Asia, the coefficient on the interaction between **Urban** and **Dict** is negative, and statistically significant at the $p < 0.001$ level. Here, support for agriculture is increasing across the range of **Urban** under democracy, from −30 percent to 84 percent, but increasing at a much lower rate under dictatorship from −7 percent to 15 percent. In Latin America, support for agriculture increases across the range of **Urban** under both democracy and dictatorship, but differences in policy outcomes are not statistically significant across regime type. In high-income countries, support to agriculture is decreasing across the range of the urbanization variable under dictatorship and increasing under democracy.

I now turn to $H_{1.3}$, that inequality is associated with declining support to agriculture under democracy compared to dictatorship. This hypothesis is based on the logic that support to agriculture implies higher food prices for consumers; as income inequality increases, poorer voters demand lower food prices from democratic governments, who provide this by decreasing their support for the rural sector. In Table 3.6, I present the results of six models, which, in addition to those in Table 3.4, give a relatively complete picture of the interaction between regime type and inequality in determining levels of support to agriculture.

Consider first Models 4.1 and 4.2 in Table 3.6, which are identical to Models 3.1 and 3.2, except they include the inequality Gini coefficients **Inequality** in the place of the **Urban** variable included in the models presented in Table 3.5. Model 4.1 shows a weak negative relationship between income inequality and support for agriculture, when its effects are not allowed to vary across democracy and dictatorship. The changes in predicted support levels are small, from 27 percent to 21 percent, when allowing the **Inequality** variable to move across its entire range from 0.25 to 0.60. The effect of inequality on **Ag Support** is insignificant in this model, though the effects of the binary **Dict** regime type indicator

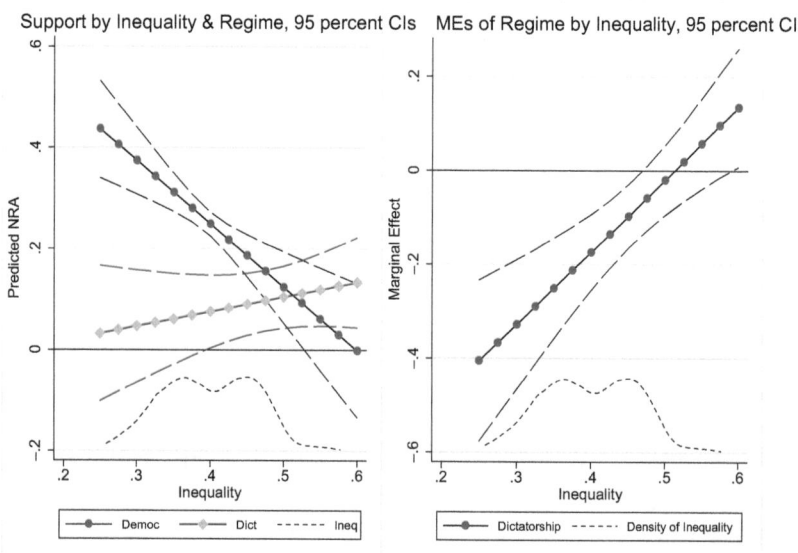

FIGURE 3.6 Effects of Inequality on Agricultural Support by Regime Type
Results are from Model 2.1, Table 3.4.

are negative and highly significant. Support for agriculture is negatively correlated with the size of the sector and international agricultural market prices and positively associated with GDP, similar to previous models.

In Model 4.2, the effects of inequality are allowed to vary by regime type, as the **Inequality** variable is interacted with **Dict**, a binary indicator of an undemocratic regime. Here, we see significant effects of inequality on agricultural support, which vary by regime type. The sign on the uninteracted **Inequality** coefficient is negative, suggesting that increasing inequality is associated with decreasing agricultural support in democracies. The size of the substantive change in policy is relatively large, from 62 percent to 13 percent as inequality ranges from 0.25 to 0.60. The effect of inequality under democracy is only significant at the $p < 0.10$ level, however. Dictatorships support agriculture significantly less than democracies, on average, in Model 4.2, but this effect is mitigated under conditions of high income inequality. Predicted support for agriculture increases from -3 percent to 21 percent across the range of **Inequality** under dictatorship, meaning that at high levels of inequality there is no statistically significant difference in agricultural policy outcomes across regime type, holding all else constant. The magnitude of the changes associated with the **Inequality** variable are much larger than those associated with changes in political institutions and similar to the size of those associated with changes in urbanization. In these models, such structural features of polities are associated with much larger shifts in agricultural policy outcomes than regime change.

The results of Model 4.2 are broadly in line with those emerging from the fully specified Model 2.1 in Table 3.4, which I graph in Figure 3.6. Controlling for the effects of urbanization and landholding inequality, these results are even stronger than those in Model 4.2. We see that predicted support levels for agriculture are weakly increasing in **Inequality** under dictatorship, but steeply decreasing under democracy. While at low levels of inequality democracies support agriculture almost 40 percentage points more than dictatorships, above a Gini coefficient of 0.45 there is no significant difference in policy outcomes between the two regime types. Although these models show increases in support for agriculture associated with greater inequality under dictatorship, Model 2.6 in Table 3.4, which includes only undemocratic country-years does not confirm this finding. In this model, although the coefficient on **Inequality** is positive, it is very small compared to those in Models 2.1 and 4.2 and does not approach statistical significance. This suggests that the main changes in policy associated with inequality are to be seen under democratic regimes, where the demands of poor food consumers for lower prices are likely to be heeded by elected governments.

I finally look at the effects of inequality on agricultural support by region in Models 4.3–4.6. In these models, the effect of inequality on agricultural support under both democracy and dictatorship is found most strongly for Asian countries in Model 4.4. In this model, support for agriculture declines by around 23 percentage points from 66 percent to 1 percent across the range of the **Ineq** variable, under democracy. Under dictatorship, support increases by around nineteen percentage points, from −34 percent to 21 percent. **Inequality** is associated with lower support under democracy in Latin America and high-income countries also, but the size of this relationship is smaller. In Africa, the signs on the **Ineq** variable and its interaction with **Dict** are the opposite to that which I hypothesize: Inequality is associated with greater **Ag Support** under democracy but lower support under dictatorship. However, these coefficients are estimated with a great deal of uncertainty, with standard errors larger than the coefficients, meaning that we cannot draw any conclusions from these results.

In sum, the results of the models presented in Tables 3.4–3.6 show, first, that the structural **Urban** and **Inequality** variables have much larger effects on agricultural policy outcomes than those capturing institutional characteristics. This finding will be repeated for landholding inequality in models discussed later. Second, they suggest that urbanization does lead to diverging policy outcomes across regime type: support is increasing in urbanization under dictatorship but at a significantly lower rate than under democracy. In Asia and Latin America, however, support is increasing in absolute terms as urbanization increases, regardless of regime type. The main results provide conditional support for $H_{1.2}$. Urbanization leads to a greater policy influence of urban interests under dictatorship not in absolute terms, but only relative to their influence under democracy. Finally, inequality is robustly correlated with lower support for agriculture, and thus lower food prices, under democracy. It is not, however, as strongly associated with policy shifts under dictatorship. As with urbanization, these results hold more strongly for Latin America and Asia than for Africa.

Rural Interests

A core element of my theory of regime type and agricultural policy is the assertion that dictatorships do not exclusively follow the policy preferences of urban interests, but instead must weigh them against those of the rural sector. Under democracy, rural interests find it easier to lobby the government for support when the agricultural sector is small and the cost of support is relatively low. Under dictatorship, on the other hand, I hypothesize in $H_{1.4}$ that landholding inequality increases the capacity of the rural sector to organize and threaten the government, leading to increased support for agriculture in response. In Table 3.7, I present the results of six models that, alongside the full models in Table 3.4, test this proposition.

In Model 5.1, I look at the simple relationship between landholding inequality and agricultural support without allowing this relationship to vary by regime type. I find that, on average, greater levels of landholding inequality are associated with more support to agriculture, holding all else constant. A two-standard deviation shift in the **Land Gini** variable from 0.45 to 0.80 results in a thirteen percentage point increase in the predicted level of **Ag Support**, from 11 percent to 24 percent. As with the **Urban** and **Inequality** variables earlier, **Land Gini** is associated with much larger changes in agricultural support than those under different types of political regime. In Model 5.1 the binary **Dict** variable is negatively and significantly correlated with agricultural support, as are the size of the agricultural sector and international food prices. Development is associated with greater support to agriculture, as in the models reported earlier.

In further models, I allow for the effects of landholding inequality to vary by regime type, by interacting it with the **Dict** indicator of an authoritarian regime. In Model 5.2, the results of this interaction are inconclusive. **Land Gini** is correlated with greater support to agriculture under both democracy and dictatorship, though the coefficients on the variable and its interaction with **Dict** do not approach statistical significance. It is when the effects of urbanization and income inequality are accounted for, in Model 2.1 in Table 3.4, that significant differences in policy outcomes across regime type emerge. As illustrated in Figure 3.7, below landholding inequality levels of 0.6 democracies support agriculture significantly more than dictatorships. Setting **Land Gini** at 0.45, one standard deviation below its mean, democracies support agriculture more than thirty percentage points more than dictatorships, increasing prices by 27 percent versus world markets on average while dictatorships decreased them by 4 percent. Moving to one standard deviation above the mean of **Land Gini**, at 0.80, dictatorships are predicted to support agriculture by around one percentage point *more* than democracies, by 23 percent versus 22 percent,

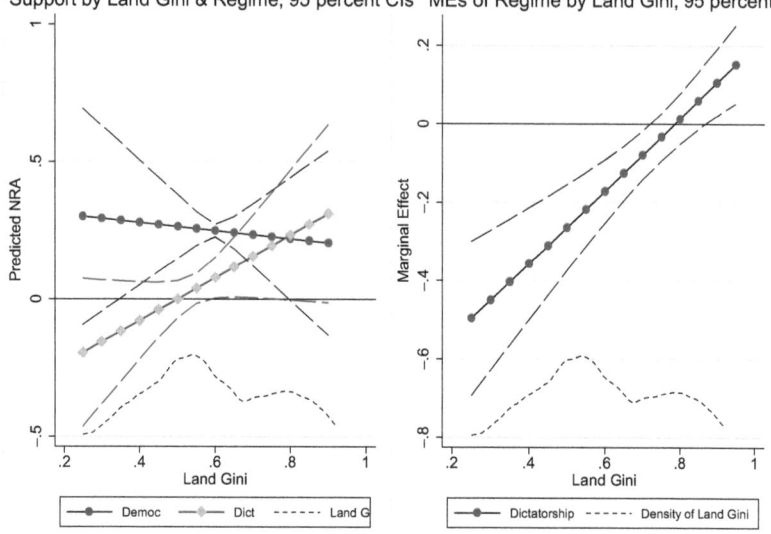

FIGURE 3.7 Effects of Landholding Inequality on Agricultural Support by
Regime Type

Results are from Model 2.1, Table 3.4.

and there is no statistically significant difference in policy outcomes across
regime type.

Restricting the model to include only autocratic country-years, and
controlling for the effects of authoritarian regime type, I find a large and
statistically significant positive relationship between landholding inequality and agricultural support in Model 2.6, Table 3.4. A two-standard
deviation shift in the **Land Gini** from 0.45 to 0.80 results in an increase
in the predicted level of **Ag Support** of 46 percentage points from −23
percent to 23 percent. This is a change in policy outcomes almost twice
the size of that resulting from Model 2.1, with the interaction between
landholding inequality and regime type. It is also a far larger shift in
predicted policy outcomes than that associated with military or party
regimes. These regime type indicators have only very small and statistically insignificant effects on agricultural policy.

I present four more models of the relationship between landholding
inequality and agricultural support, by region, in Models 5.3–5.6,
Table 3.7. These show that the positive relationship between **Land Gini**
and agricultural support holds most strongly in Asia. There, the NRA

is predicted to decrease from 100 percent to −63 percent across the observed range of the landholding inequality variable, under democracy. Under dictatorship, the same change in **Land Gini** is associated with much smaller decrease in the predicted support level from 29 percent to −37 percent. In Latin America and Africa there is no significant association between landholding inequality and policy outcomes. In high-income countries, support to farmers is decreasing in landholding inequality, but not increasing under dictatorship.

Overall, the full models in Table 3.4 lend robust support to the hypothesis that landholding inequality is associated with increases in support to agriculture under authoritarian regimes. In every model presented here, greater levels of landholding inequality are correlated with higher levels of agricultural support under dictatorship. The models in Table 3.7 are less unequivocal in their support for $H_{1.4}$. In Model 5.2, landholding inequality is positively correlated with support for agriculture under dictatorship, but this relationship is not statistically significant when the effects of income inequality and urbanization are not controlled for. In the regional models, it is in Asia that landholding inequality is robustly correlated with agricultural support under dictatorship. In high-income countries, it is more that democracies are associated with lower support for farmers as landholding inequality increases.

3.4 CONCLUSION

In this chapter, I tested four hypotheses on the institutional and structural determinants of agricultural policy outcomes. I presented robust evidence that democratization is associated with shifts toward more support for agriculture. I found that variation in socioeconomic structures is correlated with much larger shifts in agricultural policy outcomes than institutional differences are, particularly among authoritarian governments. In fact, I found only very small and statistically insignificant differences in policy outcomes across military, party, and personal dictatorships. Urbanization, income inequality, and landholding inequality, on the other hand, are associated with relatively large variation in policy outcomes. Greater levels of urbanization translate into lower support for farmers under authoritarian regimes than they do under democracies, while increases in income inequality are associated with large declines in support for farmers under democracy. Landholding inequality is associated with greater support for agriculture under authoritarianism, but not robustly correlated with changes in policy under democracy. These major findings all apply to pooled models including all country-years; separate models by region show that they are supported more in some places than in others. In particular, it seems that the relationship between landholding inequality, authoritarianism and support for farmers holds more for Asian cases than for African or developed states.

The results presented here are an important test of my theoretical argument relating to policy outcomes. They suggest that authoritarian and democratic regimes respond to different types of political incentives when making agricultural policy, leading to relatively large divergences in the treatment of the sector associated with variation in socioeconomic structures and regime type. However, the argument laid out in Chapter 2 makes the claim that the political logic behind these policies also relates to the stability of authoritarian governments, generating a series of hypotheses, which I will now go on to test in a cross-national setting. Although democracies are inherently stable and I do not expect them to experience political unrest associated with policies that increase the price of food, this is not true of autocracies. I expect that authoritarian governments support agriculture less than democracies when urbanization is high because they fear that government food taxes will be opposed by greater levels of urban unrest. I test whether food taxes are in fact a cause of urban unrest in Chapter 4. I also expect that authoritarian regimes increase support to farmers when landholding inequality is high because regime instability would result from landed elites confronted with a policy counter to their interests. In Chapter 5 I test whether the likelihood of regime collapse is significantly lower when landholding inequality is high and policy distributes rents to the rural sector.

4

Food Policy and Urban Unrest: A Global Analysis

In Chapter 2, I presented a theory of agricultural policymaking across regime type and its effects on political stability. I argued that these policies are made according to different rules under dictatorship compared to democracy and go on to have divergent effects on political stability depending on institutional context. The threat of collective opposition plays a key role in policy formation under authoritarian governments. These regimes respond to the threat of collective action against their rule by moving policy closer to the ideal point of threatening groups in order to buy their support. Under democracy, electoral incentives play the dominant role in policy formation, with governments weighing the interests of voters and well-organized interest groups. Agricultural policy has significant effects on political stability under authoritarian governments, but not under democracies, which are an inherently more stable form of political regime. Under authoritarianism, policies that increase the price of food induce the threat of unrest among consumers, particularly those in cities that find it relatively easy to mobilize and who cannot produce any food themselves. Mobilization in opposition to taxes on food is contingent on broader political opportunity structures, however, and most likely under regimes that combine a lack of democratic accountability with relatively low levels of repression.

In this chapter, I explore the link between government food taxes and urban unrest hypothesized in Chapter 2. I analyze an event dataset on social and political disorder in cities across the developing world, which I extended to include all countries covered by available cross-national data on consumer food taxes between 1965 and 2009. As in Chapter 3, much of the material covered here is technical in nature and relates to the difficulties in estimating the relationship between two phenomena, food taxes and urban unrest, which is likely to be subject to significant endogeneity. However, I have again gone to lengths to present the main elements of the chapter graphically in a way that will be accessible to readers less interested in quantitative research methods. Dynamics of the food tax data and urban unrest data that form the core of the analysis are presented in Figures 4.1–4.3, and the key results on the relationship between the two variables are presented in Figures 4.5 and 4.6.

The chapter proceeds as follows. In a preliminary step, I review recent literature on global urbanization and urban political unrest and the role of food prices and food policy in contributing to unrest in cities. I show that although government food taxes have been often cited as a cause of protests, demonstrations, and violence in cities, their role in propagating such political unrest has not been rigorously tested. I then proceed with my original empirical analysis, which fills this gap. First, I estimate panel regressions of the effect of food taxes on unrest. I find no simple relationship between food policy and political instability in cities. However, when the effects of food taxes are allowed to vary by political regime type, I find that higher taxes are significantly associated with greater levels of unrest under anocracy. Second, I estimate instrumental variables regressions, which exploit exogenous variation in the composition of a country's agricultural sector to identify the causal effect of food taxes on unrest. The results of these models align with those of the panel regressions. I find that higher food taxes are significantly correlated with greater unrest, but only under anocracies that combine a lack of democratic accountability with a relatively permissive political opportunity structure.

4.1 PREVIOUS LITERATURE

Rapid urbanization poses a significant challenge to political order and stability in the developing world. More than half the world's population currently lives in urban areas, and cities will see the vast majority of global population growth over the next thirty years (United Nations, 2014). However, the cities in the global South, which will host rapid population growth, are characterized by poverty and dramatic inequalities, which engender grievances and political instability.[1] Therefore, as the developing world becomes increasingly urbanized, sites of political contention are shifting from the countryside, in which civil wars and insurgency are

---

[1] See, for example, Beall, Goodfellow, and Rodgers (2013) and Moncada (2013).

most prevalent, to urban areas.[2] The frequency of urban unrest events increases with city size, with violence often driven by poverty and the lack of public services and security in the fast-growing periphery of cities.[3] Many scholars see urban unrest, such as that witnessed across North Africa and the Middle East in 2010 to 2012, as a real and growing threat to the stability of governments in the global South.[4]

Economic grievances, and in particular high food prices, are a significant contributing factor to urban unrest. Because the urban poor spend a large proportion of their income on food, and because they cannot raise any food themselves, food prices play a large role in determining standards of living among this group and can cause significant grievances and conflict. Bellemare (2015) shows that food price increases caused by shocks to global markets are associated with political unrest. Arezki and Brückner (2011) found that increases in international food prices lead to deteriorations in democratic institutions, increases in antigovernment demonstrations, and civil conflict. Smith (2014) studied sociopolitical unrest in African cities from 1990 to 2012 and found a link between domestic food prices and conflict. Hendrix and Haggard (2015) estimated models of social disturbances in fifty Asian and African cities between 1961 and 2010 and found that democracies and anocracies are more prone to unrest during periods of high food prices than autocracies.

For many political economists, the link between high food prices and urban unrest has clear policy implications. Governments in the developing world intervene heavily in agricultural markets via policies such as export tariffs, subsidies for inputs, food price ceilings, and transfer payments for farmers and consumers (Anderson, 2010; Swinnen, 2010b). These policies determine the final cost of food for consumers and are commonly urban-biased, decreasing prices for urban consumers in order to prevent political instability in cities. This line of argument has a long pedigree; Bates (1981, 1983) gives consumer protests a central role in explaining agricultural policy outcomes in Africa, while Wallace (2013, 2014) argues that the political threat posed by large cities causes urban bias. Hendrix and Haggard (2015), Hendrix and Brinkman (2013), and Pierskalla (2016) argue

---

[2] On rural civil wars and insurgencies, see Fearon and Laitin (2003), Kalyvas (2004), and Thomson (2016).

[3] See the cross-national studies by Urdal and Hoelscher (2012), Buhaug and Urdal (2013), and Thomson et al. (2017), and regional accounts of Brazil and Africa by Arias (2013) and LeBas (2013).

[4] For example, Goldstone (2010), Bellin (2012), and Della Porta (2014).

that food taxes are associated with urban unrest, and that urban bias is a response to the risk of such unrest by authoritarian governments.[5]

Anecdotal evidence showing that urban-biased food policies mitigate the danger of urban unrest also abounds. Cuts to food subsidy programs, such as those advocated in the 1980s and 1990s by the International Monetary Fund (IMF), have been widely associated with political unrest (Bienen and Gersovitz, 1986; Auvinen, 1996). For example, in 1977, the Sadat dictatorship in Egypt followed advice from the IMF to eliminate subsidies for foods such as bread, flour, and cooking oil. These policies had been seen as a core element in the government's strategy of maintaining political stability, and increases in the prices of these staples resulted in food riots in major cities, which posed a real threat to the regime. The government was forced to reverse its policy decision within days of its announcement and thereafter never questioned its commitment to a pro-consumer policy guaranteeing a virtually limitless supply of low-cost bread to the urban population, even at the expense of decreasing producer prices (Gutner, 2002). Similarly, in early 1985 President Blanco of the Dominican Republic announced food price increases of around 50 percent as part of a year-long austerity program implemented in consultation with the IMF. Almost immediately, large-scale strikes and resulting violence in the capital and other major cities forced the president to announce food price cuts in order to restore political stability to the country.[6]

However, empirical studies of the link between food policy and unrest are rare. Hendrix and Haggard (2015) included a measure of agricultural producer price supports in their models and found significant increases in unrest under democracy and anocracy where food taxes are higher. However, the measure of producer policy they used only imperfectly captures changes in consumption incentives caused by government policy, their data do not include cities in Latin America or the Middle East, and they do not address problems of reverse causality. Wallace (2013, 2014) argued that urban-biased agricultural policies cause unrest through their

---

[5] However, authoritarian governments in developing countries could be pursuing urban-biased policies for reasons other than preventing unrest. A lack of democratic institutions gives governments little incentive to respond to the economic interests of the relatively powerless rural population (Scott, 1985; Bates and Block, 2011, 2013). Authoritarian governments also have a strong incentive to use the taxes raised from agriculture to fund industrialization projects and distribute resources to powerful supporters (Lipton, 1977; Bates, 1981, 1983).

[6] These events were only one episode in a larger cycle of attempts at reform and political opposition in response (Keesing's, Various).

effects on urban population growth, but did not test the direct effects of urban bias on unrest.

4.2 RESEARCH DESIGN

The purpose of this chapter is to assess how food taxes affect the likelihood of urban unrest. In Chapter 2 the role of urban collective action in agricultural policymaking revolved around the interaction of economic grievances and political opportunity structures. I argue that urban unrest will result from situations where policy produces grievances, that is, where taxes increase the price of food. It is this threat of unrest that causes authoritarian governments in more urbanized polities to adopt urban-biased agricultural policies that decrease the price of food. However, mobilization against such policies depends on regime structures that promote grievance attribution and mobilization. Democracies, where consumers can influence policy through the ballot box, are unlikely to see urban unrest in response to higher food taxes. Very repressive autocracies, where the costs to mobilization are prohibitively high, are able to suppress dissent against high food taxes. I expect to see a significant effect of agricultural policy on the likelihood of urban unrest under regimes that combine a lack of democratic accountability with a relatively permissive opportunity structure. I therefore test the following hypotheses in this chapter:

$H_{2.1}$, *Urban Collective Action:* Policies that increase the price of food for consumers will be associated with greater levels of urban unrest, holding all else equal.

$H_{2.2}$, *Urban Collective Action:* The effects of food taxes on urban unrest will be greatest among undemocratic regimes with relatively permissive opportunity structures, holding all else equal.

Although several recent contributions have examined the effects of food price fluctuations on urban unrest, this is the first study that takes the relationship between food *policy* and unrest as its primary focus. I improve over previous contributions in several ways: first by using an original, expanded urban social disturbances dataset, which covers the entire postwar developing world and every nondemocratic country-year in the World Bank agricultural distortions database; second, by using a measure that more accurately captures the effects of government policy on consumer food prices; and finally, by using an instrumental variable

(IV) to account for endogeneity and estimate the causal effect of food taxes on urban unrest.

The task of identifying the effects of government market interventions on unrest is challenging because these interventions, their consequences for consumer welfare, and how they are perceived by consumers are complex. For example, the Indonesian government from the late 1960s until the late 1990s used a combination of subsidies for fertilizer and seed, import restrictions, and strategic use of buffer stocks to set domestic prices, boost production, and achieve rice self-sufficiency. This set of policies, some of which only directly affected farmers and all of which were difficult to observe for consumers, had the net effect of increasing domestic rice prices above those on world markets for most of the 1960s to the 1980s (Timmer, 1993; Fane and Warr, 2009). By contrast, through the mid-1980s the Thai government did not intervene to set domestic rice prices directly, but saw rice exports as an important source of revenue and imposed a tax on rice leaving the country while banning imports. This policy, less complex than that in Indonesia but also difficult to observe for consumers, decreased domestic prices vis-à-vis world markets (Sayamwala and Setboonsarn, 1989; Warr and Kohpaiboon, 2009). The only feasible way to capture, and just as important to compare, the net effects of such diverse market interventions as these is by relating domestic food prices to those of like products at the border (Anderson et al., 2008).

I illustrate these dynamics in Figure 4.1, which shows a world food price index as a black time-series plot and a measure of total consumer food taxes (CTE) in gray.[7] When consumer food taxes increase prices above world market levels, the CTE variable is positive, while negative CTE values indicate policy that decreases prices below international prices. Consumer food taxes in Indonesia are positive for much of the 1970s and 1980s, though they are negative in the 1990s. Note that much of the variation in Indonesian policy can be explained by world market shifts, with consumer taxes moving inversely to the food index as the Indonesian government defended its fixed domestic prices. Thai food taxes were negative through the 1970s to the 1980s and become neutral in the 1990s. They are not as highly correlated with world market prices as those in Indonesia, especially after the Thai government abandoned its policy of taxing rice exports in the 1980s.

---

[7] The CTE variable is the Consumer Tax Equivalent by Anderson and Nelgen (2012).

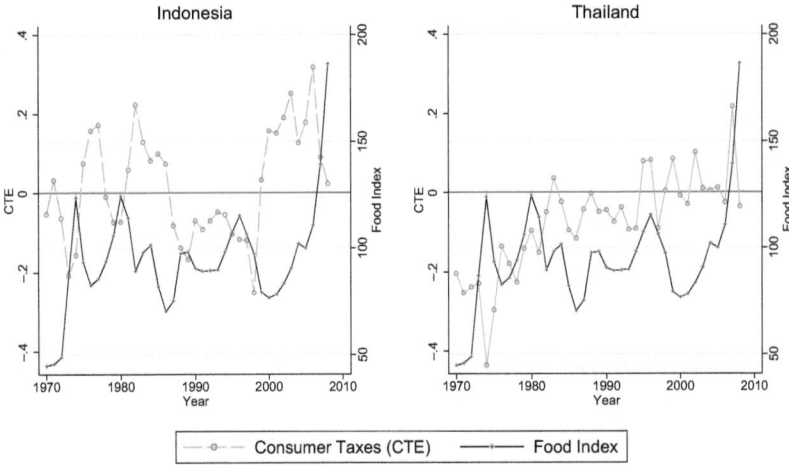

FIGURE 4.1 Global Food Prices and Consumer Taxes in Indonesia and Thailand, 1970–2010

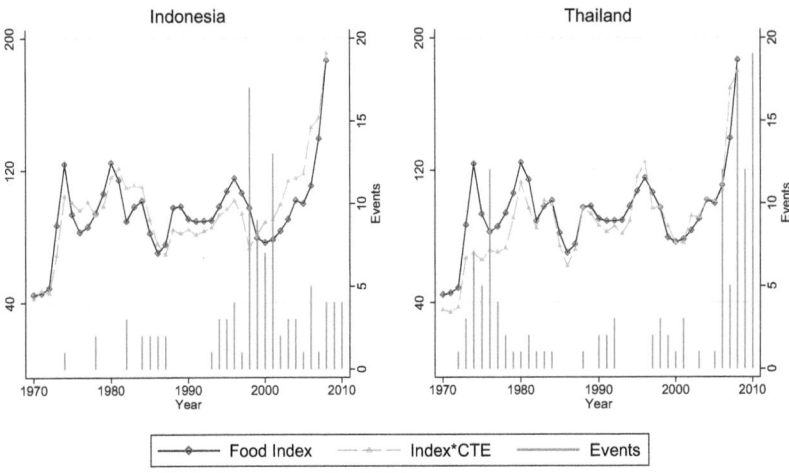

FIGURE 4.2 Global Food Prices, Consumer Taxes, and Urban Unrest in Indonesia and Thailand, 1970 to 2010

Real consumer food prices, after accounting for government market interventions, in Indonesia and Thailand are illustrated in Figure 4.2. Again, a world food price index is shown in black while domestic consumer prices, the price index multiplied by taxes, is shown in gray. The left-hand plot shows how food prices tracked slightly above those on world markets in Indonesia for much of the 1970s and 1980s, fell below world market prices from the end of the 1980s to the end of the 1990s, to rise above international market prices again after 2000. The right-hand plot shows that domestic food prices were substantially below world market prices in Thailand during the 1970s, but have been almost identical to international prices since the government removed its import tax on rice at the end of the 1980s.

Assessing the independent contribution of government policy to the likelihood of urban unrest requires estimating the effect of these policies holding world market prices constant. Was there a higher likelihood of unrest events in Jakarta after the year 2000 when government policy significantly increased food prices vis-à-vis world market levels than there was during the 1990s when policy decreased domestic food prices, *ceteris paribus*? Similarly, was the likelihood of unrest in Bangkok lower during the 1970s when the Thai government intervened to significantly decrease domestic food prices vis-à-vis world market levels, *ceteris paribus*? The unrest experiences of the two cities, as shown in Figure 4.2, paint an interesting but unclear picture. I plot the number of unrest events in each city alongside the food index and domestic food prices as gray vertical bars. In Jakarta, average levels of unrest are greater after the year 2000, when food policy tended to increase prices vis-à-vis world market prices, but these levels of unrest are low compared to the period around the collapse of the Soeharto regime in 1998. It is difficult to discern a clear association between global food prices and unrest levels in Jakarta. In Thailand, on the other hand, there is a clearer association of greater levels of unrest with the spikes in global food prices experienced in 1973 and 2008 to 2009. It also appears that the increases in unrest levels were more moderate during the food crisis of the 1970s when government interventions lowered food prices vis-à-vis world markets compared to the increase in unrest during the second food crisis, although the increases in food prices were not as great during the first food crisis, and the period after 2005 was marked by significant political instability in Thailand.

As Figure 4.2 makes quite clear, global food prices have experienced significant fluctuations since the 1960s, sinking through the early 1980s and famously spiking during the first oil crisis in 1973 and during the global food crisis of 2008 to 2009.[8] In comparison to these fluctuations, the contribution of policy interventions to consumer prices is relatively modest on average, as in the Indonesian and Thai examples earlier. Food

---

[8] It is important to note that the sorts of policies I analyze here, most notably the Soviet Union's entrance into international grain markets in 1973 and American and European subsidies for biofuels in 2008, made decisive contributions to these global price increases (Anderson, 2009, 3).

prices increased fivefold between 1970 and 2009, while the average size of government distortions to consumer prices across this period was only around 2 percent. However, policies exhibit a huge amount of variation. Some governments such as those in Zambia and Egypt intervened to decrease the price of food by over 50 percent during the late 1970s and 1980s, while market distortions in South Africa and South Korea increased food prices by over 30 percent during the same period. Because of the large effects that they have on consumer welfare in some contexts, and because urban collective action plays a central role in my theory of regime type and agricultural policymaking, it is important to analyze exactly what contribution high food taxes can make to the likelihood of urban unrest.

To this end, the relationship that I want to estimate is

$$y_{t,c} = \alpha_1 + \beta_{1f} f_{t,n} + \beta_{1x} \mathbf{X}_{t,c} + \nu_c + \varepsilon_1, \qquad (4.1)$$

where $y_{t,c}$ is the count of unrest events in a given city-year, $f_{t,n}$ is a measure of national consumer food taxes in a given country-year, $\mathbf{X}_{t,c}$ is a vector of control variables at the city- and country-year level, ν_c is a city fixed effect, α is a constant, and ε is an error term. Because I hypothesize that the relationship between unrest and food policy varies by political opportunity structure, I interact $f_{t,n}$ with variables for political regime type and also separately for democracies, anocracies, and autocracies.

There are two main challenges in estimating Equation 4.1. The first relates to the dependent variable, a count of city-level unrest events, which is a nonnegative integer. Because the mean of this variable is low, at 1.65 unrest events per year, and its distribution is right-skewed, it is more appropriate to model it using methods for count data than with standard linear regression models (Cameron and Trivedi, 2013). The second challenge relates to endogeneity, and more specifically reverse causality. Food policy is not exogenous to urban unrest. In fact, there is good reason to believe that both outcomes are mutually determined, as consumers respond to changes in food taxes by engaging in contentious collective action, and governments manipulate their policies in response to urban unrest. The resulting simultaneity problem means that estimates of the effects of food policy on unrest will be biased in standard regression models. I address this problem using an instrumental variable for food policy, based on the export orientation of each country's agricultural sector.[9]

---

[9] Angrist and Pischke (2009). On count models with endogenous regressors, see Cameron and Trivedi (2013, 385–407) and Windmeijer and Santos Silva (1997).

Identification Strategy

In my empirical analysis, I estimate models of unrest including a lagged measure of policy as an independent variable and using city fixed effects or a lagged dependent variable to control for unobserved heterogeneity and time dependence in unrest, respectively.[10] I also estimate models using an IV for food policy and including a lagged dependent variable to account for time dependence in the likelihood of unrest. Both sets of analyses have strengths and weaknesses.

The panel models have the significant advantage that the fixed effects control for unobserved characteristics of each city that could contribute to the likelihood of unrest. They also allow me to directly compare my results with studies of urban unrest by Hendrix and Haggard (2015) and Buhaug and Urdal (2013), which use a previous and smaller version of my urban unrest dataset and in the case of Hendrix and Haggard (2015) a different measure of food policy, but are also specified using city fixed effects and lagged independent variables. I do not claim that I am solving the reverse causality problem by lagging the policy measure, given potential serial correlation in unobservable confounding factors (Bellemare, Masaki, and Pepinsky, 2015). This necessitates the IV approach that I take in further models. However, finding good instruments in cross-national studies is challenging, and as I will discuss later, my IV models do not control for unobserved city-level heterogeneity as the panel models with city fixed effects do. I therefore argue that the fixed-effects models are a useful and informative step in the analysis, for controlling for city-level unobservables and facilitating comparison with previous studies. As a robustness test of the results of the fixed-effects models, I also report results of random-effects models, including a lagged dependent variable and with standard errors clustered by country.

I also use an IV approach to estimate the causal relationship flowing from food policy to urban unrest. My identification strategy here rests on the use of an instrument for my endogenous food policy variable, which is uncorrelated with the error term in Equation 4.1. To do so, this IV must fulfill two requirements. First, it must be correlated with the endogenous variable, that is, my instrument must be a good predictor of policy. Second, it must only affect the outcome of interest through the endogenous variables. My instrument therefore must only affect unrest through its effect on food taxes.

---

[10] I include a lagged independent variable, because results of autodistributed lag models indicate that the effects of food policy on unrest are significant at $t + 1$, while its effects at other time periods are insignificant. See De Boef and Keele (2008).

Finding good instruments in cross-national research is challenging. Examples include natural disasters, which have been used as instruments for international food prices by Bellemare (2015); world commodity prices, which have been used as instruments for domestic food prices by Smith (2014); oil reserves, which have been used as an instrument for national oil income by Haber and Menaldo (2011); and exogenous shocks to policy caused by programs administered by the International Monetary Fund (Auvinen, 1996). All of these variables are potentially correlated with food policy and thus potential instruments. However, they are endogenous because they are likely to have effects on unrest through their impact on exchange rates and domestic food and fuel prices, as well as through their more general effects on government spending.

I use an instrument for food policy that is based on the export orientation of a country's agricultural sector. This variable is negatively correlated with food taxes. Research on the political economy of agricultural policy has repeatedly confirmed that import-competing products are supported more than exportables, most importantly because they tend to be protected from foreign competition by import restrictions. Governments tax agricultural exports because such tariffs are a valuable source of revenue. Imports are taxed for the same reason, but also because international producers have little representation in domestic political structures, while producers of import-competing products find it easier to lobby governments for protection (Krueger, 1989; De Gorter and Swinnen, 2002; Swinnen, 2010b).

The instrument is unlikely to have effects on unrest except through its effects on policy, however, and is very unlikely to be itself affected by unrest. The level of bias toward support of import-competing producers is randomly assigned across countries due to product-specific factor endowments in the agricultural sector – such as topography, soil type, and climatic factors – which are exogenous to urban unrest and very unlikely to be affected by reverse causality flowing from unrest to the structure of agricultural production. Argentina's agricultural sector is very export-oriented, for example, as it exports practically all products that it produces. Considering its level of development, government market interventions in Argentina provide low levels of support to agriculture and low consumer prices. Indonesia, on the other hand, had only between 20 and 30 percent of agricultural production in exportable products through the 1980s and 1990s, and as we have seen, the country had policies causing relatively high consumer prices, given its level of development and political institutions.

I construct a measure of the share of a country's agricultural production made up by exportables, *Exp Index*, as an instrument for food policy,

$$ExpIndex_{c,t} = \sum_{i=1}^{p} Exportable_{p,t}\left(VOP_{p,t}/VOP_{c,t}\right), \qquad (4.2)$$

where p is an index for each product, c and t indicate the country and year of each observation, respectively, VOP is the value of production in current US dollars and *Exportable* is a dummy variable indicating whether a product is exportable. I construct this measure from the product-level data in the World Bank agricultural distortions database, using their measures of total production in current US dollars by product and their classification of each product as exportable, nontraded or import-competing.[11] The Export Index is correlated with food policy at $r = -0.33$ and correlated with my measure of unrest at $r = -0.06$. It is moderately negatively correlated with the size of the agricultural sector in a country, and its endowment of arable land, at $r = -0.27$ and $r = -0.28$, respectively.

The Export Index is assumed to be uncorrelated with unrest in the IV regression,[12]

$$y_{t,c} = \alpha_2 + \beta_{2f}\hat{f}_{t,n} + \beta_{2x}X_{t,c} + \epsilon_2, \qquad (4.3)$$

where $\hat{f}_{t,n}$ is the predicted value of $f_{t,n}$ from a first stage regression of food policy on the Export Index and all the control variables in Equation 4.1,

$$f_{t,n} = \alpha_3 + \beta_{3e}ExpIndex + \beta_{3x}X_{t,c} + \epsilon_3. \qquad (4.4)$$

The export index is negatively and significantly correlated ($p < 0.001$) with food policy in the first stage of a linear instrumental variables regression on the entire dataset. The t-statistic from the same first stage is $t = 11.11$, exceeding the conventional level of $t = 10$, which indicates a strong instrument. Assuming that the instrument is valid and effectively exogenizes food policy relative to unrest, the coefficient β_{2f} on the food policy variable in Equation 4.3 is the increase in the number of unrest events due to food policy in those years when the Export Index caused a change in policy. I estimate the IV models using both linear two-stage

---

[11] See Anderson et al. (2010), Anderson and Valenzuela (2008), and Anderson and Nelgen (2012).

[12] I am formalizing the identification strategy here using the interpretation familiar from linear two-stage least squares. The methods in count models for endogenous regressors are different; see Cameron and Trivedi (2013, 385–407) and Windmeijer and Santos Silva (1997).

least squares, which estimates local average treatment effects even for nonnegative limited dependent variables (Angrist and Pischke, 2009, 197–198), and also the generalized method of moments IV Poisson model by Windmeijer and Santos Silva (1997). It is not possible to find an instrument for policy that varies by regime type, and I cannot include interactions in the IV regression. Therefore, in order to assess how the effects of food policy vary by regime type using IV models, I split the sample and estimate separate models for democracies, anocracies, and autocracies.

The export index is a suitable instrument for food taxes because it is correlated with policy but not with unrest. However, it does not vary over time within countries as much as food policy. The trade status of each product does not change often within countries, and neither do the relative shares of products within total agricultural production. I estimate the IV models with a lagged dependent variable rather than with city-level fixed effects because of this lack of variation in the export index across different cities within the same country in any country-year and the low level of variation within countries across time. In the IV models, although I include a full set of relevant control variables, I am making the assumption that it is not time-invariant city-level characteristics that are driving the likelihood of unrest, but the level of unrest each city experienced in a previous time period. This assumption is bolstered by results of panel models including a lagged dependent variable presented in Table 4.4, which are similar to those of models including city fixed effects.

4.3 DATA

The dependent variable in all models, *Events*, is a count of urban unrest events at the city-year level from an extended version of the PRIO Urban Social Disturbances database (USD).[13] Because residents of cities cannot produce much food themselves and are dependent on markets for purchasing their daily consumption needs, using data on unrest in cities – rather than measures of civil conflict, for example – is a good way of estimating the effects of government food policy on consumer behavior, as distinct from its effects on producers. I extended the previous version of the USD data, which covered only Africa and Asia, to all major countries

---

[13] Urdal (2008) and Urdal and Hoelscher (2012). In one model, I also use a binary variable indicating whether a city-year witnessed any unrest. Summary statistics of all variables are shown in Table 4.1.

TABLE 4.1 *Summary Statistics: Unrest Models*

Variable	Mean	Std. Dev.	Min.	Max.	N
Events	1.65	2.7	0	23	2,057
Unrest Dummy	0.54	0.5	0	1	2,057
CTE $(t-1)$	0.01	0.35	−0.84	1.96	2,057
Exp Index	0.52	0.32	0	1	2,022
Anocracy	0.17	0.37	0	1	2,057
Democracy	0.47	0.5	0	1	2,057
Food Index	88.81	24.95	38.94	186.44	2,028
Ln GDP/Cap	7.92	0.92	5.73	10.38	2,057
Ln City Pop	7.66	1.09	4.35	9.81	2,057
City Growth	86.89	111.44	−264.75	668.48	2,057
Conflict	0.31	0.46	0	1	2,057
End CW	0.08	0.26	0	1	2,057
Econ Shock	0.33	0.47	0	1	2,057

in Latin America, as well as Egypt and Turkey.[14] This resulted in a total of 3,824 city-years spread over 75 cities, compared to 2,804 city-years from 52 cities in the original dataset. In my analysis, I use a total of 2,034 city-years: 651 observations from Asia, 654 from Africa, 553 from Latin America, and 176 from Turkey and Egypt. The years covered are from 1965 to 2009. I therefore have 27 percent more observations in my models of food policy and unrest than in the previous study by Hendrix and Haggard (2015).

The *Events* variable codes violent and nonviolent contentious political events, ranging from peaceful protests through strikes to shootings and terrorism, from reports in *Keesing's World News Archive*. Cities included in the final dataset were national capitals, former capitals, and large urban centers with a population over one million.[15] The USD dataset uses a consistent underlying data source and includes all relevant information on the timing, size, location, and nature of the unrest events. However, due to the nature of the underlying data source it is subject to some

[14] Given my research question of the impact of food policy and regime type on unrest, I extended the dataset to cover all countries that experienced any undemocratic country-years and that are included in the World Bank agricultural policy database, except a very small number of observations in post-1991 Russia and Ukraine. All these countries are included for the entire time period 1960 to 2010.

[15] See Urdal (2008) for more information on the African and Asian data. Not all cities with a population over one million were included, but only major population centers with political importance. In Brazil, both Rio de Janeiro and São Paulo were included alongside Brasília.

biases: authoritarian governments might restrict access to information on events within their territory, the Keesing's archive might systematically include more information on certain cities or regions due to customer demand or institutional idiosyncrasies, and improving communications technology could be systematically changing the extent of information available about unrest events. Wide searches of the database mitigate the first concern, while including city fixed effects and a time trend variable in my models mitigate concerns of bias resulting from the latter two.

The modal city-year in the dataset as used in my models witnessed no unrest; the mean city-year experienced 1.6 events, the city-year at the seventy-fifth percentile experienced two events, while the city-year at the ninetieth percentile experienced four unrest events. The *Unrest* variable is moderately overdispersed, with a variance larger than the mean: It has a mean of 1.6 and a standard deviation of 2.7. The maximum number of unrest events in a given city-year in the dataset as used here was 23, in Santiago in 1973. Of the ten most unrest-prone city-years, four are in Latin America, four are in Asia, one is in Istanbul (20 events in 2006), and one is in Cairo (18 events in 1993). Unrest is highest in Turkey and Egypt, with an average of 2.5 events per city-year, followed by Asia with 2 events, Latin America where the variable averages 1.7, and Africa where it averages 1 per city-year.

My key explanatory variable is a measure of consumer food taxes, the *Consumer Tax Equivalent (CTE)* from the World Bank agricultural distortions database (Anderson and Valenzuela, 2008; Anderson and Nelgen, 2012). The CTE measures the effects of policies that are due exclusively to governments' actions on the consumer price of agricultural produce. It is the percentage by which the domestic consumer price is above (if positive) or below (if negative) the border price of like products in a given year. Most commonly, these consumer market distortions are caused by import or export taxes and quotas, as well as domestic taxes and subsidies for produce, inputs and consumer consumption. Unlike the measure of producer support used by Hendrix and Haggard (2015) in their study of urban unrest, the CTE includes direct food consumer subsidies and taxes while excluding direct production subsidies for farmers, and thus more precisely measures the effects of government policy on consumption incentives for food. The CTE variable used in this study has a mean of 0.02, a standard deviation of 0.35, and a range of −0.84 to 1.96.

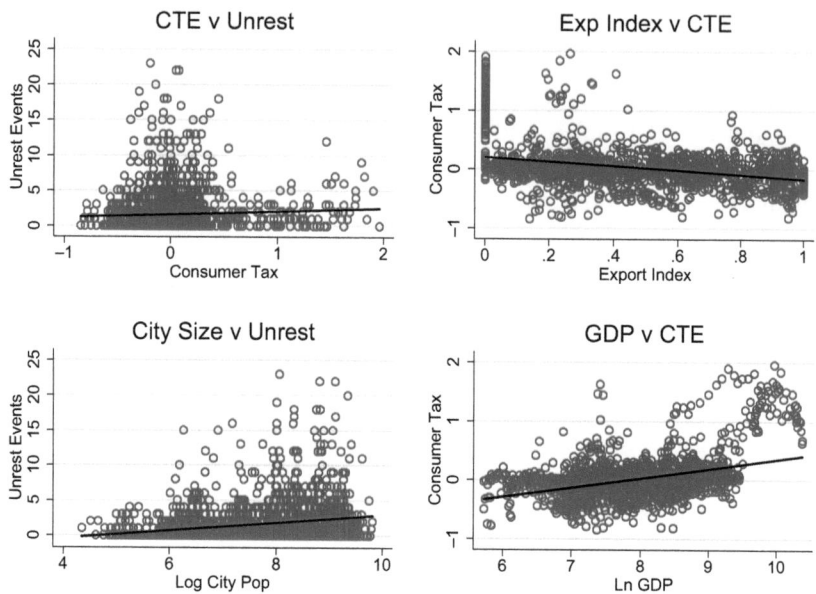

FIGURE 4.3 Unrest, Consumer Tax Data

   As I illustrate in Figure 4.3, there is only a very weak positive correlation between consumer food taxes and unrest at the city level. The
simple correlation between the two variables is $r = 0.06$. Unrest is more
strongly correlated with city size ($r = 0.22$), as illustrated in the lower-left
panel of Figure 4.3, and economic development ($r = -0.11$), but it is not
correlated with an international food price index ($r = 0.01$). The upper-
right panel of Figure 4.3 demonstrates the correlation between my *Export
Index* instrument and the consumer tax variable, which is moderately
large and negative at $r = -0.33$. Like other measures of support for
agriculture, consumer food taxes also show a tendency to be higher at
greater levels of development, as illustrated in the lower-right panel of
Figure 4.3.
   The regime type indicator used in my models is a threefold categorization of regimes as **Autocracies**, with a Polity score of -6 or lower;
Anocracies, with a Polity score between -5 and 5; and **Democracies**, with
a Polity score of 6 and above (Marshall and Cole, 2011). As I explained
more fully in Chapters 2 and 3, I use the underlying Polity score to
capture both the ability of actors to influence policy through the ballot
box and the civil liberties, which enable them to mobilize collectively

in opposition to a regime. This threefold classification indicates regimes where influence on policy runs primarily through electoral institutions (democracies), those where it runs through elections and contentious mobilization (anocracies), and those where diffuse interests can influence policy only through contentious mobilization, but this mobilization is very costly due to repression (autocracies). Following my theory, I predict that urban collective action will be associated with higher food taxes under anocracy, when governments are not able to be held fully accountable via binding elections, but the costs of collective action are not prohibitively high. There are 937 democratic city-years, 350 anocratic city-years, and 747 autocratic city-years included in the sample as used. Under all three types of regime, the modal city-year experienced no unrest. The mean autocratic city-year had 1.4 unrest events, while in both anocracies and democracies the mean city-year had around 1.8. Although anocracies experienced more unrest on average than autocracies and democracies, the maximum level of unrest in an anocratic city-year was only 14 events, while in autocracies and democracies it was 23 and 22, respectively.

I include the same control variables as Buhaug and Urdal (2013) and Hendrix and Haggard (2015) in all models also. At the city-year level, I control for the natural log of each city's population, in thousands, and the city's five-year average rate of annual population growth, in thousands. Where city population data was not available from Buhaug and Urdal (2013), I collected it from the same UN demographic yearbooks used in their study and interpolated and extrapolated it in the same manner (United Nations, Annual). I include an international food price index that takes 2000 as its base year from the World Bank (2012a). As the Indonesian and Thai examples outlined earlier show, political events such as regime change and irregular leader exits have a large effect on urban unrest, so I control for national elections (Hyde and Marinov, 2012), regime change (Marshall and Cole, 2011), and irregular leader exits (Goemans, Gleditsch, and Chiozza, 2009). I also include an indicator of ongoing conflict from the UCDP/PRIO Armed Conflict Database (Gleditsch et al., 2002), logged real GDP per capita, and an indicator of economic shocks, coded 1 when real GDP per capita decreases year-on-year (Gleditsch, 2002). I coded the years 1990 to 1992 with a dummy variable for the end of the Cold War and included a linear time trend to account for systematic changes over time, both in the likelihood of unrest and in the accuracy of reporting of events.

4.4 RESULTS

I begin my analysis by testing $H_{2.1}$, that policies increasing the consumer price of food will be associated with greater levels of urban unrest. In Table 4.2, I present five different models that estimate, using both panel and instrumental variables regressions, this unconditional relationship between consumer food taxes and urban unrest. The results across all these models are similar. Government policy that increases the price of food is only weakly and insignificantly associated with greater levels of social unrest in cities when its effects are not allowed to vary by political regime type. Only one model, that which does not include city fixed effects, finds a weak negative association between food taxes and urban unrest. Major factors that are positively correlated with unrest are unanticipated political shocks such as unplanned leader exits or regime change, and structural variables, most notably city size and regime type.

Model 1.1 is a negative binomial model with city fixed effects that estimates the unconditional relationship between food taxes and unrest. The fixed effects in this model effectively control for unobserved city-level factors, which do not vary but affect the likelihood of unrest, and this specification is very similar to previous analyses of these urban unrest data, for easy comparison. The coefficient on the lagged CTE variable in Model 1.1 is positive, but estimated with a lot of uncertainty and not statistically significant. As I illustrate in the left-hand panel of Figure 4.4, an increase in consumer food taxes from −0.34 to 0.33, a shift of two standard deviations, results only in a small increase in the predicted number of unrest events in a given city-year, from 0.10 to 0.18. In Model 1.1, international food prices are also not significantly correlated with urban unrest. A similar-sized shift in the international food index results in a very small, statistically insignificant decrease in the predicted number of unrest events in a city-year, from 0.15 to 0.13.

A number of significant predictors of urban unrest emerge from Model 1.1 and the other models presented in Table 4.2. Regime type is significantly associated with unrest; anocratic city-years experience 0.40 more unrest events than autocratic city-years, holding all else equal. Democracies experience similar levels of urban unrest to autocracies. Short-term shocks, whether economic or political, play a significant role in causing urban unrest. Recessions, as captured by the *Econ Shock* variable, are associated with significantly more unrest, as are irregular political leader exits, regime change, and civil conflict. Elections and underdevelopment are not significantly correlated with unrest, but larger cities experience

TABLE 4.2 *Results of Consumer Tax and Unrest Models*

	(1.1) NB, FEs	(1.2) NB, REs	(1.3) Logit	(1.4) IV Reg	(1.5) IV Pois
CTE $(t-1)$	0·113	−0·137	0·063	0·533	0·288
	(0·119)	(0·167)	(0·248)	(0·689)	(0·377)
Foodindex $(t-1)$	−0·001	−0·001	−0·001	−0·001	−0·001
	(0·001)	(0·002)	(0·003)	(0·003)	(0·002)
Democracy	−0·005	0·019	0·051	−0·167	−0·034
	(0·085)	(0·115)	(0·178)	(0·189)	(0·123)
Anocracy	0·400***	0·293*	0·618**	0·142	0·203
	(0·091)	(0·125)	(0·189)	(0·205)	(0·137)
Econ Shock	0·154**	0·152*	0·310**	0·195	0·137*
	(0·058)	(0·068)	(0·113)	(0·110)	(0·065)
Irreg Exit	0·578***	0·891***	1·669***	2·043***	0·748***
	(0·107)	(0·138)	(0·378)	(0·465)	(0·126)
Reg Ch	0·473***	0·377**	0·563**	0·843**	0·390***
	(0·089)	(0·130)	(0·218)	(0·309)	(0·096)
Conflict	0·323***	0·340***	0·437*	0·600***	0·392***
	(0·076)	(0·093)	(0·177)	(0·153)	(0·088)
Ln City Pop	0·177*	0·289***	0·203	0·310*	0·267**
	(0·070)	(0·075)	(0·233)	(0·130)	(0·083)
Observations	2,053	2,058	2,053	2,058	2,058

Standard errors in parentheses.
Autocracy is the base category.
All models control for GDP, time trend, and end of CW.
* $p < 0.05$, ** $p < 0.01$, *** $p < 0.001$.

significantly more unrest than smaller cities. A two-standard deviation increase in the *Ln City Pop* variable is associated with a 0.4 increase in the predicted number of unrest events in a city in Model 1.1.

I go on to specify further models of the unconditional relationship between consumer food taxes and urban unrest. Model 1.2 is identical to Model 1.1, but instead of city fixed effects, it includes a lagged dependent variable among the right-hand-side covariates. The results are similar, but not identical, to the fixed-effects model. The coefficient on the lagged CTE variable does not approach statistical significance, but is negative instead of positive. Model 1.3 is a logistic regression that takes a binary indicator of unrest as its dependent variable and includes city fixed effects. The results are also in line with Model 1.1, which takes a count of unrest events as the dependent variable. Food taxes show a very small and statistically insignificant positive association with unrest. A two

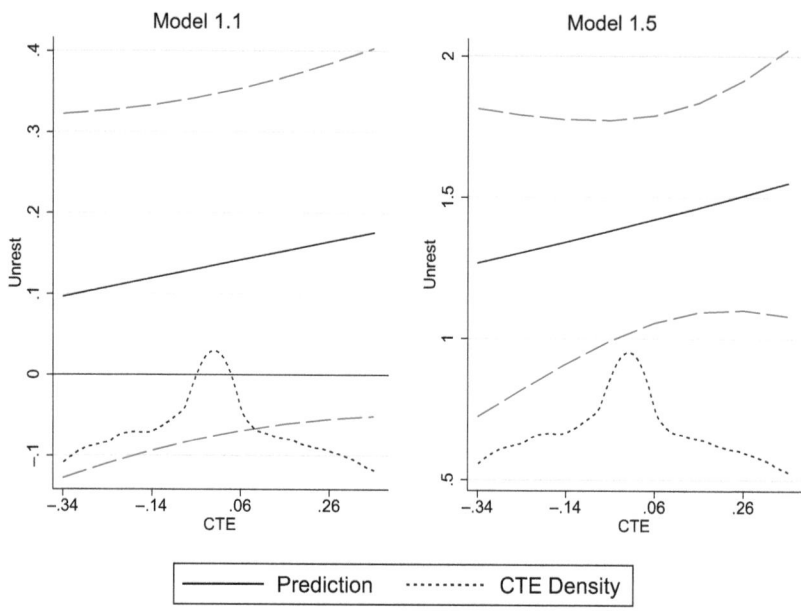

FIGURE 4.4 Consumer Tax and Unrest Model Results

standard deviation increase in the lagged CTE variable is associated with a tiny increase in the probability of unrest from 0.568 to 0.577. On the whole, then, these panel models suggest that food taxes are weakly and insignificantly associated with unrest when their effects are not allowed to vary by regime type.

Finally, I estimate two instrumental variables regressions of the effects of food taxes on unrest. Both models use the *Export Index* variable discussed earlier as an instrument for consumer taxes and include a lagged dependent variable rather than city fixed effects. Both models also cluster standard errors by city, allowing for serial correlation in idiosyncratic shocks to unrest within cities. Model 1.4 is a linear two-stage model, and Model 1.5 is a IV Poisson model, which does a better job in accounting for the right-skewed distribution of the dependent variable due to it being a count of unrest events. The first-stage regression of the CTE variable on all independent variables plus the exogenous instrument *Export Index* has a F-statistic of 11.11, and the coefficient on the *Export Index* variable is significant at the $p < 0.001$ level. Both instrumental variables models generate similar findings to the panel regressions. Consumer food taxes are positively but insignificantly associated with unrest in Models 1.4 and

1.5. In Model 1.4, an increase in the CTE variable from −0.34 to 0.36 is associated with a 0.4 increase in the predicted number of unrest events in a city. In Model 1.5 the corresponding increase is 0.3, as illustrated in the right-hand panel of Figure 4.4.

The five models presented in Table 4.2 all estimate the unconditional relationship between consumer food taxes and urban unrest. They do not allow the effects of these policies to vary by regime type. Across all the models, no significant relationship is found between the level of food taxes and the number of unrest events at the city level. Instead, the major predictors of urban unrest are sudden political and economic shocks, such as recessions, regime change or an irregular leader exit, and incoherent political institutions. I therefore cannot conclude that $H_{2.1}$ holds, and that increases in government food taxes are associated with political mobilization and instability in urban areas, regardless of regime type.

The second step of my analysis is to estimate models that allow the effects of consumer food taxes on unrest to vary by regime type. I do this to test $H_{2.2}$, that the effects of food taxes on urban unrest will be greatest among undemocratic regimes with relatively permissive opportunity structures. Again, I estimate both panel and instrumental variables regressions. The panel models interact consumer food taxes with a threefold indicator of regime type, while I estimate separate instrumental variables models for autocracies, anocracies, and democracies using the same instrument as earlier for policy. The results of all these models are reported in Table 4.3 and broadly confirm that consumer food taxes are associated with greater levels of urban unrest under anocracy, but not under democracy or repressive autocratic regimes.

Model 2.1 is a negative binomial regression, which takes a count of unrest events as its dependent variable and includes city fixed effects. I present the results of this model in Figure 4.5, where the left-hand panel shows the marginal effects of consumer taxes on unrest under each political regime type, and the right-hand panel shows the marginal effects of each regime type on unrest across a two standard deviation range of consumer taxes. In this model, consumer food taxes do not have a significant effect on urban unrest under either autocracy or democracy. As shown in the left-hand panel of Figure 4.5, the results show a very small, insignificant negative effect of the CTE variable on unrest under autocracy. A one-unit increase in consumer taxes is associated with a 0.26 increase in the predicted number of unrest events in a democratic city-year, but this increase is only significant at the $p < 0.08$ level. In the right-hand

TABLE 4.3 *Results of Regime Type, Consumer Tax, and Unrest Models*

	(2.1) NB, FEs	(2.2) NB, REs	(2.3) Logit	(2.4) IVR Anoc	(2.5) IVP Anoc	(2.6) IVP Democ	(2.7) IVP Autoc
CTE $(t-1)$	-0·177	-0·280	-0·470	3·670*	1·723*	0·023	0·564
	(0·172)	(0·179)	(0·324)	(1·745)	(0·675)	(0·394)	(0·958)
Foodindex $(t-1)$	-0·001	0·002	0·000	0·013	0·006	-0·002	0·002
	(0·002)	(0·003)	(0·004)	(0·007)	(0·004)	(0·002)	(0·003)
CTE L*Democ	0·435*	0·136	0·849*				
	(0·198)	(0·192)	(0·384)				
CTE L*Anoc	0·711**	0·495*	1·241*				
	(0·275)	(0·246)	(0·609)				
Food Ind L*Democ	-0·001	-0·006*	-0·005				
	(0·003)	(0·003)	(0·005)				
Food Ind L*Anoc	0·008*	0·002	0·014*				
	(0·003)	(0·004)	(0·007)				
Anocracy	-0·246	0·164	-0·431				
	(0·294)	(0·347)	(0·579)				
Democracy	0·119	0·538*	0·541				
	(0·241)	(0·264)	(0·452)				
Econ Shock	0·143*	0·147*	0·292*	0·227	0·231	0·017	0·074
	(0·058)	(0·066)	(0·114)	(0·354)	(0·186)	(0·100)	(0·169)
Irreg Exit	0·566***	0·903***	1·605***	2·447*	0·670*	0·681**	0·800***
	(0·108)	(0·135)	(0·377)	(1·230)	(0·336)	(0·214)	(0·122)
Observations	2,053	2,058	2,053	346	346	969	628

Standard errors in parentheses.

Autocracy is the base category. All models with full set of controls.

$* p < 0.05, ** p < 0.01, *** p < 0.001.$

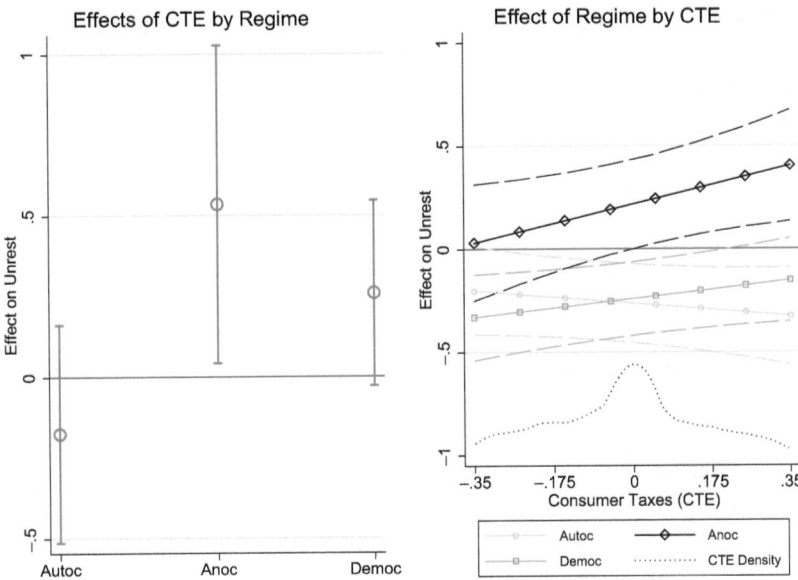

FIGURE 4.5 Regime Type, Consumer Tax, and Unrest Model Results

panel of Figure 4.5, we see that the effects of autocracy on unrest are decreasing in the level of consumer taxes, while the effects of democracy are increasing along with higher values of the CTE variable. However, the effects of these two regime types are statistically indistinguishable from one another at all levels of consumer taxes.

Consumer taxes have a significant positive effect on urban unrest under anocratic regimes, on the other hand. In Model 2.1, a one-unit increase in the CTE variable is associated with a 0.53 increase in the predicted number of unrest events in a city-year, holding all else equal. This effect is statistically significant at the 0.035 level, as shown in the left-hand panel of Figure 4.5. The right-hand panel illustrates that at low levels of consumer taxes, Model 2.1 finds no significant difference in unrest levels across the three regime types, holding all other factors constant. As the CTE variable increases across a two standard deviation range from −0.35 to 0.35, anocracies are associated with increasing rates of unrest and significant differences across regime type emerge. Above a value of zero on the CTE variable, anocratic city-years are predicted to experience significantly more unrest than both autocracies and democracies, and at high CTE levels of 0.35 cities under anocracy are predicted to experience 0.55 more unrest events per year than those under democracy, on average.

Further panel regressions that interact the CTE variable with regime type broadly confirm the result that higher food taxes are associated with greater unrest under anocracy, but not under democracy or autocracy. Model 2.2 is an identical model to Model 2.1, but includes a lagged dependent variable instead of city fixed effects and clusters its standard errors by city. Similar to the model including city fixed effects, the marginal effect of consumer food taxes is negative under autocracy and positive under anocracy, although the size of the effect is very small and insignificant under autocracy. Under anocracy, the positive effect of the CTE variable at its mean is to increase the predicted number of unrest events by 0.53 in a city-year, a similar size to the effect in Model 2.1, but it is estimated with much more uncertainty and is not statistically significant. This model also shows a very small and insignificant effect of the CTE variable under democracy.

Model 2.3 is a logistic regression, which takes a binary indicator of unrest as its dependent variable and like Model 2.1 includes city fixed effects. The results are very similar to those of the model of the number of unrest events in a city-year, but are more uncertain. The effect of a one-unit increase in consumer food taxes on unrest is negative under autocracy, positive under anocracy and small but positive under democracy. Like Model 2.1, the logistic regression predicts significant differences in the likelihood of unrest across regime type as the CTE variable increases. At low levels of CTE below −0.14, there are no statistically significant differences in the predicted probability of unrest across autocracies, anocracies and democracies. However, above this level anocratic city-years have a significantly greater likelihood of experiencing unrest. Where the CTE variable is set to −0.04, an anocratic city-year has a 0.59 probability of experiencing unrest, versus 0.44 and 0.46 in autocracies and democracies, respectively. At a CTE of 0.36, the probability of unrest under anocracy is much larger, at 0.65 versus 0.40 under autocracy and 0.49 under democracy.

I go on to estimate instrumental variables regressions of unrest, where I use the *Export Index* variable as an instrument for consumer food taxes. These models attempt to avoid problems of reverse causality and other forms of endogeneity to estimate the causal effect of food taxes on unrest. Because it is very unlikely that I would be able to find an instrument for food policy that also varied by regime type, I simply estimate identical but separate models for anocracies, democracies, and autocracies. I estimate both linear and Poisson instrumental variables models, and their results are very similar, but due to space constraints I do not report

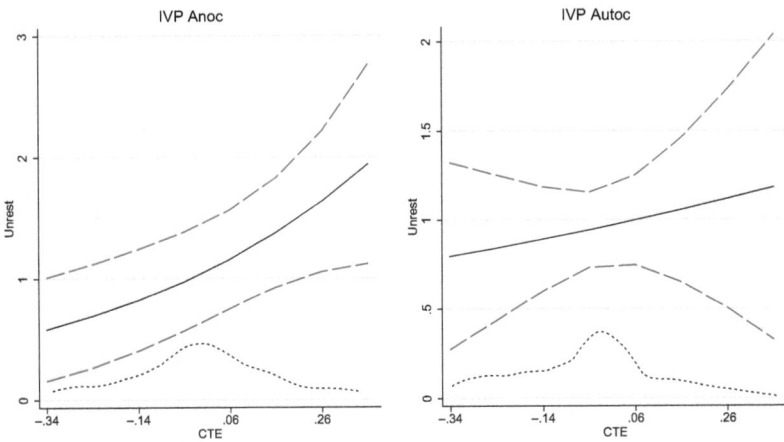

FIGURE 4.6 Regime Type, Consumer Tax, and Unrest IV Model Results

all of them in Table 4.3. I plot the results of Models 2.6 and 2.8 in Figure 4.6.

For anocracies, I report the results of both linear and Poisson instrumental variables regressions as Models 2.5 and 2.6 in Table 4.3. Both robustly confirm that increased consumer taxes are associated with greater levels of urban unrest under anocratic regimes. The coefficient on the instrumented CTE variable in the linear model is positive and significant at the $p < 0.035$ level. A two standard deviation increase in consumer food taxes from -0.34 to 0.37 results in an increase in the predicted number of unrest events from -0.06 to 2.50. Similarly, the results of the Poisson model, which I graph in the left-hand panel of Figure 4.6, show a positive and significant coefficient on the instrumented CTE variable. The same shift in this variable corresponds to an increase in the predicted number of unrest events in a city-year from 0.58 to 1.94. Like the panel data models earlier, these instrumental variables regressions find a significant effect of food taxes on unrest under anocracy. However, the size of these effects is much larger in the latter set of models. In the panel data models, a one-unit increase in the CTE variable was associated with around a 0.5 increase in the number of unrest events in an anocratic city-year. The instrumental variables Poisson model, on the other hand, predicts an increase of 1.5 unrest events for the same shift in the CTE variable. Although the instrumental variables models are imperfect, because they do not include city fixed effects or all regime types in one model, these results do give confidence in the finding that consumer taxes are associated with unrest under anocracy and suggest that the effects of food taxes might in fact be larger than the panel data models found.

For democratic and autocratic regimes, instrumental variables regressions do not find a significant relationship between consumer food taxes and urban unrest. Model 2.7 restricts the sample only to democratic city-years and uses the *Export Index* instrument for the CTE variable. The coefficient on the instrumented indicator of consumer food taxes is positive, but very small and statistically insignificant. I also estimate a linear instrumental variables model, which is not reported here, in which the coefficient on the instrumented CTE variable is of a similarly small size, also statistically insignificant, but negative. On the basis of these results, I cannot reject the null hypothesis that there is no relationship between consumer food taxes and unrest under democracy. Model 2.8 is identical to Model 2.7, but restricts the sample to autocratic city-years. I plot the effect of the instrumented CTE variable on unrest in the right-hand panel of Figure 4.6. Although the coefficient on the instrumented CTE variable is positive and much larger than in Model 2.7, it is not statistically significant, and as we can see clearly in Figure 4.6, the increases in predicted levels of urban unrest across values of the consumer food tax indicator are modest in autocratic city-years compared under anocracy. I also estimate a linear regression that is identical to Model 2.8, but its results are similar. The coefficient on the instrumented CTE variable is positive but does not approach statistical significance.

4.5 CONCLUSION

In Chapter 2, I argued that food consumers in cities are able to mobilize collectively against policies that raise the price of food. This is a key component of the threat that urban interests pose to authoritarian governments and causes them to respond by intervening in agricultural markets to decrease the price of food and stave off political instability. In this chapter, I show that the collective threat that urban food consumers pose in response to food taxes is contingent on political opportunity structures associated with regime type. Under autocratic regimes, urban unrest is suppressed through repression, while democracies are inherently stable political systems, as voters can influence policy through the ballot box. It is under anocratic regimes, which combine a lack of democratic responsiveness with relatively open political opportunity structures, that I find significantly greater levels of urban unrest in response to higher food taxes.

This is an important finding on the political economy of urban instability and civil conflict because it establishes specific grievances caused by government policy alongside general economic deprivation as a cause of political instability and conflict. Although urban food consumers are often cited as a potential source of political instability, especially when confronted with high food prices, previous studies have not attempted to disentangle the unrest effects of shifts in market prices for food from the effects of policy.

My results partially confirm the explanation of urban bias under authoritarianism laid out in Chapter 2 and explored empirically in detail in Chapter 3. The tendency for undemocratic governments to tax farmers and provide cheap food for consumers can be partially explained by the threat of urban unrest. However, my findings are also puzzling. The most autocratic governments, which I find in Chapter 3 to implement highly urban biased policies, are not faced with significant unrest in response to food taxes. Anocracies, which tax consumers more, are. The most repressive governments could therefore be argued to be undertaxing the urban sector relative to its political threat while more permissive anocracies are overtaxing it. Urban bias emerges from my analysis as more than a simple response to the threat of unrest emanating from urban food consumers. More work is need to fully understand the roots of urban bias under authoritarian regimes.

5

Agricultural Rents, Landholding Inequality, and Authoritarian Regime Durability

In Chapter 2, I laid out a theory of agricultural policymaking and political stability. I argued that policymaking revolves around the threat of collective action by rural and urban interests under authoritarian regimes, and that agricultural policy has significant effects on the stability of these governments. Democratic regimes, on the other hand, are more responsive to electoral incentives when making policy and inherently more stable than autocracies. Agricultural policy does not have significant effects on political stability under democracy. In Chapter 4, I undertook a first empirical test of the relationship between agricultural policy and political stability, focusing on urban interests and collective action in the developing world. I found that government food taxes can have significant positive effects in provoking urban unrest, but that these are contingent on broader political opportunity structures. Urban unrest in response to higher food taxes is more likely to occur under anocratic regimes than democracies and repressive autocracies.

The purpose of this chapter is to carry out further cross-national tests of the relationship between agricultural policy and political stability, but focusing on rural interests and collective action and restricting my analysis to autocracies. I examine the relationship between landholding inequality, interventions in agricultural markets and the stability of authoritarian regimes. As in previous empirical chapters, I have gone to lengths to make the quantitative analysis and the major empirical results easily understood in graphs and figures. The most important of these are Figures 5.1 and 5.2, which illustrate my original measures of agricultural rents, and Figures 5.7 and 5.6, which show the relationship between these measures, landholding inequality, and authoritarian regime collapse.

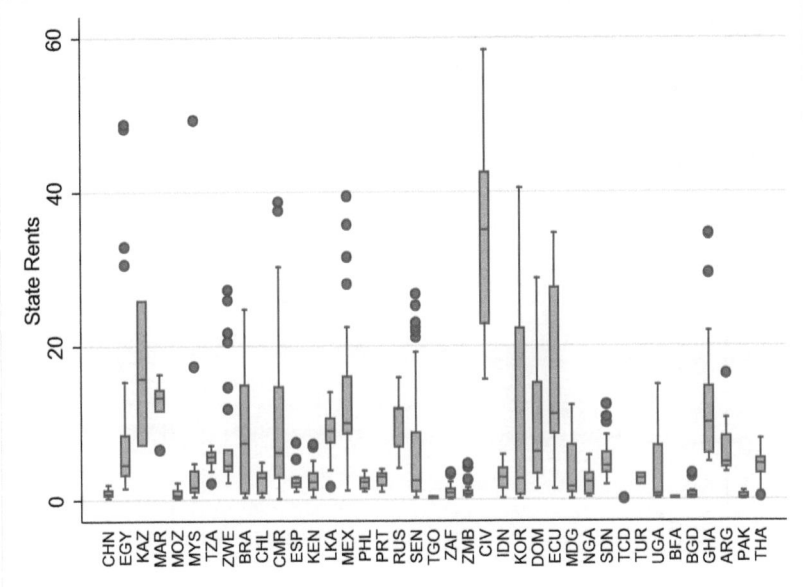

FIGURE 5.1 State Rents Per Capita, Three-Year Moving Average by Country

The chapter is laid out as follows. In an initial section, I discuss the contemporary literature on authoritarian regime durability. I argue that, on the whole, economic factors have not attracted as much interest from scholars of comparative authoritarianism as institutions. Where economics have been linked to authoritarian rule, work has focused on nontax revenues such as oil rents, foreign aid, and remittances from citizens living abroad. The agricultural sector, despite its prominence in our accounts of authoritarian rule and regime change, remains relatively unexplored in empirical work. In order to fill this gap, I construct measures of the size of rents that are generated by agricultural market distortions and distinguish between those that are distributed to producers and those that are most easily captured by the state. I show that the size of state rents is relatively small compared to producer rents, and that both forms of agricultural rents are much smaller than those originating from oil revenues, for example. I then go on to estimate a series of models of authoritarian regime durability. First, I test whether landed elites are threatening to authoritarian regimes, and concentrations of landholdings are associated with a greater risk of regime collapse. I find a weak positive relationship between landholding inequality and

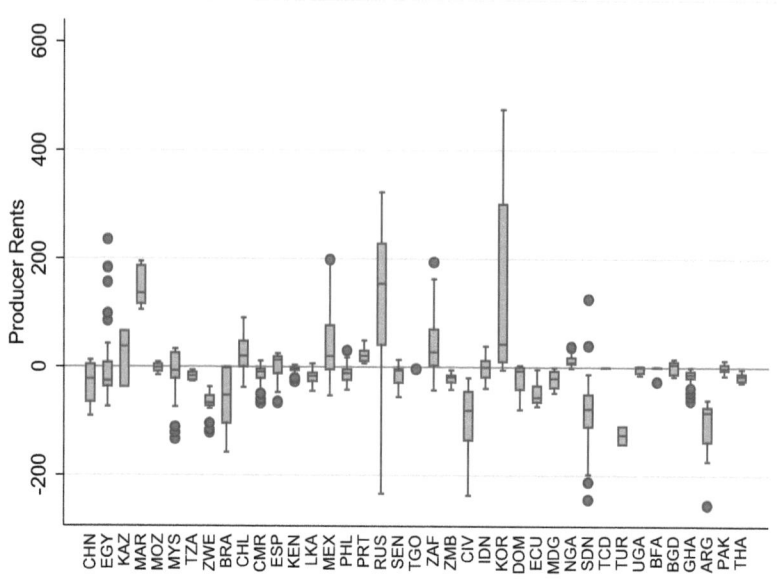

FIGURE 5.2 Producer Rents, Three-Year Moving Average by Country

the likelihood of collapse. Second, I look at the relationship between agricultural rents and regime durability. I find that rents that accrue to the state have no effect on the probability of regime collapse. Rents accruing to agricultural producers, however, do have a significant interactive effect on regime stability. Where landholding inequality is high, regimes that distribute greater rents to the agricultural sector are significantly less likely to break down.

5.1 PREVIOUS LITERATURE

In this chapter, I make a significant empirical contribution to our understanding of the political economy of authoritarianism. First, I estimate the effects of landholding inequality on authoritarian regime durability. This is important, because although landed elites play a central role in theories of authoritarian politics, the effects of landholding inequality on regime durability – rather than transitions to democracy – have not been previously explored cross-nationally. Second, I estimate the effects of agricultural rents on the probability of authoritarian regime collapse. This is important, because although a long-standing literature argues that agricultural market distortions follow a distinct political logic, there have been no empirical studies investigating its effects on the stability of authoritarian governments. Previous studies have highlighted the role of economic rents in perpetuating authoritarian rule, but have focused on oil, foreign aid, and remittances as sources for these rents. They have not examined agriculture as a source of rents with consequences for authoritarian politics and regime stability. Before I proceed with my empirical analysis, I will first situate it within the broader contemporary literature on authoritarian politics.

In the growing literature on comparative authoritarianism, economic factors play a subordinate role to institutions in explaining regime outcomes.[1] In her seminal contribution, Geddes (1999) discussed the tendency for single-party dictatorships to be much more long-lived than military and personalist regimes. Parties help dictators establish durable power-sharing arrangements among elites and to create mass support for the regime, having significant positive effects on regime durability.[2] A broad literature has also established that other nominally democratic institutions, in particular multiparty legislatures and elections, help authoritarian regimes stabilize their position in power (Pepinsky, 2014). They serve as a form of concession to restive groups at large, and prevent revolutionary upheaval.[3] They can help regimes co-opt rival elites and larger groups in society and facilitate the distribution of patronage to supporters.[4] The results of elections also signal levels of support for the regime, providing vital information on the location of strongholds and weak spots for the regime.[5]

Research on authoritarian regime durability has neglected economic policymaking. Policies such as those in agriculture played a central role in canonical accounts like that of Bates (1981). However, recent work has focused on nontax revenue flows that are not generated by government policy, whether they be from natural resource endowments, foreign aid, or remittances. These nontax revenues are seen as distinct and especially important tools of authoritarian rule. They impose no direct costs on the citizenry, but still provide the fiscal means for governments to

---

[1] This is partly due to the criticism of modernization theory implicit in much work on authoritarian politics. Economic factors obviously play a predominate role in the former literature. See, for example, Przeworski et al. (2000), Boix and Stokes (2003), and Ansell and Samuels (2014).

[2] See, for example, Slater (2003, 2010) and Magaloni and Kricheli (2010) for a review.

[3] Schedler (2006), Levitsky and Way (2010), and Gandhi and Przeworski (2007).

[4] Boix and Svolik (2013) and Gandhi and Przeworski (2006).

[5] Brownlee (2007), Malesky and Schuler (2011), and Miller (2015).

appease threatening groups and thus prevent political instability.[6] Natural resource rents, in particular those derived from oil production, have been found to stabilize authoritarian regimes for several reasons. They allow them to distribute welfare and patronage and fund increased spending on repression. They also provide an incentive for authoritarian elites to cling doggedly to power in the face of challenges, as they seek to maintain access to the flows of resources that oil revenues provide.[7] Similarly, foreign aid has been found by some scholars to increase the resources at dictators' disposal to remain in power and decrease their incentives to move toward democratic governance.[8] Finally, remittances sent home by workers abroad form a further source of nontax revenue, which can be used by authoritarian governments to fund patronage and prevent political instability.[9]

Research on economic policymaking under authoritarianism, on the other hand, remains relatively underdeveloped. In particular, similar to my analysis in Chapter 3, it tends to treat economic policy as an outcome of authoritarian politics, rather than a cause of regime stability. Steinberg and Malhotra (2014), for example, find that regimes with smaller selectorates are more responsive to selective interests and more likely to follow a fixed exchange rate. Relatedly, Hankla and Kuthy (2013) find that more institutionalized regimes follow open trade policies because they are less likely to favor selective interests and more likely to favor policies promoting long-term growth. These studies do not take the step to explicitly model the effects of policy on regime durability.

Economic policy in general thus remains a blind spot in the new literature on comparative authoritarianism, but the agricultural sector stands out as a particularly important, but neglected, area for research. We know from canonical studies that landed elites have particularly antidemocratic interests, that they wield considerable influence under

[6] For a discussion, see Morrison (2009).

[7] See, for example, Ross (2001, 2012), Dunning (2008), and Wright, Frantz, and Geddes (2015). The link between oil and authoritarianism is disputed by Haber and Menaldo (2011) but confirmed for the post-1970 period by Andersen and Ross (2014).

[8] Bräutigam and Knack (2004). However, this argument is hotly contested. Dietrich and Wright (2015) argue that economic aid promotes democratization, Dunning (2004) finds that aid promoted democracy in the post–Cold War era, and Wright (2009) argues that the effects of aid are conditional on authoritarian coalition structure.

[9] Ahmed (2012) and Abdih, Chami, and Dagher (2012). Escribá-Folch, Meseguer, and Wright (2015) dispute this finding, arguing that remittances are qualitatively different from other forms of nontax revenue because they accrue to individuals and not the government. They find no effect of remittances on democratization on average and democratic effects under single-party regimes.

authoritarian governments and block moves toward democracy.[10] A similarly important body of literature also examines the effects of authoritarian politics on the agricultural sector. It suggests that agricultural policy plays a significant role in authoritarian regime durability. However, this role revolves around placating threatening urban interests rather than landed elites.[11] Undemocratic governments impose urban-biased policies that decrease the price of farm produce and food in order to privilege these urban interests and prevent political instability. There is an obvious puzzle here: If landed elites are such powerful proponents of authoritarian government, why are they so disadvantaged by agricultural policy under autocracy? The urban-bias thesis only tells half the story of agricultural policy under authoritarian governments. As I showed in Chapter 3, we obscure considerable variation in policy outcomes by taking an urban-biased stance and ignoring the role of producers. Where landholding inequality is high, indicating the presence of a powerful landed elite, authoritarian governments intervene in agricultural markets to increase returns to farmers.

In this chapter, I explore the role of landed elites and agricultural policy in authoritarian regime durability. I account not only for urban bias but also the trade-off between urban and rural interests in agricultural policymaking when making predictions on the consequences of these policies for authoritarian politics. This is a novel contribution. Bates (1981) describes the ways in which government market interventions in Africa are used to distribute rents and cement urban support coalitions for authoritarian rulers and to fragment the rural opposition through the provision of selective benefits. He explains these policies as instruments in the accumulation of political influence that help governments retain power (Bates, 1983, 125–133). However, policy enters the analysis predominantly as a tax on agriculture and as an outcome to be explained, not as a cause of regime stability. Similarly, Wallace (2013) argues that urban-biased agricultural policy affects regime stability, but only through its positive effects on urban migration, which leads to the growth of large and unstable urban agglomerations.

---

[10] This is argued by influential theories of democratization such as those by Boix (2003), Acemoglu and Robinson (2006), and Ansell and Samuels (2014). It is also shown in subnational studies such as those by Ziblatt (2008a, 2009), Thomson (2015), and Baland and Robinson (2012).

[11] See the seminal works by Lipton (1975, 1977), Bates (1981, 1983), and Scott (1985), but also more recent research such as Wallace (2013, 2014), Olper and Raimondi (2011), and Bates and Block (2013).

This chapter makes the first systematic attempt to explore the effects of agricultural policy, and specifically rents extracted from the agricultural sector, on authoritarian regime durability. I argue that the effects of rents depend on the underlying threat structures facing an authoritarian regime. Resources derived from agricultural market interventions significantly decrease the likelihood of authoritarian regime collapse when they are directed toward threatening groups. When landholding inequality is high, indicating the presence of a powerful and threatening landed elite, regimes minimize the likelihood of regime collapse by distributing rents to the agricultural sector. Conversely, when landholding inequality is low, indicating that threats emanate primarily from the urban sector, regimes minimize the threat of regime collapse by stripping rents from the agricultural sector and redistributing them to urban interests.

5.2 DATA: MEASURING AGRICULTURAL RENTS AND AGRICULTURAL PRODUCER POWER

My theory of agricultural policy, regime type, and political stability laid out in Chapter 2 generates three hypotheses related to the relationship between agricultural rents and authoritarian regime durability. First, because landed elites find it relatively easy to mobilize and influence or oppose authoritarian governments, landholding inequality will be associated with political instability under authoritarianism:

$H_{3.1}$, *Rural Collective Action:* Landholding inequality will be associated with an increased probability of authoritarian regime failure, holding all else equal.

Second, agricultural market distortions generate rents that can be appropriated by authoritarian elites and used for their own political purposes. They attract challenges from rival elites and rural interests, increasing the risk of political instability:

$H_{3.2}$, *State Rent-Seeking:* Policies that provide greater state access to agricultural rents will be associated with a greater risk of regime collapse, holding all else equal.

Finally, rents generated by agricultural distortions do not accrue only to the state but to the broader rural sector. They can therefore be used to buy off landed elites and mitigate the threat that they pose to the regime:

$H_{3.3}$, *Rural Collective Action:* Policies that distribute rents to agricultural producers will be associated with a lower likelihood of authoritarian regime collapse when landholding inequality is high, holding all else equal.

My arguments relating agricultural rents to authoritarian regime durability differ from those in previous studies of natural resource rents because they do not focus exclusively on rents accruing directly to states or rents that do not require taxation of citizens. Instead, the agricultural policies that I examine here do clearly impose costs on citizens – both farmers and food consumers – while generating politically relevant rents that accrue both to the state and farmers, depending on the product and policy instrument. To differentiate between types of rents, I construct variables capturing rents accruing to the state and a separate variable capturing those affecting the value of agricultural production and thus farmer welfare. Because my theory does not revolve solely around state rents, and because no data are available that measure directly how much of the rents derived from agricultural market distortions accrues to the state, I do not use a measure of fiscal reliance or the share of agricultural rents in government revenue (Haber and Menaldo, 2011). My measures of rents capture the population-weighted value, in constant US dollars, of government market distortions. They are similar to measures of total oil income per capita used elsewhere in the resource curse literature.[12] They are constructed from World Bank product-level market distortion data by Anderson and Valenzuela (2008).

Measures of Agricultural Rents

The first variable measuring agricultural rents in this chapter, **State Rents**, captures the rents most easily and directly captured by the state from the agricultural sector. These are those derived from restrictions to trade in agricultural commodities. Rents can emerge from policies that impose lower domestic prices than world markets for export commodities. In this case the state pays farmers a low price for their produce, receives a higher price for exports on world markets, and captures the difference. Rents can also emerge from policies that impose higher domestic prices than world markets for imported commodities. In this case the state pays a low price on world markets, receives a higher price from domestic consumers, and captures the difference. These sorts of policies are often implemented

---

[12] See, for example, Dunning (2008) and Ross (2012).

by state agricultural marketing and export boards, which can divert the resulting windfalls to government coffers.

The variable that I construct to measure the size of these rents is the sum of the total market distortion generated by policy measures implemented *at the border*, such as tariffs or quantity controls. This total market distortion is computed for all traded agricultural products in a given country-year and weighted by total population to give a measure of state rents in constant US dollars,

$$\textit{State Rents}_{c,t} = \frac{\sum_{i=1}^{p} Q_{p,c,t} \times BP_{p,c,t} \times BMS_{p,c,t}}{\textit{Population}_{c,t}}, \quad (5.1)$$

where Q is the volume of exports in the case of exportable products, and the volume of imports in the case of importable products; BP is the undistorted border price of like products in a given country-year; and BMS is the border price support, the percentage by which trade measures increase or decrease domestic prices vis-à-vis world market prices.[13] In the case of exports, the BMS in this equation is the percentage (in absolute terms) by which domestic prices are decreased compared to world market prices; in the case of imports, the BMS is the percentage by which domestic prices are increased compared to world market prices. The BMS therefore captures the magnitude of the distortion from world market prices caused by government agricultural policy, and when multiplied by the volume of trade for each commodity it captures the size of rents resulting from market interventions. Because the value of state rents can fluctuate significantly from year to year due to shifts in world market prices and exchange rates, I use a three-year moving average of the variable in all my analyses here. In addition to the population-weighted **State Rents** variable presented here, I also construct a GDP-weighted measure, which I will use as a robustness test in my analyses.

The variable **State Rents** only captures positive rents, not any possible fiscal burdens imposed by policy. Agricultural policy can impose fiscal costs on states, but it does so relatively rarely because the costs of policy are mostly passed on to consumers in the form of higher food prices, while rents generated by trade policy can be relatively easily captured by the government. **State Rents** only captures the effects of border measures because the resulting rents are those most easily generated and appropriated by the state. Domestic policy measures such as input or con-

---

[13] To relate the BMS to variables used in Chapters 3 and 4, it is the portion of the Nominal Rate of Assistance which is caused by trade restrictions for each product.

sumption subsidies do not generate rents that so clearly accrue to the government and its agents. Border policy measures, on the other hand, are applied either directly by the state or by parastatal organizations such as producer marketing boards or food logistics agencies whose resources are relatively easily appropriated by the government.[14] I do not claim that the entire value of these market distortions is captured by the state. However, restrictions on trade have long been recognized as a widespread and lucrative source of rents. Although some rents from border policy measures are captured by private importers and exporters, particularly those resulting from quotas, the proceeds of export and import tariffs accrue to the state and are a significant source of government revenue in the developing world.[15]

To illustrate the measure, in 1981 Argentina was ruled by a repressive military dictatorship. Its pampean ranchers produced approximately 4.5 million tons of beef that year, which was worth around $1520 per ton on the world market.[16] The country has a comparative advantage in pastoral agriculture and is highly competitive in beef production, so 16 percent of this beef was exported, about 720,000 tons.[17] These exports were subject to a border price support of −36 percent, meaning that Argentine farmers were paid around $550 less than world market prices per ton for their beef, due to government trade restrictions. The magnitude of the price distortion to beef in 1981 was very high by global standards and compared to distortions in Argentina of less than 5 percent from 1990 to 2005. To a certain extent, the policy outcome was caused by the large increases in international agricultural prices during the period, which were not being passed on to Argentinian farmers. However, it was not very different from average distortions of over 20 percent in the 1970s and 1980s, when Argentina experienced considerable political instability. Argentine policy since the Second World War has imposed export taxes on agriculture in order to protect industrial interests and provide easy fiscal

---

[14] See the depictions of African agricultural marketing boards in Bates (1981, 11–29) and of the rice logistics agency BULOG in Indonesia by Timmer (1993).

[15] See Krueger (1974) on quotas and export licenses and Bates (1981) on the state revenue imperative behind policy. Unfortunately, the World Bank agricultural distortions data do not decompose the effects of border policy measures into those due to quantity restrictions versus tariffs.

[16] This discussion is based on data from Anderson and Valenzuela (2008) and the study of Argentinian agricultural policy by Sturzenegger and Salazni (2008). See also O'Donnell (1978) and Richardson (2009). The prices given here are all in 2000 US dollars.

[17] The logic of the **State Rents** for importable products is simply the reverse of that for exportable products: Rents are generated by the difference between a higher domestic price and a lower international price, multiplied by the quantity imported.

TABLE 5.1 *Summary Statistics: Regime Durability Models*

Variable	Mean	Std. Dev.	Min.	Max.	N
Failure	0.06	0.23	0	1	970
St Rents/Cap 3y	6.88	14.62	0	159.23	970
Pr Rents/Cap 3y	−9.37	68.86	−474.61	658.58	970
Land Gini	0.57	0.16	0.23	0.98	970
Oil Inc/Cap	59.99	140.87	0	1,059.93	970
Ln GDP	6.52	1.04	4.36	9.06	970
Civil War	0.1	0.3	0	1	970
Reg Democ	16.36	16.28	0	95.45	970
Military	0.2	0.4	0	1	970
Party	0.51	0.5	0	1	970

revenues for the government. These were successful in generating rents accruing to the state. The total dollar value of trade restrictions to beef – the difference between world market prices and the price paid to farmers, multiplied by the total quantity exported – amounted to over $396 million in Argentina in 1981. The total value of trade restrictions to agriculture is the sum of these values across all traded products. I weight this figure by a state's population or GDP to create the **State Rents** variable.

In Figure 5.1, I present a box plot of the **State Rents** data by country, including all authoritarian country-years, which are in this chapter's empirical analysis. This is a three-year moving average of the variable as depicted in Equation 5.4, excluding a small number of outliers. Countries are listed on the *x*-axis by number of regime failures during the period included in the analysis, 1963–2006. Therefore, China and Egypt are at the extreme left of the plot because these regimes persisted for this entire period, Chile is in the center of the *x*-axis with one regime failure, and Pakistan and Thailand are at the extreme right of the *x*-axis with five failures each. The average regime had annual state rents of only $7 per capita in the entire dataset, the variable has a standard deviation of $26, and values above $60 are very rare. There is no clear association between state rents and the proclivity of a country to experience regime failure observable in this plot. There is relatively wide variation in the size of per capita rents generated by border policy measures across the spectrum of regime instability, with the greatest within-country variation seen in countries such as Ivory Coast, South Korea, and Ecuador. Summary statistics of the key variables used in this chapter's analysis are presented in Table 5.1.

The second variable that measures agricultural rents in this chapter, **Producer Rents**, captures the impact of government market distortions on farmers rather than the value of rents accruing to the state. This variable is the sum of total assistance to farmers across all products in a given country-year. I weight total assistance by the agricultural population to generate a figure in constant US dollars,

$$Producer\ Rents_{c,t} = \frac{\sum_{i=1}^{p} VOP_{p,c,t} \times NRA_{p,c,t}}{Agricultural\ Population_{c,t}}, \tag{5.2}$$

where *VOP* is the undistorted value of production, by product and country-year, in constant US dollars; and *NRA* is the nominal rate of assistance, or the percentage by which government policy measures increase or decrease domestic prices vis-à-vis world market prices for like products. The NRA includes all market interventions, both at the border and domestically. Because government policy can both increase and decrease farmers' incomes vis-à-vis world market prices, **Producer Rents** can be both positive and negative.

To illustrate, consider the Argentinian example outlined earlier. In this case, all government policies affecting beef farmers were imposed at the border and had the net effect of decreasing domestic producer prices by around 36 percent versus border prices. Because beef was exported in large quantities, these policies generated rents derived from the gap between domestic and international prices, which could be captured by the state. However, these rents were generated at the expense of Argentinian beef producers, leading to a negative total value of the **Producer Rents** variable for this product in 1981, of around −$396 million. Consider, by contrast, beef policy under the authoritarian South African government in the same year.[18] Since the formation of the country in 1910, the South African regime had followed policies that privileged white farmers. Increasingly isolated internationally by the early 1980s, it continued its stance, which implemented significantly higher prices for farm produce compared to those on world markets. Faced with the same international prices as the Argentinian regime, but without a comparative advantage in beef production, South African policies had the net effect of increasing domestic beef prices by 75 percent compared to those on world markets. Given total production of around 600,000 tons that year, the total value of this policy to beef producers was around $585 million. The **Producer**

---

[18] This very brief description is based on Kirsten, Edwards, and Vink (2009) and Kirsten, van Zyl, and Vink (1998).

Rents is the sum of all such policy-generated rents, whether positive or negative, weighted by the size of the agricultural population.

In Figure 5.2, I present a box plot of the **Producer Rents** data by country, showing a three-year moving average on the *y*-axis and listing countries by the number of regime failures on the *x*-axis and excluding a small number of outliers as in the plot of state rents in Figure 5.1. Unlike the outcomes depicted in the Figure 5.2 plot, producers can be affected both positively and negatively by policy, so I include a horizontal line at zero on the *y*-axis to show a neutral policy as a reference point. The average regime followed policies that decreased returns to agriculture by $21 per person working in the sector, though the **Producer Rents** variable has a much larger variance than the **State Rents** variable with a standard deviation of $355. Values above $500 and below −$350 are very rare in the data. Similarly to trends in the **State Rents** variable, there is no clear association between the size of the rents distributed to farmers and regime instability distinguishable in Figure 5.2.

In Figure 5.3, I present histograms of all measures of agricultural rents and also of the Haber and Menaldo (2011) data on oil income per capita. The size of both forms of agricultural rents is considerably smaller than per capita natural resource income as measured by Haber and Menaldo (2011). In oil-producing countries, these incomes typically run into the hundreds or even thousands of dollars per capita per year. In Norway, they increased from zero to over $5000 per year in the first two decades following the discovery of oil; in Mexico, natural resource income was around $500 per capita in the year 2000. Both measures of **State Rents**, whether weighted by population or GDP, are skewed toward zero. The mean level of these rents per capita is only $7, and levels more than one standard deviation above the mean, over $33, are quite rare. Ivory Coast had very high levels of state rents per capita, between $35 and $160, from the 1970s through 2009. Malaysia had very high levels of state rents accruing from trade restrictions during the international food crisis of 2007–2009, reaching the maximum level seen in the dataset of $525 per capita in 2009. However, these cases are rare exceptions. Rents as a share of GDP follow a similar pattern to those calculated per capita, with the mean level of rents around 1 percent of GDP and values above 3 percent relatively rare. The largest values on this variable are observed in states with relatively large agricultural distortions and low levels of development. Ivory Coast, along with several other West African regimes such as Ghana and Senegal, each had several years of state rents above

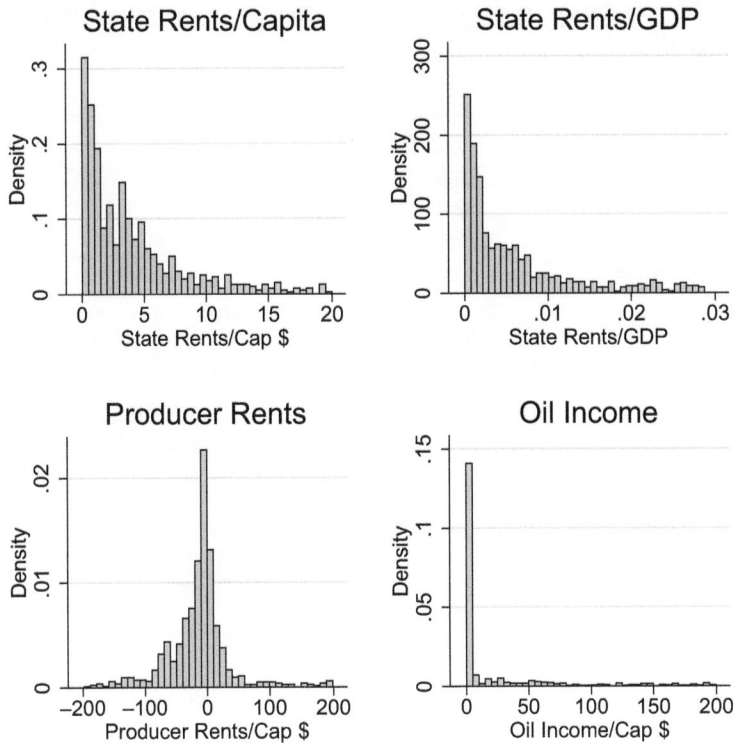

FIGURE 5.3 Rent Variables, Histograms

5 percent; the highest levels of rents as a share of GDP observed the dataset were 15 percent in Ivory Coast and Ghana in 1978. **Producer Rents** weighted by agricultural population have a mean value of −$622 in the dataset. As illustrated in the histogram in the lower-left panel of Figure 5.3, values of the variable are clustered densely around the mean. Although the standard deviation of the variable is $359, rents per capita of less than −$100 and greater than $50 are relatively rare. Countries with large negative values on the **Producer Rents** variable include the Argentinian case discussed earlier, from the mid 1970s to the early 1980s, Ivory Coast, Malaysia during the 2007–2009 food crisis, and Sudan from the early 1980s to the late 1990s. Countries with large positive values on the variable include Chile under the Pinochet regime in the late 1980s, South Korea under military rule from the early 1970s to the late 1980s, and the South African case discussed earlier, from the mid 1980s to the mid 1990s.

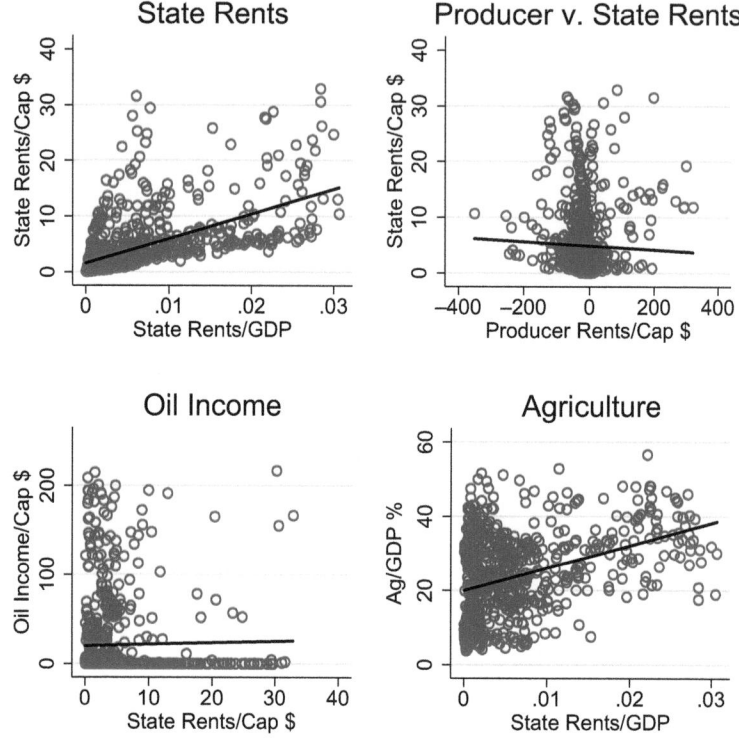

FIGURE 5.4 Rent Variables, Simple Correlations

In Figure 5.4, I present scatter plots that illustrate the simple correlations between the rent variables, oil income, and the share of agriculture in total output. The top-left panel shows that there is a strong positive correlation ($r = 0.80$) between the **State Rents** variables, that weighted by total population and that weighted by GDP. There is a slight negative correlation between **Producer Rents** and **State Rents**. Producer rents are the net effects of all policies affecting the agricultural sector and can be either positive or negative. State rents are derived from trade restrictions and can only be positive. The simple correlation between the **Producer Rents** variable and state rents weighted by population is -0.09, the correlation with the GDP-weighted measure is -0.25. As illustrated in the lower-left panel of Figure 5.4, there is no correlation between oil income and the rents measures ($r = 0.06$ with state rents per capita, shown here). There is a positive ($r = 0.17$) correlation between the GDP-weighted **State Rents** variable and the share of agriculture in GDP, as illustrated in the lower-right panel of Figure 5.4. However, the correlations with the population-weighted measure and **Producer Rents** are much weaker at $r = -0.09$ and $r = 0.02$, respectively. Simple regressions of the population-weighted **State Rents** and **Producer Rents** variables on indicators of authoritarian regime type show no significant differences in levels of these variables across party, military, and personalist dictatorships, when controlling for per capita GDP.

Landholding Inequality and Agricultural Producer Power

The effects of agricultural rents on authoritarian regime durability are conditional on the threats facing these regimes. When farmers pose a significant threat to regime stability, this threat can be mitigated via policies that distribute rents to agricultural producers. Conversely, when farmers are not a threatening group, regimes maximize their chances of survival by redistributing rents to more threatening urban interests.

Testing this argument requires a measure of the power of agricultural producers. Following my account of authoritarian policymaking in Chapter 2 and analysis in Chapter 3, I use a Gini coefficient of landholding inequality to capture the ability of farmers to threaten the stability of an authoritarian government. Greater levels of landholding inequality are an indicator of rural interests' political power because as land is concentrated in the hands of fewer individuals, this group is more likely to be able to act collectively to lobby and oppose the regime; it is more likely to be able to withhold production and use this threat when making demands for an advantageous policy, and large landowners often hold considerable local political power, which regimes seek to enlist in maintaining political order in the countryside.

Data on landholding inequality used in this chapter are Gini coefficients collected in national agricultural censuses coordinated by the Food and Agriculture Office of the United Nations (FAO).[19] Because these data are collected at ten-year intervals, at the best, I inter- and extrapolated from them to generate a comprehensive country-year dataset on land inequality. The variable **Land Gini** ranges from 0.23 to 0.98 as used in the present analysis and has a mean of 0.58. In some models, I use the variable **Interpolated LG**, which includes only land Ginis interpolated between two data points, excluding extrapolated values and countries with only one observation. This variable has an identical range to **Land Gini**, but its

---

[19] For more details on this data, see Chapter 3.

mean is slightly higher, at 0.62. The lowest levels of landholding inequality are in Asia and West Africa, which are characterized by smallholder agriculture. The highest levels of landholding inequality are in Latin America and South and East Africa. Levels of landholding inequality change relatively slowly over time; in Brazil the land Gini changed only from 0.84 to 0.83 from 1965 to 1985, while in Egypt it changed from 0.46 to 0.69 between 1975 and 2000.

Dependent Variable: Regime Collapse

In this chapter, I am interested in assessing the consequences of agricultural policy for the stability of authoritarian regimes. Therefore, analysis in this chapter is restricted to undemocratic political systems only, whereas in previous chapters I examined comparative evidence across regime type. Authoritarian regimes are distinct leadership groups, which make the most important decisions on policy and political leadership within a country, but are not chosen through democratic elections. Often these groups are dominated by ruling parties, the military, or an ethnic group. Political conflict in these types of regimes focuses on control of the executive and the ability to nominate the ultimate leadership of the regime.[20] It therefore can result both in a change in the individuals represented in government, or in the rules used to choose the government. Political instability under authoritarianism results from an inability to effectively manage conflicting claims to power and can have four possible outcomes: no leadership transition and the continuation of the current regime; the continuation of the current regime under new leadership; the collapse of the regime and its replacement with democracy; or the collapse of the regime and its replacement with a new authoritarian coalition. Following established definitions of regime collapse, only when the ruling leadership group is replaced with another can we speak of an authoritarian regime collapse. When a leadership group persists, even in the face of a change in key individuals, a regime is not deemed to have collapsed.

The indicator of regime collapse used in this chapter is from the data published by Geddes, Wright, and Frantz (2014, elsewhere GWF). Authoritarian regimes in this dataset are determined primarily on procedural grounds, that is, whether they achieved power via free, fair and competitive elections in which at least 10 percent of the total population was entitled to vote. This represents something of a deviation from the

---

[20] See, for example, Geddes, Wright, and Frantz (2014) and Svolik (2009, 2012).

coding of dictatorship in previous chapters, which was based on the Polity dataset and included restrictions on civil liberties. However, the differences are not large, and I use the GWF dataset because, unlike previous cross-national regime type datasets such as Polity, it explicitly codes authoritarian regime collapses as such, rather than coding only transitions between autocracy and democracy.[21] These data cover a total of 280 autocratic regimes from 1946 to 2010, which ended with a transition to democracy in 102 cases and a transition to another authoritarian regime in 112 cases. They also code each dictatorship as a monarchy, when power is held by a single ruling family; a military regime, when it is dominated by the army or other branch of the armed forces; as a single-party regime, when power is in the hands of a dominant party; and as a personalist regime when the government is controlled by a narrow group surrounding a single dictator. Single-party regimes have been the most common form of authoritarian regime since the end of the Second World War, though they are no longer much more common than personalist regimes. Military regimes were very numerous during the Cold War but have declined in number since 1990. Monarchies have made up a relatively small but unchanging proportion of authoritarian regimes since 1946.

Control Variables

My models control for all major variables that have been found to influence authoritarian regime durability. I include the natural log of per capita GDP from the World Development Indicators (World Bank, 2012b) in all models, and a measure of total oil income per capita from Haber and Menaldo (2011). All models also include controls for time dependence following Beck, Katz, and Tucker (1998), civil wars and the diffusion of democracy at the regional level from Haber and Menaldo (2011). Some models include a larger set of controls including indicators for military and party dictatorships from Geddes, Wright, and Frantz (2014) and political liberalization using the Polity score by Marshall and Cole (2011).

---

[21] An alternative dataset on authoritarian regime durability, rather than democratization, is that by Svolik (2012). I use the GWF data here, in order to ensure comparability of results with many other empirical analyses that use their coding of authoritarian institutions.

5.3 MODELS AND RESULTS

The general empirical approach in this chapter is similar to many previous studies of authoritarian regime durability.[22] I model the likelihood of an authoritarian regime collapse, where a regime collapse entails the replacement of one authoritarian leadership coalition either with a democratic regime or another leadership group. I do so using the data on autocratic breakdowns and regime transitions by Geddes, Wright, and Frantz (2014) described earlier. Democracies are explicitly excluded from the sample in this analysis. I am interested in the relationship between agricultural rents, the power of agricultural producers, and regime durability.

I begin my empirical analysis by testing $H_{3.1}$, that greater concentrations of landholdings are associated with an increased probability of authoritarian regime failures, by estimating models of the effect of landholding inequality on authoritarian regime durability,

$$ln\left(\frac{Pr(y_{i,t})}{1 - Pr(y_{i,t})}\right) = \beta_1 + \beta_2 LandGini_{i,t} + \beta_3 X_{i,t} + \epsilon_{i,t}, \qquad (5.3)$$

where $y_{i,t}$ is a binary variable indicating whether a regime collapses in a given country-year, **Land Gini** is the data on landholding inequality discussed earlier, and $X_{i,t}$ is a vector of variables that control for other factors influencing regime durability, including time dependence. Because of the limited coverage of my land inequality data, I estimate two sets of models. One includes all the land Ginis interpolated and extrapolated from the FAO agricultural census data (the **Land Gini** variable) and has around 2,800 observations. A second includes only those interpolated between two observations, excluding extrapolated values and countries with only one land Gini observation (the **Interpolated LG** variable) and has around 1,100 observations. Equation 5.3 is modeled using logistic regression, and I specify the standard errors $\epsilon_{i,t}$ to be clustered by country. The results of these landholding inequality models are reported in Table 5.2.

Two further sets of models estimate the effects of agricultural rents on regime durability. The first tests $H_{3.2}$, that state access to rents from the agricultural sector will be associated with a greater risk of regime failure. These models are identical to the land inequality models but include the **State Rents** variables and are specified,

$$ln\left(\frac{Pr(y_{i,t})}{1 - Pr(y_{i,t})}\right) = \beta_1 + \beta_2 StateRents_{t,c} + \beta_3 X_{t,c} + \epsilon_{t,c}. \qquad (5.4)$$

---

[22] For example, Wright, Frantz, and Geddes (2015), Escribá-Folch, Meseguer, and Wright (2015), and Wright (2009).

TABLE 5.2 *Results, Landholding Inequality, and Authoritarian Regime Stability*

	(1.1) Land G	(1.2) Land G	(1.3) Land G	(1.4) IP Land G	(1.5) IP Land G
Land Gini	0·91 (0·56)	−1·63 (2·83)	1·31* (0·70)		
Land Gini Sq		2·11 (2·20)			
Interpolated LG				0·58 (0·91)	1·57 (1·13)
Military			0·58** (0·26)		−0·35 (0·42)
Party			−1·40*** (0·31)		−2·22*** (0·52)
Polity			0·21*** (0·03)		0·26*** (0·04)
Oil Inc/Cap	−0·00 (0·00)	−0·00 (0·00)	−0·00 (0·00)	0·00 (0·00)	0·00 (0·00)
Ln GDP	−0·15 (0·14)	−0·16 (0·14)	−0·30* (0·17)	0·16 (0·23)	0·05 (0·31)
Civil War	0·89*** (0·22)	0·91*** (0·23)	0·45 (0·34)	1·16*** (0·30)	0·48 (0·38)
Observations	2,769	2,769	2,738	1,085	1,071
AIC	1155.08	1156.40	949.83	483.55	382.23

Standard errors in parentheses.
All models include regime age, temporal splines, and regional democracy.
* $p < 0.10$, ** $p < 0.05$, *** $p < 0.01$.

I estimate two models including the population-weighted **State Rents** variable and two including the GDP-weighted **State Rents/GDP**. The first set of models is reported in Table 5.3.

The second set of models tests $H_{3.3}$, that policies that distribute rents to agricultural producers will be associated with a lower likelihood of authoritarian regime collapse when landholding inequality is high. They are the same as those listed earlier, but interact the land Gini with the **Producer Rents** variable described earlier,

$$ln\left(\frac{Pr(y_{i,t})}{1 - Pr(y_{i,t})}\right) = \beta_1 + \beta_2 ProducerRents_{t,c} + \beta_3 LandGini_{t,c}$$
$$+ \beta_4 ProducerRents_{t,c} \times LandGini_{t,c} + \beta_5 X_{t,c} + \epsilon_{t,c}. \quad (5.5)$$

TABLE 5.3 *Results, Producer Rents, State Rents, and Authoritarian Regime Stability*

	(2.1) St Rents	(2.2) St Rents	(2.3) Pr Rents	(2.4) Pr Rents	(2.5) PR Land G	(2.6) PR Land G	(2.7) PR IP LG
State Rents	0·01 (0·01)	0·02 (0·01)					
Producer Rents			−0·00 (0·00)	0·00 (0·00)	0·01*** (0·00)	0·01** (0·00)	0·01** (0·01)
Land Gini		2·37** (1·17)		2·13* (1·25)	0·83 (1·21)	1·83 (1·20)	
Interpolated LG							0·94 (2·44)
Pr Rents*LG					−0·02*** (0·01)	−0·02** (0·01)	
Pr Rents*IP LG							−0·03*** (0·01)
Military		1·50*** (0·50)		1·44*** (0·45)		1·40*** (0·46)	
Party		−1·64** (0·71)		−1·70* (0·74)		−1·56** (0·73)	
Polity		0·28*** (0·05)		0·27*** (0·05)		0·27*** (0·05)	
Oil Inc/Cap	−0·00 (0·00)		−0·00 (0·00)	0·00 (0·00)	0·00 (0·00)	0·00 (0·00)	0·00 (0·00)
Ln GDP	−0·01 (0·24)	−0·55** (0·25)	−0·04 (0·21)	−0·57** (0·24)	−0·35 (0·26)	−0·67** (0·27)	−0·52 (0·41)
Observations	885	828	961	877	886	877	468
AIC	384.09	281.71	420.84	305.31	392.40	305.02	237.63

Standard errors in parentheses.
Controls: regime years, temporal splines, and regional democracy.
* $p < 0.10$, ** $p < 0.05$, *** $p < 0.01$.

These models are presented in Table 5.3. By including the measures of agricultural rents and their interactions with landholding inequality, I can test my hypotheses that the effects of rents have significant effects on regime durability, conditional on the political power of farmers. However, because the coverage of the World Bank agricultural distortions dataset is not as broad as that of the land inequality data, these models have a maximum of around 1,000 observations compared to 2,800 for the land inequality models.

Results: Landholding Inequality

I turn first to the results of the models, which include landholding inequality without its interaction with agricultural rents, and test $H_{3.1}$. These are presented in Table 5.2 and graphed in Figure 5.5. I argue that because it is an indicator of a powerful landed elite, landholding inequality will be associated with a greater risk of authoritarian regime collapse, though its unconditional effects excluding agricultural rents are only suggestive of the total relationship between land inequality and regime stability. As I outlined earlier, although landholding inequality has been found in previous studies to have a negative effect on democratization, this is the first cross-national study of its effects on authoritarian regime durability. There are four models reported in Table 5.2 and Figure 5.5. The first three use the full **Land Gini** dataset and include around 2,800 observations. Model 1.2 tests for a nonlinear relationship between landholding inequality and regime collapse by including the squared term of **Land Gini**. Models 1.4 and 1.5 use the smaller **Interpolated LG** dataset and include only around 1,100 observations. Only GDP, oil income, civil conflict, previous regime failure, and regional democratic diffusion are included as controls in Models 1.1, 1.2, and 1.4, while Models 1.3 and 1.5 also control for authoritarian regime type and the Polity score.

The models presented in Table 5.2 find a positive relationship between landholding inequality and authoritarian regime collapse, although this relationship is only statistically significant at the $p < 0.10$ level in Model 1.3. The association between landholding inequality and regime instability appears to be monotonic, as Model 1.2 does not find a statistically significant relationship between **Land Gini**, its squared term, and regime collapse. In Model 1.1, which includes the full **Land Gini** data and a relatively sparse set of control variables, the coefficient on the **Land Gini** variable is positive but significant only at the $p < 0.104$ level. Moving

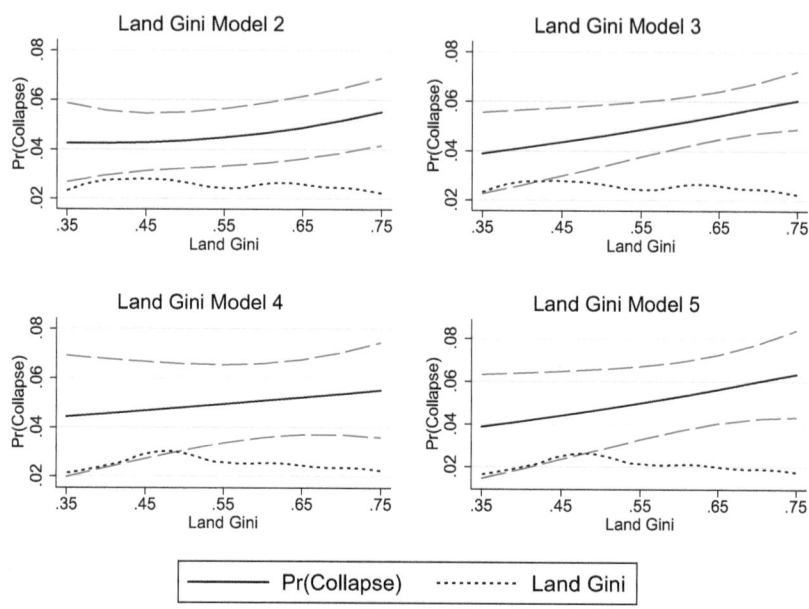

FIGURE 5.5 Landholding Inequality and Regime Collapse

across a two standard-deviation range of **Land Gini,** from 0.40 to 0.75, generates an increase in the predicted probability of regime collapse in a given year of around 1.5 percentage points, from 0.042 to 0.057. By comparison, a two standard-deviation shift in the **Ln GDP** variable results in a slightly smaller decrease in the predicted probability of regime collapse, from 0.063 to 0.048, while the incidence of a civil war increases the likelihood of regime collapse from 0.050 to 0.111. Model 1.2, which includes the squared term of **Land Gini,** generates almost identical increases in the predicted probability of regime collapse to those from Model 1.1, but these are estimated with greater uncertainty. As illustrated in the upper-left panel of Figure 5.5, moving across a two standard-deviation range of the variable increases the probability of collapse from 0.043 to 0.055.

Model 1.3 in Table 5.2 includes controls for military and party regimes and the Polity score and finds larger substantive effects of landholding inequality on regime failure. This model finds a positive relationship between landholding inequality and regime failure, which is statistically significant at the $p < 0.061$ level. The effect of the land Gini on regime collapse in Model 1.3 is graphed in the upper-right panel of Figure 5.5. Moving from 0.4 to 0.75 on the land Gini variable increases the probability of regime failure in a regime-year by slightly more than two percentage points, from 0.039 to 0.061. This is around a one-third larger effect than that seen in Model 1.1 with a more sparse set of control variables. By comparison, a two standard-deviation shift in **Ln GDP** in Model 1.3 results in a decrease in the likelihood of regime collapse of around the same magnitude, from 0.068 to 0.043, and the incidence of a civil war in a country increases the probability of regime failure by around two percentage points from 0.050 to 0.073. Model 1.4 also includes controls for authoritarian regime type and democratization. Military regimes are significantly more likely to collapse in this model, with a failure probability of 0.046 versus 0.075 for personalist regimes in a given country-year. Party regimes are significantly more stable, with a predicted probability of failure of 0.082 versus 0.024 for personalist regimes. The Polity score is also a significant predictor of regime instability, with an increase in the Polity score from −6 to 5, or from full autocracy to a highly open anocracy, associated with an increase in the probability of regime collapse from 0.03 to 0.21.

Models 1.4 and 1.5 include the **Interpolated LG** variable, which restricts the land Gini data to those interpolated between two observations from the FAO dataset. This excludes all extrapolated observations and regimes with only one land Gini datapoint in my dataset. The results of Models 1.4 and 1.5 are graphed in the lower two panels of Figure 5.5. Model 1.4 includes **Interpolated LG** and the smaller set of controls. This model finds a smaller and statistically insignificant relationship between landholding inequality and regime failure. In Model 1.3, a shift from a land Gini of 0.35 to 0.85 results in an increase in the probability of regime failure of slightly less than two percentage points from 0.041 to 0.059. As in Model 1.1, civil war remains a major predictor of regime failure in this model. The incidence of civil war is associated with an increase in the predicted probability of regime failure from 0.052 0.146. Model 1.5 is identical to Model 1.3, but includes the **Interpolated LG** variable. The coefficient on **Interpolated LG** in this model is similar in size to that on **Land Gini** in Model 1.3, but it is not statistically significant ($p < 0.17$). The predicted increases in regime failure associated with a shift in the **Interpolated LG** variable in Model 1.5 are very similar to those generated by Model 1.3, from 0.041 to 0.064. In this model, party regimes are more durable than personalist dictatorships, and those with a higher Polity score are more likely to collapse. However, in Model 1.5 military dictatorships are not more likely to fail than personalist dictatorships, as in Model 1.3.

The five models presented in Table 5.2 and Figure 5.5 give a picture of the simple relationship between landholding inequality and regime collapse, leaving aside the role of agricultural policy and rents. In sum, they indicate that landholding inequality is positively and monotonically associated with authoritarian regime instability, but this association is very uncertain. As landholding inequality varies, the substantive size of changes in the predicted likelihood of regime collapse is not trivial. It is similar in magnitude to shifts in economic development and to the effects of civil war and some institutional characteristics of autocracies. However, it is estimated with a lot of uncertainty, barely reaching statistical significance in one of the five models. Institutional variation among autocracies, most importantly party institutions and restraints on the executive measured by the Polity score, have much larger and statistically significant effects on regime durability. This suggests that there is no significant, simple relationship between landholding inequality and authoritarian regime durability. In the remainder of this chapter, I will explore how this relationship changes when controlling for, and interacting with, rents created by government intervention in the agricultural sector.

Results: Agricultural Rents

I turn now to the effects of agricultural rents on regime durability. I begin by testing $H_{3.2}$, that greater state access to agricultural rents will be associated with a greater risk of regime collapse, holding all else equal. In Table 5.3 I present the results of two models including **State Rents**, weighted both by population, as a predictor of regime failure.[23] As with the landholding inequality models in Table 5.2, I estimate one set of regressions with a relatively sparse set of controls before including variables to account for more possible confounding factors.

In Model 2.1, agricultural rents accruing to the state have no effect on regime failure. The coefficient on the **State Rents** variable is positive but statistically insignificant. The predicted change in the likelihood of regime collapse in a given regime-year as the **State Rents** is increased from zero to $60, a change of around two standard deviations, is from 0.05 to 0.07. This is a substantively larger change in the likelihood of regime collapse compared to that associated with variation in landholding inequality, but it is estimated with a great deal of uncertainty; across

---

[23] I also estimated a model (unreported) using the natural log of the population-weighted state rents variable, and the results were unchanged.

the range of **State Rents**, the 95 percent confidence intervals around the predicted probability estimate overlap, and at high levels of the variable they span zero. Model 2.2 also estimates the effects of **State Rents** on regime failure, but controls for landholding inequality, institutional characteristics of autocracies, and the Polity score. The coefficient on **State Rents** in this model is larger than in Model 2.1 and is estimated with more certainty, but nonetheless does not reach statistical significance ($p < 0.12$). The shifts in the predicted probability of regime failure associated with a two standard-deviation increase in **State Rents** are large in Model 2.2, from 0.05 to 0.11, but they are not statistically significant. Similar to the landholding inequality models reported in Table 5.2, military regimes are more likely to collapse than personalist regimes, party regimes are less likely to collapse, and the Polity score is positively associated with regime collapse in Model 2.2. However, in Model 2.2 **Land Gini** is positively and more significantly associated with regime collapse than in previous models; a two standard-deviation shift in the variable generates an increase in the probability of collapse from 0.04 to 0.07. I also estimate two further models that are identical to Models 2.1 and 2.2, but they include a **State Rents/GDP** variable, which is weighted by total GDP rather than by population. I do not report these results in Table 5.3. Similar to the previous models, they find a positive but insignificant association between these rents and regime collapse, though the magnitude of the effects found in these models is smaller.

These four models of **State Rents** and authoritarian regime failure do not give reason to reject the null hypothesis of $H_{3.2}$, that greater state access to agricultural rents is not associated with the risk of regime collapse. Although the substantive size of the relationship between **State Rents** is not trivial in Models 2.1 and 2.2, it does not reach statistical significance. In models that include the GDP-weighted **State Rents** variable, the size of the relationship between it and regime failure is very small and does not approach statistical significance.

I now move on to testing $H_{3.3}$, that policies that distribute rents to agricultural producers will be associated with a lower likelihood of authoritarian regime collapse when landholding is high, holding all else equal. The first model presented as Model 2.3 in Table 5.3 includes only a sparse set of control variables and finds no simple relationship between **Producer Rents** and regime failure. The coefficient on the variable is small, negative, and statistically insignificant. Moving from −85 to 65 on the **Producer Rents** variable, a shift of two standard deviations, results only in a small decline in the probability of failure from 0.062 to 0.049. Model 2.4

includes controls for institutional characteristics of authoritarian regimes and still finds no significant relationship between rents distributed to the rural sector and regime instability. The coefficient on the **Producer Rents** variable is positive, but very small and does not approach statistical significance. The predicted change in the probability of regime collapse associated with a two standard-deviation shift in the producer rents variable is negligible, at around one-third of one percentage point. As in previous models, in Model 2.4 military regimes emerge as significantly more likely to collapse then personalist regimes, party regimes are significantly less likely to fail, and regimes with higher Polity scores also are significantly more likely to collapse. The coefficient on the **Land Gini** coefficient is also positive and significant at the $p < 0.09$ level in Model 2.4.

In Table 5.3, I also present the results of two models that include an interaction between the **Producer Rents** variable and the **Land Gini**. These models test whether the effects of rents distributed to the agricultural sector on regime stability are conditional on the power of rural interests. Model 2.5 includes the interaction with a smaller set of control variables. The results suggest that rents distributed to agricultural producers are significantly associated with regime instability when interacted with landholding inequality. The coefficient on the **Producer Rents** variable is positive, the coefficient on **Land Gini** is positive, and the interaction term between the two variables is negative. A joint test of all three coefficients is highly significant ($p < 0.001$), meaning that I can reject the null hypothesis that there is no relationship between these three variables and regime instability. The signs of these coefficients indicate that distributing rents to the agricultural sector is positively associated with regime collapse at low levels of landholding inequality and negatively associated with regime collapse at high levels of landholding inequality. I graph the average marginal effects of **Producer Rents** from Model 2.5, surrounded by 95 percent confidence intervals, in the left-hand panel of Figure 5.7. They indicate that at a land Gini of 0.40, one standard deviation below the mean of the variable, producer rents are significantly positively correlated with regime failure. This relationship quickly becomes statistically insignificant at levels above 0.45, and at land Ginis above 0.65 there is a significant negative correlation between **Producer Rents** and regime failure. Expressed in terms of predicted probabilities, setting the land Gini at 0.40 and allowing **Producer Rents** to vary two standard deviations from −85 to 65 results in a 2.3 percentage point increase in the predicted probability of regime failure, from 0.034 to 0.057. Setting the land Gini at 0.75 and allowing **Producer Rents** to vary by the same amount results in a 4.6 percentage

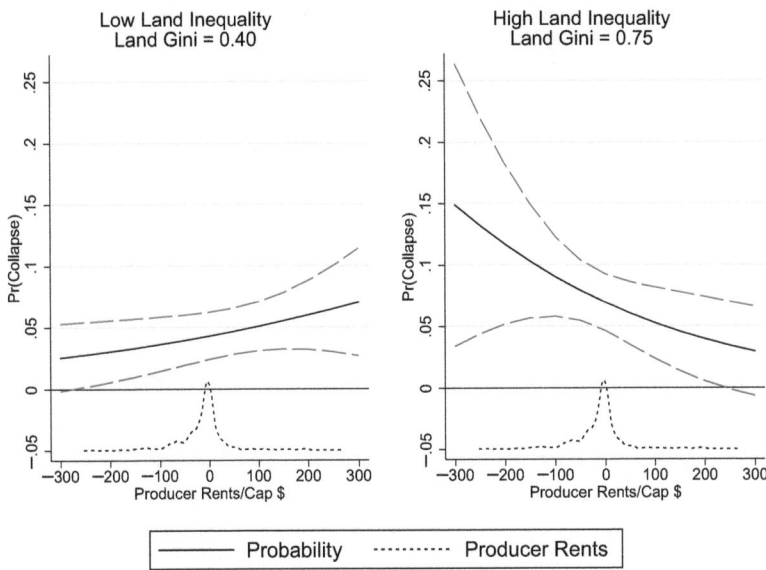

FIGURE 5.6 Producer Rents and the Probability of Regime Collapse, Model 2.6

point decrease in the predicted probability of regime failure from 0.090 to 0.044. In Model 2.5, changes in the predicted probability of regime failure are much greater at high levels of landholding inequality, around double the magnitude of those seen at low levels of this variable.

Model 2.6 in Table 5.3 is identical to Model 2.5, but includes the more complete set of control variables familiar from earlier: military and party institutions and the Polity score. The results are similar to those in Model 2.5. Producer rents and landholding inequality are positively associated with regime collapse, while the coefficient on the interaction between the two variables is negative. A joint test of the significance of the coefficients on the two variables and their interaction is significant only at the $p < 0.05$ level, meaning that there is more uncertainty around the relationship than in the results of Model 2.5. This is reflected in the marginal effects plot presented in the right-hand panel of Figure 5.7. The average marginal effect of the **Producer Rents** variable is positive at low levels of landholding inequality and negative at land Ginis above 0.50, but it is not significantly different from zero. Variation in predicted probabilities generated from Model 2.6 is also less than in Model 2.5. Setting the land Gini at 0.40 and allowing **Producer Rents** to vary two standard deviations from −85 to 65 results in a 1.1 percentage point

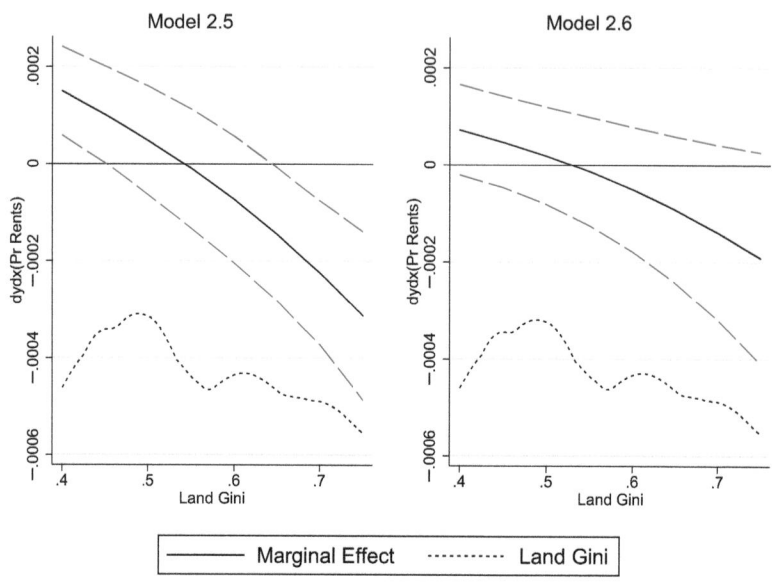

FIGURE 5.7 Marginal Effects of Producer Rents by Land Gini, Table 5.3

increase in the predicted probability of regime failure, from 0.037 to 0.048. The variation in Model 2.5 was around double this magnitude. Setting the land Gini at 0.75 and allowing **Producer Rents** to vary by the same amount results in a 2.9 percentage point decrease in the predicted probability of regime failure from 0.087 to 0.058. The variation predicted by Model 2.5 in this case was a little more than 50 percent greater. I graph the variation in predicted probabilities from Model 2.6 across almost the entire range of the **Producer Rents** variable in Figure 5.6.[24] This clearly illustrates the much larger magnitude of the relationship between rents and regime instability at greater levels of landholding inequality. In the left-hand panel of Figure 5.6, I set the **Land Gini** variable at 0.40, and the predicted increase in the probability of regime collapse across the range of **Producer Rents** is 4.4 percentage points, from 0.026 to 0.070. In the right-hand panel I set **Land Gini** at 0.75, and the corresponding decrease in the probability of regime collapse is almost three times as large, 11.9 percentage points from 0.149 to 0.030.

I estimate one final model of producer rents and regime durability, presented as Model 2.7 in Table 5.3. This model includes only the restricted sample of landholding inequality data, which is interpolated between two

---

[24] The full range of the variable is from −475 to 659.

values, excluding all extrapolated values and countries with only one land Gini in the dataset. Model 2.7 therefore only has around 470 observations versus some 885 in Model 2.5. It also includes only the smaller set of control variables as in Models 2.3 and 2.5. The results of Model 5 are very similar to those of Model 2.5. At low levels of landholding inequality, where the **Interpolated Land Gini** is below 0.65, there is no significant relationship between **Producer Rents** and regime collapse. Unlike in Model 2.5, the marginal effect of the variable is negative but only significant at the $p < 0.09$ level at low levels of the **Interpolated Land Gini** in Model 5. At land Ginis of 0.65 and above, there is a significant negative correlation between **Producer Rents** and regime collapse. Setting the **Interpolated Land Gini** at 0.75 and increasing the variable from −85 to 65 results in a seven percentage point decrease in the predicted probability of regime collapse from 0.115 to 0.045. This is a 65 percent larger substantive effect than that seen in Model 2.5, which included the complete sample of land Gini data.

5.4 CONCLUSION

This chapter is a cross-national test of my hypotheses relating to rural collective action, agricultural rents, and political stability under authoritarian governments. The main finding is that landholding inequality and agricultural rents have an interactive effect on the likelihood of authoritarian regime collapse. Unequal concentrations of land at the national level are weakly associated with regime failure, but where governments distribute greater rents to the rural sector, this effect is mitigated, and these policies significantly decrease the likelihood of collapse. The substantive size of the effects of agricultural rents are large at high levels of land inequality; they are comparable to the differences in the probability of regime failure seen across party and military dictatorships, for example. This is a novel empirical contribution to the literature on authoritarian regime durability, and a central element of the argument that I present in this book. Agricultural policy does not only affect the urban sector and the likelihood of protest in cities, as I showed in Chapter 4. Here I show that the rural sector can threaten an authoritarian government when it is characterized by high levels of landholding inequality. Agricultural policy plays an important role in mitigating this threat and is not biased solely toward powerful interests in cities.

The cross-national evidence presented in the preceding three chapters illustrates that the theoretical logic laid out in Chapter 2 holds in general terms when including as many cases as possible in the analysis. It is also very useful for comparing the effects of agricultural rents on regime stability to those of confounding factors, which vary at the national level, particularly institutional features of autocracies. However, it is also abstract, giving little insight into the precise causal link between structural variables and outcomes in the form of policy, and political stability. It also suffers from weaknesses inherent in cross-national statistical analysis: Although my models control for the most important confounding factors, bias due to an omitted variable or other endogeneity give cause to be careful in taking a causal interpretation of my results. For this reason, I present case studies of the relationship between threats, agricultural policy and regime durability in Imperial Germany and Malaysia in Chapters 6 and 7. In these case studies, I can more clearly trace out the ways that structures of landholding inequality and agricultural employment lead to authoritarian regimes' stances in agricultural policy, and how these policy stances affect regime stability.

6

Agricultural Policy and Authoritarian Regime
Durability in Germany, 1878–1890

6.1 INTRODUCTION

In Chapter 2, I laid out an account of agricultural policymaking across
regime type and its effects on political stability. I argued that government interventions in the agricultural sector play a significant role in promoting authoritarian regime stability. Using policy to reduce food prices
can mitigate the likelihood of unrest among urban food consumers, particularly under anocracy, as I showed empirically in Chapter 4. Where
landholding is high, and rural elites pose a significant threat to an authoritarian regime, this threat can be mitigated by policies that distribute
rents to the rural sector. I tested this argument in Chapter 5. My cross-
national statistical analysis in that chapter does not illustrate the exact
causal mechanism linking landholding inequality, agricultural policy, and
regime stability, however. It is not clear, for example, what sort of political dynamic the positive correlation between landholding inequality and
authoritarian regime collapse in my models is capturing. Similarly, the
threat of a landed elite could have effects on the policymaking process
at different points, for example within the executive or in authoritarian
legislatures. In previous chapters I have illustrated these correlations anec-
dotally, for example, by describing the coup mounted by landed elites
against Chávez in Venezuela in 2002. In this chapter, I use a case study
of Imperial Germany to probe these causal mechanisms in more detail.
Germany lies outside the temporal scope of my analysis in Chapter 5,
showing that my arguments have traction beyond the post-1945 world. It
is particularly useful for tracing the causal mechanisms behind my cross-
national findings because it is typical for, and confirmatory of, the theory

laid out in Chapter 2. Germany also occupies a theoretically prominent place in the literature on development and democratization, making this chapter relevant to a wide range of existing scholarship.

I examine the political causes and consequences of a protectionist shift in agricultural policy that took place in the late 1870s in Imperial Germany and significantly increased domestic food and agricultural produce prices. Embedded within a qualitative discussion of the broader institutional setting and political process leading to the adoption of the famous 1879 "iron and rye" tariff, I analyze an original dataset on the characteristics of German electoral districts, delegates to the Reichstag, and their voting patterns on the protectionist bill. I show that the impetus for the shift to protection was an exogenous shock: sinking international grain prices, which shifted the policy preferences of landowning *Junker* elites away from free trade by around 1877.[1] The threat of the rural sector within the regime was strong, as the unelected Chancellor who steered the policymaking process was an agent of landed elites with historical links to the monarchy and a well-organized lobby. I estimate two empirical models to show that the link between landholding inequality and the political threat posed by the rural sector ran not only through aristocratic networks of influence, but also through the legislature. High levels of landholding inequality in German electoral districts were correlated with disproportionate representation of aristocratic landowners and rural conservatives in the Reichstag, while urban interests – and particularly food consumers – had little influence. Models of Reichstag delegates' votes on the 1879 tariff bill show that representatives of districts with strong preferences for lower food prices were opposed to the protectionist policy shift. However, landowners and conservative representatives voted overwhelmingly for protection, formed a larger group within the legislature, and were able to form a coalition with the Catholic *Zentrum* to pass the bill. Subsequent gains from the protectionist trade policy fell disproportionately on areas dominated by the Prussian aristocracy and characterized by higher levels of landholding inequality. Agricultural policy thus played a key role in ensuring the aristocracy's political support for the Chancellor for the duration of his tenure.

---

[1] In fact, the central role played by international market forces in this case study presents an important driver of policy that I essentially bracket in Chapters 4 and 5 by controlling for international food prices in my cross-national regressions. However, the question of how international market fluctuations *interact* with domestic political structures and policy environments to create political outcomes is one deserving of a more complete treatment. See, for example, Gourevitch (1977).

6.2 PREVIOUS LITERATURE: AUTHORITARIANISM AND AGRICULTURAL PROTECTION IN NINETEENTH-CENTURY EUROPE

Embodied most famously in the repeal of the Corn Laws in Britain in 1846, there was a secular shift toward liberal trade policies in Europe, including agricultural trade, from the beginning of the nineteenth century until the 1870s.[2] Indeed, major trading nations such as Great Britain, France, the Netherlands, and Belgium had no tariffs restricting trade in grain from the 1860s through 1900, with only France imposing import restrictions to protect farmers in the 1880s. In Britain and the Low Countries, industrialization and the diversification of elites' assets had led to the waning of the political power of landed interests, and with it support for protection, which increased food prices. France's larger and more homogeneous agricultural sector was able to overcome initial resistance from the government and was protected against falling international grain prices by tariffs starting in the 1880s.

In Germany, the move to protection came more swiftly and decisively than in the rest of Europe, starting in 1879 with the infamous "iron and rye" tariff which is the centerpiece of this case study. Agricultural policy in the German Empire made a dramatic shift from free trade to protectionism, with restrictions on grain and livestock imports being steadily increased, and the domestic prices of staples such as wheat and rye rising significantly above world market prices. By 1880, German policies had increased domestic wheat prices to 13 percent above international levels, while in France they were only 6 percent above those on world markets. In 1890, the countries' respective levels of support for wheat prices were 27 percent and 18 percent.[3] I argue that German policy, which was significantly more interventionist and pro-producer than those followed by other European nations, was not a simple function of economic interests. Instead, it was the result of an authoritarian survival strategy, which secured the support of powerful agricultural interests at the expense of relatively powerless food consumers.

The argument that protectionism in agriculture was a tool by which the Imperial German regime sought to remain in power is not new. Beginning in the 1870s, a steep decline in the price of imported grain buffeted Prussian agricultural elites economically and threatened to erase them from the political landscape through a wave of bankruptcies and estate sales.

---

[2] See, for example, Kindleberger (1975), Schonhardt-Bailey (2006), and Swinnen (2009).
[3] These figures are from Swinnen (2009, 1505).

German liberals such as Brentano (1911) recognized at the beginning of the twentieth century that the protectionist response of the government to the existential crisis of the landed Junkers was not only an important shift in policy. It was also part of a strategy by which Bismarck sought to secure the position of the monarchy by propping up its core aristocratic support base and co-opting it into supporting the regime, at the expense of urban food consumers. For later historians such as Gerschenkron (1943), the imposition of grain tariffs in 1879 "meant the perpetuation of the feudal element in German society through preservation of the traditional economic basis of the Junkers." Similarly, Rosenberg (1967, 178–188) noted that through agricultural protectionism, Bismark was able to "freeze" the rural class structure and distribution of land ownership in the face of an economic crisis, safeguarding the political support of agricultural elites for the existing regime while at the same time extending the power of the state in economic affairs and securing the Empire.

Political scientists have approached the German move to protectionism in agriculture from a different angle, regarding it more as an empirical testing ground for theories on the political consequences of international economic integration than as a case study of an authoritarian survival strategy.[4] Rogowski (1989, 38–43) famously explains the "iron and rye" coalition in Germany as one between land and capital, or scarce economic factors of production as predicted by the Stolper-Samuelson theorem (Stolper and Samuelson, 1941). Brawley (1997) notes that Rogowski's approach cannot explain the persistence of protectionism in Germany despite considerable capital accumulation during the last part of the nineteenth century and argues that the coalitions formed around trade policy are better explained by a model allowing for factors of production to have varying degrees of mobility. Schonhardt-Bailey (1998) emphasizes the role of political ideology, and political parties, as intervening variables that affected the impact of economic interests on German trade policy after 1878.

As informative as these analyses are, they implicitly assume that the country was a parliamentary democracy, and that political parties in the

---

[4] Berman (2001, 442) is a notable exception; using the Imperial German case to illustrate the strengths and weaknesses of modernization theory, she briefly notes Bismarck's tariff policies as a mechanism by which he attempted to "lock in" the support of landed interests and large industrialists for the monarchy. Gourevitch (1977) also makes note of "political explanations" of protectionism after 1873, but does not give due credit to the authoritarian nature of the German political system at the time. Economic historians also approach the "iron and rye" coalition without an eye to authoritarian politics; see, for example Klug (2001).

Reichstag made the critical decisions over tariffs. As I will explain in more detail later, the Imperial German political system was a complex structure over which the Kaiser and his Chancellor exercised decisive authoritarian influence. Therefore, although patterns of party support or legislative voting can illustrate the links between economic dynamics and some of their political effects, they were only a small part of a larger mechanism by which policy was made in the Empire.

Rather than a testing ground for political-economic theory, I take the Imperial German case as a source of valuable material illustrating authoritarian politics, economic policy under authoritarianism, and the politics of a pro-producer authoritarian agricultural policy. This case study focuses on the founding Imperial regime, that of Kaiser Wilhelm I and his Chancellor Otto von Bismarck, from the time directly before the imposition of the first protective tariffs (1878) until the death of the Kaiser (1888) and subsequent dismissal of Bismarck (1890). I choose to limit my analysis to this time period in order to restrict the unit of analysis to one "regime" under a concrete set of actors. The extension of the case study to include Kaiser Wilhelm II and his governments would create several extra layers of complexity while not providing much in the way of extra insight into the role of agricultural policy in authoritarian regime survival.

6.3 SETTING THE STAGE: INSTITUTIONS AND POLITICAL THREATS TO THE IMPERIAL GERMAN REGIME

Imperial Germany in the late nineteenth century was not a parliamentary democracy, but an authoritarian monarchy in which the unelected executive was responsible to the Kaiser, not the legislature. It was a constitutional regime that would today be described as "competitive" or "electoral" authoritarianism, where nominally democratic institutions play an important – though not decisive – role in maintaining and exercising political authority.[5] The autocratic power of the monarch and his Chancellor was moderated, especially by the lower house of the Imperial legislature, the Reichstag, which was elected by universal male suffrage and had veto power over legislation. However, influence was still heavily concentrated with the Kaiser, his political appointees, and the Prussian aristocratic elites. The Kaiser stood completely aloof from parliamentary politics and had the capacity to dissolve the Reichstag at will. Neither the Chancellor nor his Ministers were responsible to parliament, and Bis-

---

[5] See Levitsky and Way (2010) and Schedler (2006).

marck regarded the Reichstag with contempt when it attempted to moderate the power of the executive, using all the tactics and resources at his disposal to achieve his policy goals. For these reasons, the German regime considered here, despite the centrality of its elected parliament to my account, fits within the categorization of an authoritarian regime as defined in this book.

As in many authoritarian regimes, policymaking was a decidedly top-down process in Imperial Germany, but unlike many authoritarian regimes, agricultural interests predominated at its center. Imperial government ministries were never established after the unification of Germany, so domestic policy remained the primary preserve of the Chancellor and his Prussian state bureaucracy. It was also subject to considerable influence by the agricultural interests politically dominant in that part of the country, as Prussian landowners held influential positions within the regime. For example, the landed aristocrat Otto Stolberg-Wernigerode became Bismarck's Imperial Vice Chancellor in 1878 after serving as President of the Prussian House of Lords and was able to advocate the adoption of a protectionist policy stance the following year (Jacobs, 1908). Botho Wendt zu Eulenburg, a descendant of ancient Saxon nobility and the owner of a large estate in the east of present-day Poland, was Prussian Minister of the Interior between 1878 and 1881 (Born, 1959).

Despite the influence of agricultural interests, the elected Reichstag did have the power to modify and strike down any legislative proposals by a simple majority. Creating supportive majorities at this crucial veto point was a difficult battle for Bismarck from the beginning of his tenure and became more difficult as it proceeded, driving him to craft shifting coalitions between his loyal Conservative supporters and other parliamentary factions. The Chancellor's task of creating supportive majorities was made considerably easier by the composition of the Reichstag, which despite Conservative party members' lack of an absolute majority was nonetheless comprised predominantly of aristocratic landowners and white-collar professionals. The parliament was thus a gathering of elites, particularly agricultural elites, and proved receptive to their interests rather than those of the general population, who barely featured among their members. I collected data on the occupations of every member of the Reichstag at the time of the passage of the protectionist agricultural tariff bill in 1879. These data are displayed in Table 6.1 and show that aristocratic landowners were not confined to the ranks of the Conservative parties, but were also represented in Liberal

TABLE 6.1 *Members of the Reichstag, 1879, by Occupation and Party Group*

Occupation	Conservative	Liberal	Zentrum	SAPD	Regional	Total
Landowner	77	21	32	0	20	150
Professional	28	77	48	3	13	169
Businessman	8	27	10	4	5	54
Farmer	1	3	1	0	1	6
Industrialist	1	10	1	0	0	12
Total	115	138	92	7	39	391

Source: Election results from 1878 election were published by the Statistisches Reichsamt (1879), occupations from biographical handbooks by Haunfelder (1999, 2004, 2010), Schröder (1995), and the Database of Reichstag Deputies (Hirth, 1878, 115–259).

parties, the Catholic Zentrum, and regional minority parliamentary groups such as that of the Polish minority in Silesia. They made up a remarkable 38 percent of the total members of the Reichstag in 1879, although they comprised a vanishingly small proportion of the Empire's total population. The largest group in the Reichstag by occupation was that of professionals such as lawyers, doctors, teachers and professors, who made up 43 percent of the total membership. Businesspeople, farmers, and workers were notably absent from the parliamentary benches, making up barely 15 percent of the Reichstag together. The few exceptions, such as the famous Social Democrat August Bebel who had apprenticed as a carpenter and joiner in Leipzig, serve to illustrate the dominance of economic elites in the membership of the Reichstag.

Despite the constitutional authority of the Kaiser, the Imperial German regime was not inherently secure; it faced political threats to its future viability, in particular from rising urban interests, but also indirectly from established rural elites. Biographers of Wilhelm I and Bismarck agree that their primary goal in government was the the preservation of the Prussian monarchy in the face of domestic challenges "from below" – that is, variously, from liberal professional elites, the Catholic church, or Social Democrats and the working class. Bismarck's position and success as Chancellor were derived from his dedication to, and political skill in achieving, this end (Steinberg, 2011).

A policy that supported agriculture was favored by the regime for two reasons. On the one hand, for the Chancellor, if not for the Kaiser, there was the risk of being replaced in his position by rival elites, or a problem of "authoritarian power-sharing" (Svolik, 2012). On the other hand, for the entire regime the economic and social position of the Prussian landowning class was essential for the perpetuation of the monarchy. Threatened by plummeting grain prices, the Junkers needed government support in order to preserve their role in the political system. Thus, a pressing threat originated from the Prussian rural sector, which was sufficient to compel the Chancellor to follow an agricultural policy that privileged this group over urban food consumers.

Rural elites, who were more reactionary than Bismarck and saw political compromise with liberals as a betrayal of their interests, had been the Prussian economic and social ruling class for hundreds of years. Their large estates dominated vast swathes of the East Elbian countryside, giving them dominant positions in local life as landlords and employers, which even in the nineteenth century were akin to those of feudal lords (Schissler, 1980). Landowners formed a large and loyal group of deputies in both the Prussian state parliament and the Reichstag. These aristocratic Junkers also had a large degree of formal and informal influence over the Kaiser, who actively sympathized with the Junkers. They dominated the Prussian and later Imperial army and also had a large influence on military policy and administration in the Kaiser's Military Cabinet (Schmidt-Bückeburg, 1933). Playing such a central role in the Imperial political system, aristocratic Prussian landowners were nonetheless threatened by cheap grain imports from North America and the Russian Empire by the end of the 1870s. This economic threat to their social and political standing was an implicit threat to the stability of the monarchy itself. For Bismarck, the risk of being replaced by an untraconservative Prussian rival was real, especially after his break with the Junkers' parliamentary wing, the *Altkonservative Partei*, in 1866. In 1872, for example, in response to Bismarck's progressive policies, which posed a threat to the social position of the large landowners in East Prussia, both the Prussian General von Moltke and the Ambassador in Paris, Count Arnim von Roon, were considered as replacements for Bismarck by conservative elements in Prussia. As a concession to the Junker elites, the Kaiser forced the Chancellor to give up his position as Prussian Minister President for a year, but to his longtime political ally von Roon rather than his archconservative rival Moltke.

6.4 SOCIOECONOMIC STRUCTURES, POLITICAL THREATS, AND THE COMPOSITION OF THE 1879 REICHSTAG

The lack of a strong socioeconomic position in the Empire was a significant determinant of the weak political position of the German urban sector in the 1870s and the corresponding strength of the rural sector. Low levels of urbanization and associated inequality implied a population of food consumers who did not pose an immediate threat of political unrest, and these socioeconomic factors also weakened the presence of antiprotection parties in the Reichstag. At the same time, high levels of landholding inequality perpetuated the social and political status of the regime-friendly Prussian aristocracy, including its position within the critical veto point of the Reichstag.

Industrialization in Germany, which drew huge numbers of migrants in search of work from the countryside to the cities, had begun to have a large impact on the demographics of the Empire by the 1870s. The earliest census data available, from 1882, show that the proportion of employment in agriculture was 44 percent, with industry, trades, and mining making up 34 percent and middle-class professions such as commerce, banking, and professional services 11 percent.[6] As peasants – food producers, if not necessarily on a large capitalist scale – moved out of agriculture and became industrial workers, the number of food consumers grew in Germany, and it continued to grow through the course of the 1880s (Berman, 2001, 442). However, urbanization was still in its early stages in the 1870s, with the proportion of the population living in large towns and cities with over 20,000 inhabitants only around 12.5 percent in 1871, although this figure was to grow swiftly to 34.7 percent by 1910 (Grant, 2005, 56–67). Therefore, large concentrations of food consumers, who would find it easier to organize in violent or conspicuous political opposition to higher food prices, and thus pose a threat to the regime, were not yet a feature of the Imperial German landscape in the 1870s. Food consumers did not occupy a dominant economic position within Germany, with agriculture still making up almost one-third of national income (Hoffmann, 1965). Urban migration in Germany also carried with it economic risks to the urban population, which left many of them impoverished and politically disenfranchised. Reflecting contemporary accounts that describe precarious, unsafe working conditions in large industrializing cities such as Berlin, Grant (2002, 4) shows what he describes as a "hollowing out" of the income distribution in Prussia in the course of the nineteenth century. Simultaneous increases occurred in the number of rich individuals paying the highest tax rate, and in the number of the very poor who were excused from paying any income tax whatsoever.

---

[6] Census data are from Statistisches Reichsamt (1884).

Inequality was significantly higher in urban areas versus rural areas, with an average Gini coefficient for income of 0.43 versus 0.35 in 1896.[7]

The socioeconomic position of food consumers in Germany in the 1870s was not one that gave them the resources to organize in overt and direct political opposition to higher food prices, in the form of protests or food riots. Furthermore, low levels of urbanization and inequality weakened the position of the working class and food consumers in parliamentary politics. As I will show in more detail later, these factors of a broader structural transformation in the German economy were driving support for Liberal parties and the Social Democrats, but examination of voting returns from 1878 show that the Social Democratic movement (the only party that proved to vote en masse against higher food prices) was still very weak, winning only 2 percent of seats in the Reichstag and about 13 percent of the popular vote. Huge electoral victories for the Social Democratic movement came only after 1890, as a consequence of continued urban migration, industrialization, and the expiration of the repressive Antisocialist Laws (Pack, 1961; Berman, 2001).

The socioeconomic foundation of the rural sector's power in Imperial Germany, on the other hand, was strong. It lay in the ownership of land, particularly large estates owned by a very small Prussian agricultural elite. Royal and aristocratic families owned the majority of large farms in eastern Germany in the late 1800s, with the ruling Hohenzollern family and the Prussian state the largest two landowners (Eddie, 2008, 86–122). The size of agricultural holdings in Prussia was large, averaging nine hectares in 1882 compared to 7.6 hectares in the Empire overall.[8] I collected data on the size and distribution of land holdings in the Empire and calculated Gini coefficients for each administrative district (*Verwaltungsbezirk*).[9] The mean of this measure of land inequality is 0.72 across the whole of Germany, well above levels of land inequality found in contemporary OECD countries and similar to levels found in the Middle East or Latin America today. It ranges from 0.43 in the southwestern district of Karlsruhe to 0.93 in the East Prussian district of Danzig. I also compared these data to Ziblatt's (2008b) landholding Gini coeffcients calculated from the 1893 agricultural census returns. The high correlation between

---

[7] This is the earliest figure given by Grant (2002). It must be noted that overall levels of inequality in Germany were much lower than in the United Kingdom throughout the course of the nineteenth century (Grant, 2002, 8).

[8] All 1882 data on the distribution of land are from agricultural census returns published at the administrative district level by the Statistisches Reichsamt (1885).

[9] The data definition of a land holding or "agricultural unit" are given by the Statistisches Reichsamt (1885, 1*–107).

the two variables ($r = 0.87$) shows that the inegalitarian distribution of land in Germany did not change to a great degree in the latter part of the nineteenth century, and that this important source of producers' socioeconomic power remained throughout the period of interest in this study.

Large landholdings did not simply give East Elbian agricultural producers a stable economic base and thus a large degree of independence and political influence, but also a powerful social position as landlords and employers, which led to gross political inequality and the privileging of Junker interests over those of others. These "bread lords" (Anderson, 2000) had a large influence over the inhabitants of their estates and neighboring areas. The Junkers and their deputies dominated local government, running local schools, electoral boards, tax collection, poor relief, and often the village Lutheran church. They also served as members of the Landtag and Reichstag themselves, as illustrated in Table 6.1. The Junkers were able to compel locals to follow their political positions through traditional relationships of authority and subservience, but also through threats and violence as necessary. Crucially, this was the case even after the institution of universal male suffrage in 1871, and a key cause of the high correlation between landholding inequality and support for Conservative candidates found by Ziblatt (2008a) for Prussia and confirmed below for the whole Empire. For example, workers were routinely fired for voting for the "wrong" (i.e., liberal or Social Democratic) candidate, a practice that was widely seen as employers' right (Anderson, 2000, 159). Districts characterized by higher levels of landholding inequality also had higher levels of electoral fraud (Ziblatt, 2009). The prestige and authority commanded by aristocratic landowners allowed them to place considerable pressure on local politicians to follow their preferred policies, even if those politicians were not members of Conservative parties (Thomson, 2015).

The low levels of urbanization and high levels of landholding inequality that characterized the German Empire in the 1870s had *direct* political effects. Without reaching a critcal mass of concentration in cities, food consumers did not pose the risk of threatening demonstrations or food riots, while Junkers' positions as landlords, employers, and traditional elites gave them considerable influence over local politics. This gives a first set of structural reasons to suspect that the rural sector's interests would be weighed more heavily than those of food consumers in policymaking by the authoritarian regime. However, these socioeconomic structures also had important *indirect* effects on national politics. They did so by having a significant impact on the constitution of the Reichstag, its members' occupations, and members' party affiliations. Thus, urban interests were relatively weak even at this critical veto point where they had the greatest chance of pushing policy toward lower food prices due to their enfranchisement via universal male suffrage.

Socioeconomic Structures and the Composition of the 1878 Reichstag

I estimate two multinomial logistic regressions taking the categorical occupation and party data laid out in Table 6.1 as dependent variables. These models predict the log odds of an occupational group or party group winning a Reichstag mandate in the 1878 election directly preceding the 1879 tariff bill vote. The dependent variables were constructed by taking the original roll-call vote on the first protectionist tariff bill in July 1879 and matching the names of the voting members to the results of the 1878 election.[10] By combining these two sources, I created a dataset including the name of each member, which district they were elected by, how they voted on the bill, and what political party they belonged to. These data were then matched to socioeconomic data on each district.

The indicator of the Reichstag members' occupations is coded as **Landowners**, who were described as an aristocratic landowner (*Rittergutsbesitzer*), administrator of an estate or titled members of the aristocracy (*Majoratsbesitzer, Fideikomissbesitzer, Majoratsherr*); **Farmers** who were not included in the preceding category; **Industrialists**, owners of companies who would directly benefit from the protectionist iron tariff such as owners of companies in the iron, steel, machine-building, or railway industries; **Professionals**, lawyers, doctors, professors, teachers, civil servants, priests, and journalists; **Businessmen** not included in category 3, workers, and others. I also construct indicators, used in the roll-call analysis of the tariff bill vote below, of members' previous affiliation with the **Prussian Army** or membership of the **Prussian Upper House,** or House of Lords.

For the party model, I created the dependent variable by grouping the party affiliations of all Reichstag members into five categories: **Conservative**, German Conservative Party (DKP) and German Reich Party (DRP); **Liberal**, National Liberals (NLP), Progressives (DFP), German Peoples' Party (DVP) and independent liberals; **Zentrum**, Catholic Center party; **SAPD**, Social Democrats; **Regional**, Poles, Alsatians, Danes, and Welfs.

The independent variables in the occupation and party models were collected primarily from census data published in government statistical

---

[10] The roll-call vote is in Deutscher Reichstag (1879), and the results of the 1878 electioin are from Statistisches Reichsamt (1879).

yearbooks.[11] **Landholding Inequality** is a Gini coefficient calculated from an 1882 census at the administrative district level. The mean of this variable is 0.72, the range is from 0.43 to 0.94, and standard deviation is 0.12. **Economic Inequality**, the ratio of unskilled wages to total GDP per worker in each administrative district, is derived from 1882 occupational census data at the administrative district level. The mean of this variable is 0.50, the range is from 0.43 to 0.59, and standard deviation is 0.03. **Urbanization** is the proportion of workers in an electoral district who are not employed in agriculture, from 1882 occupational census data at the administrative district level. The mean of this variable is 56, its range is from 4 to over 99, and standard deviation is 19. **Catholic**, the proportion of the population self-identifying as Catholic in each administrative district, is from an 1880 population census. The mean of this variable is 38, the range is from 0.29 to 100, and standard deviation is 33.

The results of the multinomial occupation and party models are reported in Table 6.2, and I also graph the effects of landholding inequality and urbanization on delegates' occupations in Figure 6.2. The occupation model shows large and statistically significant correlations between electoral districts' levels of landholding inequality and urbanization, and the occupations of the Reichstag deputies representing those districts. As shown clearly in the left-hand panel of Figure 6.2, districts characterized by high levels of landholding inequality were significantly more likely to elect landowners to the Reichstag than members of other professions, *ceteris paribus*. At a Gini coefficient of 0.60, one standard deviation below the mean, professionals are most likely to be elected, and landowners were no more likely to be elected than businessmen. Average levels of landholding inequality of around 0.70, led to landowners being more likely to be elected than businessmen but still not as likely to be elected as professionals. However, at very high levels of landholding inequality above 0.70 landowners were even more likely to be elected than professionals. The map of landholding inequality in Figure 6.1 shows that almost all of Prussia's electoral districts had a land Gini of 0.65 or above, making them likely to elect landowners over other occupational groups. As shown in the right-hand panel of Figure 6.2, urbanization had the opposite effects on the occupational make-up of the Reichstag to those of landholding inequality, holding all else equal. At levels of urbanization around 40 percent, one standard deviation

---

[11] Statistisches Reichsamt (1883, 1884, 1885). Data on wages are from Hoffmann (1965). For detailed descriptions of these variables and sources, see Thomson (2015).

TABLE 6.2 *Reichstag Member Models of Occupation and Party, 1878*

	Occupation Model				Party Model			
	Professional	Businessman	Farmer	Industrialist	Liberal	Zentrum	SAPD	Regional
Land Gini	−5·38***	−9·25***	−9·58***	−6·33	−6·33***	−3·64**	−14·68***	−0·71
	(1·37)	(2·07)	(2·79)	(4·01)	(1·73)	(1·67)	(4·70)	(2·03)
Inequality	0·46	10·14*	−4·28	30·45***	−2·14	9·19*	45·36***	10·14**
	(4·40)	(6·08)	(10·50)	(11·37)	(5·24)	(5·24)	(13·42)	(5·10)
Urbaniz.	0·47***	0·08***	−0·02	0·06***	0·05***	−0·003	0·15***	−0·02
	(0·01)	(0·01)	(0·02)	(0·02)	(0·01)	(0·01)	(0·04)	(0·01)
% Catholic	−0·002	0·001	−0·03***	0·002	−0·02**	0·05***	−0·04*	0·03***
	(0·004)	(0·01)	(0·01)	(0·01)	(0·01)	(0·01)	(0·02)	(0·01)
Constant	1·36	−4·05	7·56	−17·54***	1·31	−4·80*	−25·88***	−5·83**
	(2·20)	(2·81)	(6·17)	(5·93)	(2·54)	(2·85)	(6·57)	(2·37)
Obs.	391				392			
Pseudo R2	0·1498				0·28			
Wald Chi-sq	118·46				184·41			
Prob. > Chi-sq	<0·001				<0·001			

Landowner is base category in Occupation Model; Conservative is base category in Party Model.

Standard errors in parentheses.

* $p < 0.10$, ** $p < 0.05$, *** $p < 0.01$.

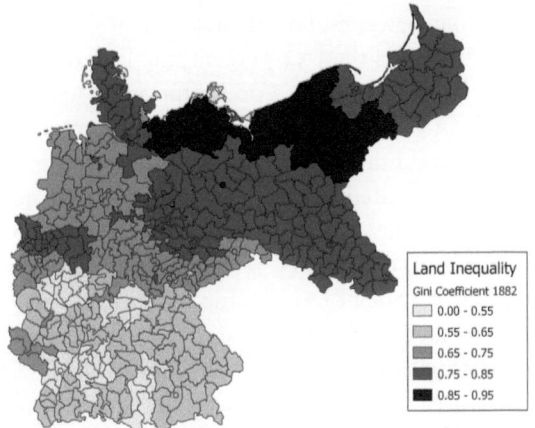

FIGURE 6.1 Landholding Inequality in Imperial German Electoral Districts, 1882

Source: 1882 data collected from Statistisches Reichsamt (1885). Data matched with QuantumGIS to the map vector layer by Ziblatt (2007).

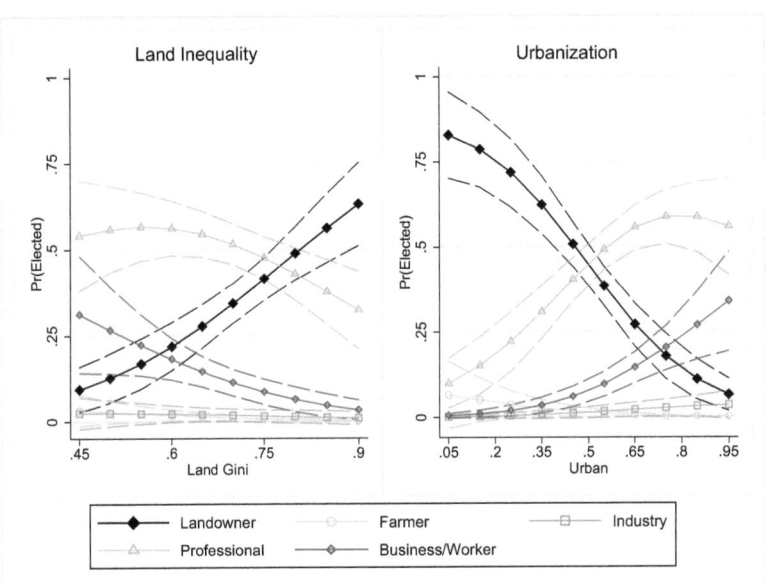

FIGURE 6.2 Predicted Occupations of Reichstag Members by District Characteristics

below the mean, professionals were no more likely to be elected to the Reichstag than landowners. However, at high levels of urbanization above 70 percent, both professionals and businessmen were more likely to be elected than landowners. Given that half of German districts had a level of urbanization less than 54 percent, the lack of highly urbanized electoral districts led to the underrepresentation of urban interests and played a large role in weakening opposition to protectionist agricultural policies, which increased the price of food.

The party model presented in Table 6.2 also shows the negative impact low levels of urbanization and high levels of landholding inequality had on the chances for food consumers' representation in the Imperial legislature. The free-trading Social Democratic and liberal party groups were not strongly represented in the Reichstag due to these structural factors. In those areas where urbanization was high, liberals and Social Democrats were more likely to be elected, *ceteris paribus*. At levels of urbanization above 50 percent, liberals were more likely to be elected than members of all other party groups. Conservatives' chances declined along with increasing urbanization and, in exclusively urban districts such as those in Berlin, were no more likely to win mandates than Social Democrats. Similarly, at low levels of landholding inequality, liberals were more likely to be elected to the Reichstag than conservatives. Only at levels of landholding inequality above 0.70 were conservatives more likely to be elected than liberals, holding all else equal. The Catholic Zentrum was guaranteed a stable support base in southern and western Germany, where the majority Catholic population regularly supported its candidates.

Food consumers were not in a socioeconomic or institutional position to pose a threat to the Imperial German regime in the 1870s. They were divided by inequality and diverging economic interests, spread across the Empire in a way that was not conducive to collective action, and neutered by a constitution that allowed them them the vote (if they were male), but not a powerful position in the complex web of institutions that made Imperial policy. Agricultural producers, on the other hand, occupied a number of powerful and threatening positions within the same institutional web that made them dangerous to the Chancellor. The Prussian aristocratic landowning class dominated the armed forces and the bureaucracy, making them both wielders of force in the Empire and policy veto players at least twice over. Also, the Junkers' ownership of large estates gave them a relatively autonomous economic position and a social status akin to feudal lords. In what follows I will show how this skewed balance of power in favor of agricultural producers had the effect of dictating the regime's choice of a protectionist agricultural policy in the 1870s.

6.5 POLICY PREFERENCES OF RURAL AND URBAN INTERESTS

The Imperial German regime in the 1870s was confronted by political threats from both the urban and rural sectors and did not face the question of its future rule complacently. However, the threat posed by rural elites was greater and was translated by the regime into a policy that supported agriculture, and by which it sought to secure its tenure in power. A rural-biased policy in the late 1870s involved state intervention in agricultural markets in order to guarantee returns to farmers, who during previous decades of relatively high international prices for their produce had been in favor of free trade. The change in agricultural policy seen in Germany in the late 1870s was a result of this shift in policy preferences among agricultural elites.

Europe was gripped by a severe economic crisis beginning in 1873, which in Germany quickly led to loud demands for protectionist tariffs on textiles, iron, and machinery. These demands were articulated by newly formed lobby groups such as the Central Association of German Industry (*Centralverband Deutscher Industrieller*, CVDI), and found sympathy with the Kaiser, but were initially ignored by the broader regime around Bismarck, with the government eliminating the last of its protectionist tariffs by 1877 (Torp, 2005, 148–149). Not as easily ignored was the impact of cereal imports from the United States and Russia, which led to decreases in the prices of grain by around 20 percent between the beginning and the middle of the 1870s. Rather than affecting industrialists, who did not yet belong to the core of the Prussian elite or make up a large group in the Reichstag, these price shifts affected the dominant Junker political class. A long-term structural shift in world agricultural markets was making itself felt in Europe; effectively, by being linked to the North American prairies and the Ukranian steppe by railroads and steamships Germany went from being a country of relative land abundance to relative land scarcity. Large-scale German agriculture would never be competitive again.[12] As the domestic market price of grain dropped in the face of increased foreign supply, agricultural interests in Germany began to abandon their free-trading stance – which in any case was merely a function of previously high prices – in favor of tariffs that would protect them from the competition of imported grain (Lambi, 1963, 131–149).

[12] See Figure 6.3, or for a more detailed account of national variation in agricultural prices, see O'Rourke (1997).

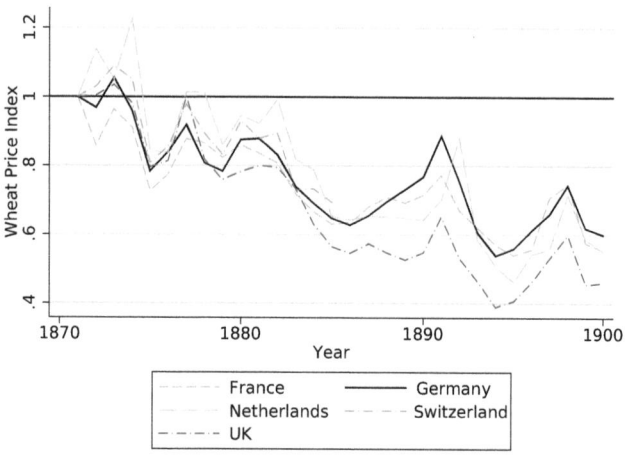

FIGURE 6.3 Wheat Prices in Europe, 1870 to 1900

Source: Index calculated from annual averages in national currency units published by Földes (1905).

Already burdened by high levels of debt, low productivity, and increasing wages due to increased labor demand through industrialization and urban migration, the Junkers were in dire economic straits. Because of the size of their estates and the relatively poor quality of the soils, they were not able to easily adjust to changing prices by shifting production to more profitable commodities such as dairy or meat (Schissler, 1980, 106–107). The lifestyle demanded by their social status was expensive, and most estates were heavily mortgaged in order to support large domestic staffs; residences in Posen, Danzig, or Berlin; and other trappings of aristocratic life (Pflanze, 1990, 11). In sum, in the mid-1870s the Junker aristocracy stood before an existential challenge, confronted with the danger of bankruptcies, foreclosures, and the division of their great estates into a number of small farms: a reversal of the agricultural consolidation process from which they themselves had profited in the eighteenth century. Their demands of the regime for protection from foreign competition were thus undergirded with a real sense of urgency and concern for the durability of their political and economic positions.

    The interests of the German rural sector stood in stark opposition to those of urban food consumers. Any increases in returns to farmers carried bitter consequences for the real incomes of the rapidly growing, impoverished urban proletariat, who as a consequence were required to pay more for food. Bad harvests in 1879 and 1880 already had driven food prices to record highs in Germany before the effects of the protectionist tariffs arrived (Pflanze, 1990, 44). In addition, the pressure of increasing living costs on wages for industrial companies meant that sector was, in principle, in favor of free trade in agriculture (Torp, 2005). Therefore, it is critical to examine exactly how the Imperial German regime came to privilege the interests of the rural sector over food consumers after 1878, how it was able to craft the coalition of "iron and rye" against the interests of workers and industrialists, and how this policy was part of an authoritarian survival strategy that responded to the acute political threats posed by rural elites but not to the lesser threat posed by urban consumers.

6.6 MAKING POLICY: FORMULATING AND PASSING THE 1879 TARIFF BILL

Agricultural policy was an important piece in the complex political puzzle that Bismarck manipulated to shape both domestic and international developments and maximize the stability of the Imperial German regime. After 1877, the government took a decisive, repressive turn in domestic policy recognized by historians as the "second founding" of the German Empire. This shift in policy included the repression of Social Democrats through the Antisocialist Laws and the elimination of more liberal elements within the Imperial bureaucracy (Tipton, 2001; Thomson, 2015). The third element of Bismarck's authoritarian second founding of the Empire was the famous protectionist tariff on grain and iron imports. Not by coincidence, these came in 1879, on the heels of the depression and the collapse of German grain exports, and as rural elites organized and lobbied in favor of protectionism. In 1876, 481 aristocratic Prussian landowners met in Berlin to establish the Association of Tax and Economic Reformers (*Vereinigung der Steuer- und Wirtschaftsreformer*, VSW). The VSW was a modern mechanism for the representation of the traditional elite: Around 450 of the 481 total members were estate owners, as were three-quarters of the Association steering committee and the entire executive committee. Eleven members of the VSW were members of the Prussian House of Lords (Gottwald, 1986, 358–360).

The goal of this organization was the preservation of the economic, social, and political status of the Prussian landowning aristocracy, although they cynically framed their arguments as promoting Christian economic policy in the public interest. Initially calling for the reduction of taxes on land, as well as for increased indirect and capital taxation, the VSW quickly became the most influential champion of protectionist agricultural policies to increase the incomes of famers (Torp, 2005, 151). The VSW lobbied the government in favor of protectionism, but also worked hard in the provinces to convince small farmers – who until recently had been convinced free-traders – of the importance and virtues of a tariff on grain imports and to mobilize voters to support the conservative parties, which shared their views. In October 1877 meetings were held between the VSW and the CVDI, which aligned the Junkers' demands with those of industrialists along the exact lines of the eventual iron and rye policies enacted by Bismarck only two years later (Gottwald, 1986, 361–362).

Rural elites did not have to go far in order to access the highest levels of the Imperial and Prussian bureaucracy and advocate their preferred policies; in some cases, they themselves comprised the highest levels of the bureaucracy. To take only one prominent example, Otto zu Stolberg-Wernigerode, Bismarck's Vice Chancellor and Deputy Prussian Minister President at the time of the passage of the first tariff law, was the founding Chairman of the VSW and a former President of the Prussian House of Lords (Jacobs, 1908). He was Bismarck's deputy and advisor in the highest affairs of state, including both domestic and foreign affairs. In the question of tariff reform, Bismarck consulted Stolberg-Wernigerode for his opinion on how best to guarantee the returns to domestic industries in the face of foreign competition and protectionist policies (Canis et al., 2008, 604).

Considering the place of the rural sector within the Imperial regime, it is unsurprising that Bismarck swiftly became a passionate advocate of the VSW's policies of support for agriculture and increased food prices for urban residents. During 1878 he became aware of the role a protectionist tariff could play in increasing the returns to grain-growers, and he was prepared to grant industrialists protection in return for the same in the case of grain imports (Rosenberg, 1967, 183). He also became convinced by the positions of the VSW on land taxation, complaining that landowners were compelled to pay "double" taxes, on both their land and their income from farming (Pflanze, 1990, 45). It cannot be overlooked that the Chancellor himself, as an estate owner, was also a victim of the sinking grain prices. In October of the same year Bismarck gave the following response to the question of whether he intended to buy a Bavarian estate:

A Bavarian estate! I have not the least intention of buying one. I lose enough on the one I bought in Lauenburg, where the mortgage eats up the income of the whole property. How could an estate yield anything, when a bushel of corn is sold at the present low price? ... It is ruining our entire agriculture. There will be no remedy until there is an increase in railway rates or a duty on grain.[13]

In general, the Chancellor's official correspondence in the last third of 1878 shows an increasing sensitivity to the international competitiveness of German industries, and particularly the relative position of agricultural producers. He complained repeatedly to his highest officials of hearing reports of sick cattle being allowed across the border from Austria, despite an Imperial ban on the import of livestock suspected of illness (Canis et al., 2008, 613, 617). The Chancellor's concern for animal health in fact had its roots in a desire to prevent competition from the East and was later expanded into a full-blown ban on meat and livestock imports for hygenic reasons (Hunt, 1974). He also suspected that government railway policies were giving Russian and Austrian grain exporters an advantage in the German market (Canis et al., 2008, 608–609). On the other hand, he displayed a callous disregard for the interests of food consumers, writing in August 1880 about the complaints of liberal politicians over the increasing price of food,

We must not yield to the screaming of the progressives, if we do not want to ruin our election chances with the rural population. The latter expect *their* minister, more than any other, to protect agrarian interests, and doubtless they have a right to expect that.[14]

Bismarck did not believe that lower food prices would be conducive to the stability of the Empire; on the contrary, he refused to consider poor relief for urban workers struggling to afford food and was of the opinion that the government must be concerned with the welfare of "producers, not consumers" (Pflanze, 1990, 44).

The Junkers and the VSW were supporters of Bismarck and his policies. However, they were also the very same class that posed the greatest threat to his position; the Prussian landowning aristocracy also dominated the military and civil service and had plotted to remove Bismarck from office in 1872. In the end, rural interests had been converted to the cause of protectionism at least a year earlier than the Chancellor, had organized to advocate protectionist policies, and cut a deal with industrialists to create

---

[13] Quoted in Lambi (1963, 165).
[14] Quote from a letter to Prussian Minister of Agriculture Robert Lucius von Ballhausen, reproduced in Pflanze (1990, 44). Italics in the original.

TABLE 6.3 *Parties in the Reichstag, 1879, and Votes on July 12 Tariff Law*

	Conservative	Liberal	Zentrum	Social Democrat	Regional	Total
No	2	93	1	7	14	117
Absent	4	11	9	0	17	41
Abstain	0	0	2	0	0	2
Yes	107	21	79	0	6	213
Total	113	135	91	7	37	373

Source: Party affiliation from 1878 election results (Statistisches Reichsamt, 1879), roll-call vote from Deutscher Reichstag (1879).

a majority for them. Bismarck came around to his protectionist stance only *after* lobbying by the VSW – industrialists had been clamoring for a tariff for years for no avail – and as a move to shore up the political support base of the regime, the East Elbian agricultural producers who would fade into insignificance without moves to increase grain prices, and could replace the Chancellor with a more amenable politician (for example, his deputy) should he not respond to their needs.

Passing the Tariff Bill in the Reichstag: Elite Politics, Voter Preferences, and Economic Interests

The influence of rural elites on the Imperial German regime did not end with their powerful position within the institutions of the empire and Prussia, or with their ability to organize and lobby the government to propose protectionist legislation to the Reichstag. The presence of large numbers of landowners in the legislature also assisted the passage of the protectionist tariff bill in the Reichstag. In this section, I present quantitative analyses of deputies' voting patterns on the bill in 1879 and show that its passage was the result of a complex mix of elite bargaining, the personal interests of Reichstag members, and those of voters and economic actors in the Empire.

I estimate ordered logistic regressions, which examine the correlates of votes for the 1879 tariff bill on the floor of the Reichstag. I model outcomes on an ordered dependent variable, which can take on the values 0, indicating a "No" vote on the protectionist bill; 1, indicating a member being absent from the vote; 2, indicating an abstention; or 3, indicating a "Yes" vote on the tariff bill. I present a summary of this variable by party group in Table 6.3. When the Chancellor presented the iron and rye tariff bills to the Reichstag on July 12, 1879, it was carried by the rural-based

Conservative parties and the Catholic *Zentrum*, as is shown in Table 6.3. Less than 2 percent of Conservative and Zentrum Reichstag members voted against the bill, while 70 percent of Liberals, all Social Democrats and around half the members of regional parties such as the Poles and Alsatians voted against protectionsim and in favor of lower food prices.

As independent variables in my models of the vote I include the data on party affiliation and member occupation reported in Table 6.1 and discussed earlier. I also collected data from official government statistical yearbooks to create the following variables, in addition to those used in the models in Section 6.4, measuring the socioeconomic characteristics of electoral districts, and matched them to each Reichstag deputy: **Hec. Rye/Cap**, the number of total hectares planted in rye in 1879/80 divided by the total population of each administrative district. The mean of this variable is 0.13, the range is from 0 to 0.31, and standard deviation is 0.08[15]; **Cattle/Capita**, the total number of cattle counted in each administrative district in the 1883 livestock census, divided by the administrative district's total population. The mean of this variable is 0.36, the range is from 0 to 0.81, and standard deviation is 0.15[16]; **Light Ind.**, the proportion of workers employed in textile production, woodworking, and printing in each administrative district. The mean of this variable is 0.07, the range is from 0.02 to 0.37, and standard deviation is 0.06[17]; **Heavy Ind.**, the proportion of workers employed in mining and metalworking in each administrative district. The mean of this variable is 0.05, the range is from 0 to 0.30, and standard deviation 0.05; **Commercial**, the proportion of the population of each administrative district employed in the banking and commercial sector. The mean of this variable is 0.06, the range is from 0.03 to 0.22, and standard deviation 0.03; **Free Trade El. Support**, the share of votes at the 1878 election won by Social Democrats and Left Liberals who vocally campaigned on an antiprotection platform.

I estimate six ordinal logistic models, the results of which are reported in Table 6.4. These models weigh up the effects of district-level structures, Reichstag member interests, and party affiliation on the passage of the tariff bill. Model 1 examines the effects of the structure of the local economy on Reichstag member voting; I predict that a greater presence of those sectors privileged by the tariff bill, agriculture and industry, in a member's district will be associated with greater support for the tariff

---

[15] Statistisches Reichsamt (1880). I use the figures for winter rye.
[16] From the 1883 livestock census (Kaiserliches Statistisches Amt, 1884b).
[17] Data for industry composition are all from the 1882 occupational census (Statistisches Reichsamt, 1884).

TABLE 6.4 *Results of Ordered Logistic Regressions Estimating Votes on Tariff Bill, 1879*

	(1) Mass	(2) Mass	(3) Occ	(4) Party	(5) Comb	(6) Comb
Landowner/ Arist.			0.68***		0.68**	
			(0.25)		(0.29)	
Farmer			−0.69		−0.92	
			(0.79)		(0.84)	
Industrialist			0.57		0.28	
			(0.64)		(0.70)	
Businessman/ Worker			−0.40		−0.34	
			(0.30)		(0.34)	
Pr. Army			0.54		0.44	
			(0.36)		(0.38)	
Member Pr UH			1.09**		1.30***	
			(0.44)		(0.48)	
Cons. MP				4.70***		5.01***
				(0.47)		(0.52)
Zentrum MP				3.75***		3.83***
				(0.37)		(0.45)
Free Trade El. Supp.		−0.022***			−0.019***	0.0027
		(0.0040)			(0.0042)	(0.0050)
Inequality	−6.31	−5.71			−7.65	12.0
	(6.45)	(6.63)			(6.96)	(9.23)
Urbaniz.	−0.031***	−0.026***			−0.019**	−0.020**
	(0.0073)	(0.0076)			(0.0081)	(0.0094)
Land Gini	−0.22	0.54			−1.15	−1.54
	(1.56)	(1.63)			(1.73)	(2.11)
Hec. Rye/ Capita	0.82	0.60			−0.017	−0.45
	(2.43)	(2.51)			(2.63)	(3.17)
Cattle/Capita	0.77	0.11			0.46	0.19
	(1.07)	(1.10)			(1.15)	(1.42)
Light Ind.	5.36**	5.01**			5.80**	3.41
	(2.20)	(2.27)			(2.31)	(2.73)
Heavy Ind.	11.3***	8.79**			10.6***	3.06
	(3.87)	(3.90)			(4.06)	(4.74)
Commercial	−0.14	0.97			3.51	−3.07
	(6.38)	(6.42)			(6.67)	(8.69)
Observations	373	373	372	373	372	373

Standard errors in parentheses.
* $p < 0.10$, ** $p < 0.05$, *** $p < 0.01$.
0 is No; 1 is Absent; 2 is Abstain; 3 is Yes.
Professionals are the base category for Models 3 and 5.

bill. Without controlling for members' occupation or party affiliation, the presence of industries that benefited directly from the protectionist tariff is positively correlated with support for the bill. Areas with lower levels of urbanization, and thus higher levels of agricultural employment, were significantly more likely to have their member vote for protection, although interestingly no differences are seen between grain-growing areas and those with greater levels of pastoral agriculture. Members from industrial areas, whether employment was concentrated in light or heavy industry, were more likely to vote for protection from foreign competition through the iron tariff.

Model 2 weighs these economic interests against those of electors by including a variable measuring total support for free-trading parties in each district. I predict that support for free-trading parties will be associated with a lower likelihood of protectionist bills as members respond to the preferences of their constituents. The highly significant negative coefficient on this variable indicates that mass preferences for free trade were indeed reflected by members' voting patterns, as they were less likely to vote for protection where these parties had greater electoral support. As in Model 1, members representing urban areas are significantly less likely to support the bill, and members from industrial areas are significantly more likely to support protection.

These two models show the direct correlations between structural features of electorates and their members' voting patterns. However, the reader will recall that these same structural features had an impact on the composition of the Reichstag in terms of members' occupations and party affiliations, as shown in Figure 6.2. Therefore, their direct effects on voting patterns should be considered alongside their indirect effects through these characteristics of the members. Model 3 examines the correlation between the occupations of members and voting behavior. I expect members with a personal interest in higher food prices – landowners, and to a lesser extent small-scale farmers – to be more likely to vote for protection, while businessmen with an interest in lower food prices will be less likely to vote for protection. The indirect effects of structural features of electoral districts, through the occupations of members elected and their party affiliation, are significantly correlated with voting patterns on the tariff bill. Aristocratic landowners are far more likely to vote for protection than professionals such as lawyers and doctors and significantly more likely to vote for higher food prices than small-scale farmers and businessmen. Members of the Prussian House of Lords were also more likely to vote for protection. Model 4 shows the impact of Bismark's coalition of Conservative and Zentrum party members on the tariff bill votes. The protectionist coalition was, to a certain extent, the result of Bismarck's bargaining on the Junkers' behalf: he had recently repealed many of the most discriminatory anti-Catholic measures of the *Kulturkampf*, which prepared the ground for an alliance with the Catholic parliamentary faction. Members of these parties were far more likely than liberals, Social Democrats, or regional minority members to vote for protection.

Model 5 compares the occupational model against the effects of free trade party support and broader economic interests from Model 2. It shows that deputies from more agrarian and industrial districts were still significantly more likely to vote for higher food prices after controlling for their occupation. The preferences of the electorate for free trade and lower food prices were also significantly correlated with votes against the bill. However, in Model 5 both landowners and members of the Prussian House of Lords are significantly more likely to vote for protection for agriculture after controlling for district characteristics, showing how both district structures and elite networks played a role in the passage of the bill. Model 6 compares broader mass interests to the effects of party affiliation, rather than member occupation. Including dummy variables for conservative and Zentrum members overwhelms the effects of most district structures, in particular the level of support for free-trading parties. In Model 6, the only district structure that is significantly correlated with voting patterns after controlling for party affiliation is urbanization.

The models presented in Table 6.4 allow me to conclude that the passage of the tariff bill was the result of a complex mix of district structures' indirect and direct effects, electoral signals, as well as political bargaining and elite political preferences. Through determining the composition of the Reichstag, socioeconomic structures in electoral districts had major effects on the passage of the protectionist bill. However, the ability of Bismarck to bring the Catholic Zentrum into the protectionist coalition along with rural conservatives and the personal preferences of the members due to their occupations also had important effects on voting patterns. Members from urban areas were less likely to vote for protection even after controlling for party affiliation, but the preferences of the electorate for free trade, as shown in their support for free trading parties, had a weaker association with votes against the bill.

6.7 THE EFFECTS OF AGRICULTURAL PROTECTION AFTER 1879

The protectionist tariff enacted in 1879 could not stop the steady decline of grain prices in Germany; prices continued to drop through the decade until the Kaiser's death in 1888 and reached their lowest point in the early 1890s. However, the government's policies were able to have a significant effect on the *relative* incomes of German farmers compared to their competitors overseas and a corresponding effect on the real incomes of food consumers in the Empire compared to those in free-trading countries. The initial 1879 tariff of 10 Marks per ton of wheat, rye, and oats examined in detail earlier was increased to 30 Marks in 1885 and then 50 marks in 1887. By the end of the 1880s grain prices, even in cereal-exporting East Germany, were above those in the free-trading United Kingdom; prices in the cities of western Germany were significantly higher.[18] East German grain exports sank rapidly as domestic prices increased above those on world markets; exports of wheat from the Empire shrank from almost 180,000 tonnes in 1880 to 1,100 tonnes in 1888 after the imposition of the 50 Mark tariff (Teichmann, 1955, 196). New markets in the growing cities of western Germany were found for the Junkers' grain. Simultaneously, bad harvests in Germany in 1879 and 1880 interacted with the new tariffs to create something of a food crisis in German cities from 1879 to 1881, when wholesale prices for rye – the staple of German bakers – increased by almost 50 percent from 132.8 to 195.2 Marks per ton (Pflanze, 1990, 43).

German rural interests were therefore the winners of the protectionist tariffs first introduced in 1879, and food consumers were the losers. However, even within the ranks of farmers the gains from the protectionist regime were unequally distributed and concentrated among the large landowners most loyal to the monarchy. Consider Figure 6.4, which shows the relationship between regional landholding inequality and a weighted measure of agricultural price support from the 1879 to 1880 growing season directly following the first tariff bill.[19] Here, areas where landowners made up more than half of members of the Reichstag are

---

[18] See Teichmann (1955), Jacks (2006), and Kaiserliches Statistisches Amt (1881, 1884a).

[19] The weighted agricultural price support measure is the sum of the production of four protected grains (wheat, oats, barley, and rye), multiplied by their Nominal Rate of Assistance, or the percentage by which their price was increased by the tariff bill. I then weighted this by the total agricultural workforce, $\frac{\sum_{i=1}^{n=4} Production_i \times NRA_i}{AgWorkforce}$. Data was only available to construct this measure by administrative district, not electoral district. I am grateful to Jan Pierskalla for sharing his method for constructing this variable.

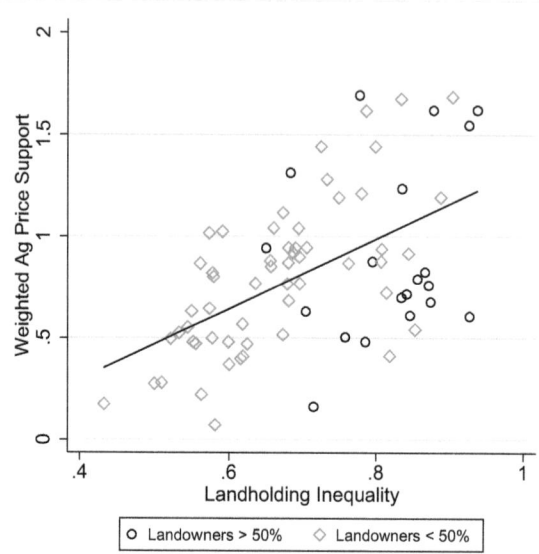

FIGURE 6.4 Landholding Inequality and Weighted Agricultural Price Support Level, 1879–1880

shown as diamonds, while other districts are shown as circles. This graph shows that the areas of the Empire characterized by large average land-holdings, the same areas dominated by the landed Junkers as discussed at length earlier, received disproportionately large increases in rents from the protectionist tariff per agricultural worker.

This finding corresponds with Rosenberg's (1967, 183–187) argument that the large Prussian landowners were the main economic benefactors of Bismarck's legislation, and as a consequence they did not experience the degree of economic distress they would have during this first "great depression" without trade protection. Without the extreme declines in grain prices seen in previous agricultural depressions, forced land sales were not endemic, farm values remained relatively stable and allowed the Prussian aristocracy to borrow against them to maintain their social and political position in the country. In this economic variant of the *Sonderweg* argument, by passing the protectionist tariffs, Bismarck was attempting to stabilize the "endangered traditional political and social power hierarchy" in the face of the depression of the 1870s (Wehler, 1969, 105). In the long term, by freezing the agrarian class structure of Imperial Germany, the protectionist grain tariffs of 1879 laid the foundation for the continuation of the monarchy until the First World War. For Gerschenkron (1943, 47) the increases in grain prices were even a direct economic cause of autocracy and Fascism in Germany until the 1940s: "at every stage of their development in the Hohenzollern monarchy as well as in the Weimar Republic the forces of democracy were hamstrung by the opposition of the East Elbian aristocracy." The political consequences of the protectionist agricultural tariffs for Bismarck personally were more nuanced. They certainly marked the beginning of a consolidation of his position after the crisis of the depression. The parliamentary liberal parties were divided through the passage of the tariff bill and no longer represented a threat. Having defeated the more progressive wing of the party, Bismarck was able to dismiss many liberals from his cabinet, which he stacked with conservatives, giving him an even freer hand in policymaking (Steinberg, 2011, 384–387). He became, in the words of the famous author Theodor Fontane, "a despot."[20] He retained his position as Chancellor until the death of the Kaiser and his replacement by Wilhelm II in 1890. However, the nature of this position changed. As Wehler (1969, 105–111) argues, Bismarck's concessions to large industrialists by including them in the tariff marked the beginning of pluralist politics in Germany and the need for government policy to respond to demands from interest groups rather than simply respect the wishes of the sovereign. Balancing the competing demands of powerful industrialists and the growing working class was the main task of the rest of his term as Chancellor, one that he approached by seeking colonial export markets for industrial goods while implementing social welfare reform to placate restive urban workers.

6.8 CONCLUSION

In this chapter, I traced the political and socioeconomic roots of Bismarck's shift to support for German agriculture in 1879. I have shown that the policy shift was caused by the bias within the German political system toward rural interests, which made them a significant threat to the Chancellor and political stability. The unequal distribution of land in the countryside gave landed elites their traditionally powerful political position, as well as an inordinate number of mandates in the Reichstag. This rural bias reached even further, to the degree that all branches of the government were dominated by the Junkers, from the Kaiser through

---

[20] Cited in Steinberg (2011, 398).

the Chancellor to the Cabinet and Prussian military and bureaucracy. By intervening in agricultural markets to support the incomes of rural elites, Bismarck was able to secure his own position in power, as well as prop up the aristocracy and authoritarian monarchy, maintaining political stability in Germany.

Imperial Germany remains the canonical example of a rural-biased authoritarian regime, where government policy was an expedient tool to placate powerful rural interests and maintain political stability. As I show in Chapter 3, the interactions between political threats and regime type illustrated by this case are also important for explaining the politics of agricultural policy globally. As I show in Chapter 5, agricultural policy under authoritarian regimes does not only serve the purposes of placating urban food consumers and industrialists with an interest in low wages, as it arguably did in England in the post-Corn Law era. It also serves as a tool of power sharing that addresses the threats of elites and powerful rural interests. Including this – rural and elite – side of the story helps explain agricultural policy outcomes and their effects on authoritarian regime stability explored in previous chapters of this book. I further explore the causal mechanisms linking the political power of rural interests, agricultural policy, and political stability in Chapter 7. I show how rural interests in Malaysia came to threaten the stability of the ethnic coalition ruling the country by defecting to the opposition at the 1969 parliamentary elections. During the subsequent period of intense regime instability, the regime used interventions in agricultural markets as a mechanism to placate the restive rural groups that threatened to impose a single-party dictatorship in the country. In this way, agricultural policy was an important tool promoting regime stability in 1970s Malaysia, which has been overlooked by previous scholars of authoritarianism in the country.

7

Agricultural Policy and Authoritarian Regime Durability in Malaysia, 1969–1980

7.1 INTRODUCTION

In the previous chapters of this book, I laid out a theory of regime type, agricultural policymaking and political stability and tested the empirical implications of this theory using cross-national data. A key element of this theory relates to the power of the rural sector. I argued that landholding inequality facilitates collective opposition to authoritarian governments by rural interests and found that it was correlated with greater levels of support to agriculture under authoritarianism in Chapter 3. In Chapter 5, I showed that landholding inequality is correlated with authoritarian regime instability, except when government policy distributes rents to the rural sector, when it is associated with stable authoritarian rule. Using a detailed case study of Germany in the 1870s and 1880s, in Chapter 6 I traced the causal mechanisms linking landholding inequality, agricultural policy, and authoritarian regime durability. I showed that high levels of landholding inequality gave rural elites powerful positions within both the executive and the legislature. When global grain prices declined, that power was translated into a protectionist policy that supported agriculture, perpetuated the position of landed elites, and maintained the stability of the authoritarian monarchy.

Germany is a historical case, but typical and confirmatory for my theory of agricultural policy, regime type, and political stability. In this chapter, I present evidence from an atypical, but nonetheless confirmatory case, which, unlike Imperial Germany, lies within the temporal scope of my cross-national analysis. I will trace in detail the causal mechanisms linking landholding inequality, agricultural policy, and regime stability in Malaysia from 1969 to 1980. The Malaysian case is atypical for my theory because the role of landholding inequality in the political economy of the country was confounded by deep ethnic and religious cleavages between the rural, Malay population and urban, Chinese interests. Furthermore, the institutional setting and dominant position of the ruling elite make it more difficult to observe the effects of landholding inequality and urban interests on agricultural policymaking, as could be done through analysis of voting returns and roll-call votes in the German case.

Nonetheless, my account of regime type and agricultural policymaking sheds light on the dynamics of the Malaysian government during a crucial period of political instability in the late 1960s and early 1970s. The Malaysian ruling coalition in the 1960s depended on the support of rural, Malay elites who dominated the United Malay National Organization (UMNO). Economic policymaking, however, was determined by a bargain between rural, Malay and urban, Chinese interests, which resulted in a non-interventionist stance toward agricultural markets. Rural Malays became increasingly dissatisfied with the economic policies of the government in the face of stagnation and poverty in the countryside, and northern rice-growing areas were increasingly mobilized by the opposition Pan-Malaysian Islamic Party (PAS). In this chapter, I analyze an original, constituency-level dataset on the correlates of support for the ruling Alliance at the 1969 parliamentary election. I show that landholding inequality was robustly correlated with support for the Alliance, even when controlling for ethnicity and development. However, rice-growing areas abandoned the Alliance for the opposition in 1969, and in these areas there is no significant relationship between landholding inequality and support for ruling coalition candidates. This important shift in mass politics led to contentious developments within the elite, which significantly strengthened rural, Malay interests in the ruling coalition. The position of the Malaysian Chinese Association (MCA) was significantly weakened in the wake of the election and subsequent rioting in the capital, Kuala Lumpur, and the position of UMNO and its rural wing was strengthened. In the course of the following year, a major restructuring of the Malaysian economy was begun through the New Economic Policy (NEP). Although the NEP touched all sectors, an important component was a pro-rural agricultural policy reform, which increased the incomes of Malay rice farmers at the expense of urban food consumers. This policy played an important role in placating rural interests and heading off their demands for a complete reorganization of the political system as a single-party dictatorship under UMNO. Thus, the power shift within the ruling coalition led to a more rural-biased policy, which in turn ensured regime stability.

7.2 PREVIOUS LITERATURE: AUTHORITARIANISM AND AGRICULTURAL POLICY IN MALAYSIA

Malaysia is not a fully fledged democracy. It belongs to the relatively large set of contemporary regimes that share many institutional features with democracies without allowing for full accountability of the government to the electorate (Case, 2004). Although it experienced relatively democratic government in the immediate postcolonial period, it has not experienced a decisive transition since 1989, as have its neighbors Indonesia, Thailand, and the Philippines. Malaysia has a relatively long history of elections and a well-established party system. Each of the major political parties in Malaysia was established along ethnic or religious lines, as shown in Table 7.1, and these cleavages have only begun to weaken very recently (Pepinsky, 2009b). However, it is regarded as an authoritarian regime by most political scientists because of collusion among parties, which has prevented the opposition from taking power since independence.[1] Elections in Malaysia were until recently dominated by a coalition of parties known first as the Alliance, later as the *Barisan Nasional* (National Front), which has formed every government since independence. The dominant party within Alliance/BN is the United Malay National Organization (UMNO), though its hegemony has not gone continually unchallenged.

Because it is a relatively wealthy country, Malaysia's lack of democratic reform is an anomaly for modernization theory. It has been explained by scholars of democratization and authoritarian politics by pointing to the remarkable level of cohesion among Malaysian elites, particularly within UMNO. Case (1996a), for example, argues that members of the ruling coalition have strong incentives to manage competition and preserve stable semidemocratic rule, and that this stability has been only periodically punctured by crises driven by mass politics. Brownlee (2007) and Levitsky and Way (2010) point to Malaysia as a canonical case of stable authoritarian rule through a dominant party, UMNO. Pepinsky (2009a) argues that because the Malaysian regime's support coalition of Malay business elites and poorer citizens had unified interests in reform during the Asian financial crisis in the late 1990s, it was able to implement

---

[1] Przeworski et al. (2000) and Marshall and Cole (2011). The opposition won its first electoral victory shortly before the time of writing in 2018, making Malaysia's future as an electoral authoritarian regime uncertain.

TABLE 7.1 *Malaysian Political Parties, 1960s–1980s*

Party	Ethnicity/Religion	Rural/Urban	Alliance/BN
United Malays National Organization (UMNO)	Malay/Islamic	Rural	1952–present
Malaysian Chinese Association (MCA)	Chinese	Urban	1952–present
Malaysian Indian Congress (MIC)	Indian	Urban	1957–present
Malaysian People's Movement (Gerakan)	Chinese	Urban	1972–present
Pan-Malaysian Islamic Party (PAS)	Malay/Islamic	Rural	1973–1978
Democratic Action Party (DAP)	Chinese	Urban	—

Source: Means (1976, 1991).

policies that promoted both political and economic stability. Slater (2010) sees strong intra-elite cohesion, party institutions and state capacity in Malaysia as a response to ethnic violence in the late 1960s and the key explanatory factors behind the lack of democratic reform in the country.

A large literature has also examined the role played by the Malaysian government's New Economic Policy in maintaining the stability of the regime. The NEP was an ambitious set of government initiatives begun in 1971 with the goal of eliminating economic inequality across ethnicities in the country (Faaland, Parkinson, and Saniman, 1990). The NEP entailed a dramatic shift from *laissez-faire* to a highly interventionist stance, which, through a series of economic plans, aimed to rapidly transform society to the advantage of ethnic Malays, or the *bumiputera*. It entailed massive growth in the size of the bureaucracy, state-owned enterprises, state support for Malay-owned companies, and social policies benefiting Malays (Pepinsky, 2009a, 64–66). Pervasive state intervention in the economy to benefit Malays has ensured their reliable support for the regime at elections. The NEP has also created a wealthy and powerful Malay business class that has close links to ruling elites within UMNO (Gomez and Jomo, 1999). By creating elite and mass interests dependent on state patronage, the NEP has played an important role in cementing the position of the regime in Malaysia, and particularly the core element of UMNO.

My account of economic policymaking and regime stability in this chapter follows a similar approach to these previous studies of Malaysian politics, with a novel focus on agriculture. I examine the role of the rural–urban cleavage in the Malaysian regime's implementation of the NEP. The policies included in the economic plans increased prices for farm produce in Malaysia much further above world market levels than those of its neighbors, in particular for import-competing foodstuffs such as rice (Jenkins and Lai, 1989). Similar to accounts such as those by Case (1996a), Pepinsky (2009a) and Slater (2010), I find that intra-elite politics are critical for understanding the trajectory of agricultural policy and the stability of the Malaysian regime. However, at critical moments such as the 1969 parliamentary election the political equilibrium within the Malaysian elite was disrupted by mass politics. The erosion of support for the ruling Alliance came to a head at these elections, leading to significant gains for the Islamic opposition and a crisis within the regime. Like Pepinsky (2009a) and Gomez and Jomo (1999), I see the support for agriculture contained within the NEP as a means to secure the backing of rural Malay interests and restore the regime's stability in the wake of this crisis. In this chapter, I build on existing literature on the political economy of the Malaysian regime by tracing in detail the links between the influence of the rural sector, agricultural policy, and regime stability. I also make a contribution with analysis of an original dataset on electoral district characteristics and outcomes of the contentious 1969 election.

7.3 SETTING THE STAGE: INSTITUTIONS AND POLITICAL THREATS TO THE MALAYSIAN REGIME

Politics in Malaysia are dominated by elites within the ruling coalition, which governed continuously from independence until very recently. In this section, I describe the institutional setting of Malaysian politics and the balance of power that existed at the elite level in the 1960s between rural, Malay and urban, Chinese interests. During the period under analysis in this chapter, UMNO was the largest party and had strong links to rural Malay elites and its main electoral base in the countryside. The MCA represented urban, Chinese interests and, although a smaller party within the coalition, held significant power over economic policymaking until the 1969 election. This uneasy balance of power between rural and urban interests ensured a hands-off stance toward the agricultural sector.

Malaysia is, by appearances, a parliamentary democracy, but its constitution in fact provides very few checks on the power of Cabinet and the Prime Minister, making this very small elite group decisive for policy-making.[2] Due to a line of stable coalition governments in Malaysia under the Alliance and BN, intracoalition politics are decisive for understanding economic policymaking and the stability of authoritarian rule in the country. Following the British tradition, the lower House of Parliament carries the primary legislative authority in Malaysia. Members of the House, or *Dewan Rakyat*, are elected in single-member constituencies for five-year terms. These elections are widely regarded to be run fairly. Without a directly elected President or an effective veto for the Senate, power is concentrated in the Dewan Rakyat and, as in any Westminster system, with the Prime Minister and Cabinet. Where Malaysia diverges from the majoritarian model, however, is in its stable coalition governments under the Alliance and BN and lack of an effective opposition. Under a stable coalition government dominated by UMNO and with a sizable majority in the House, the Malaysian political system effectively devolves into a one-party regime more similar to Mexico under the PRI than to British two-party democracy (Case, 1996b).

Cooperation between the dominant communal parties, UMNO and the MCA, can be traced back to the first Kuala Lumpur municipal elections in January 1952. In a pattern that has continued under the Alliance and *Barisan Nasional* to the present day, UMNO candidates contested Malay-dominated districts while the MCA fielded candidates in predominantly Chinese districts. This political strategy advocates coexistence and cooperation between largely separate ethnic-based parties, rather than the formation of inclusive parties that practice noncommunal politics (Means, 1976). Through this cooperation, the UMNO-MCA Alliance secured its dominance in the House and thus its hegemonic political position in Malaysia, as is shown by the Federal election results presented in Table 7.2. Comfortably winning the inaugural Federal elections in 1957, the Alliance and its successor the *Barisan Nasional* enjoyed the two-thirds majority required to make constitutional amendments continuously through the 1960s and 1970s, with the sole exception being the period following the contentious 1969 election examined in detail later.

---

[2] Case (1996b, 121) notes that due to its dominance within the Alliance/BN, the UMNO party elections are regarded as Malaysia's "real" elections.

TABLE 7.2 *Results of Elections to House of Representatives, Malaysia,*
1964–1978

	1964 Seats (% Votes)	1969 Seats (% Votes)	1974 Seats (% Votes)	1978 Seats (% Votes)
Alliance (*Periakatan*)	89 (59%)	66 (45%)		
Barisan Nasional (BN)			135 (61%)	130 (57%)
Persatuan Islam Sa-Malaya (PAS)	9 (15%)	12 (21%)		5 (16%)
Democratic Action Party (DAP)		13 (12%)	9 (18%)	16 (19%)
Other Parties	8 (36%)	45 (18%)	10 (21%)	1 (4%)
Independents		1 (2%)		2 (5%)
Total	104	144	154	154

Source: NSTP Research and Information Services (1999). 1969 results are for Peninsular Malaysia only.

In 1960s and 1970s Malaysia, UMNO and the MCA largely represented rural and urban interests, respectively. Rural interests, primarily Malay rice-growers, formed a large and powerful political constituency within UMNO, while urban food consumers and businesses were predominantly Chinese and relied on the politically weaker MCA for the defense of their interests within the ruling coalition. As the balance of power within the Alliance/BN shifted after the 1969 election, it moved toward a rural-based faction within UMNO and led to policies that favored their interests over those of urban areas. These policies placated Malay hardliners within the elite as well as the rural Malay electorate, and supported the stability of the regime.

UMNO was founded in 1946 and built upon existing Malay elites and social structures, which were predominantly rural. The Malay aristocracy, civil servants, village headmen, school and religious teachers provided leadership at both the national and grassroots level (Mauzy, 1983). Voters' existing loyalties to the royal families and aristocratic elites were utilized for support at the polls, as was the authority and organizational capacity brought to the party by the numerous civil servants in its ranks. UMNO's base in traditional Malay society gave it close links to rural interests, and rice growers in particular. Because it reached into most villages in peninsular Malaysia, UMNO was a party rooted in the countryside and responsive to the needs of these areas that are generally afforded so little influence in undemocratic political systems (Kuhonta, 2011). Also, the first generation of party leaders had grown up in what was primarily a rural colonial society, with Malaysia's second Prime Minister Razak spending his early years helping in rice paddies and attending a village school with local children from rice farming and fishing families, for example (Shaw, 1976, 12–25). Shamsul (1986, 85–86) notes that, for UMNO leaders "rice cultivation represented the 'true' Malay traditional village life," in contrast to plantation agriculture, which was viewed as an alien, capitalist venture imposed on Malaya by European colonialists. As Scott (1985) shows, the overlap of large rice farmers, the leaders of the local Farmers' Association, and prominent UMNO members was so complete that these were essentially the same set of local political elites. In the village studied by Scott, all members of the local farmers' association except one were members of UMNO, and of the richest ten families, six were large landowners and eight were members of UMNO. Therefore, in rice-growing areas the hold of large producers over the party was strong, and such areas were an important power base for the party. In fact, two of the first three Malaysian Prime Ministers, Rahman and Mahathir, were from the rice-bowl state of Kedah studied by Scott (Miller, 1959; Wain, 2009).

In the 1960s and 1970s, Malaysian urban interests were politically organized in the MCA, UMNO's junior partner in the Alliance. Conservative Chinese were organized into the MCA in 1949, in an attempt to consolidate these traditional elites' positions in opposition to the ongoing Communist insurgency in Malaya. The MCA incorporated leaders of the various Chinese chambers of commerce, ethnic, and clan associations into a truly Malayan party for the first time, with the goal of defending Chinese cultural values and capitalist interests in the face of the political uncertainty of the time. With national leadership drawing on established economic and cultural institutions, the MCA was able to quickly become an effective political party and social organization. The membership of the MCA consisted of those who had the greatest interest in lower food prices: lower-income urban residents and rubber-tappers or tin miners who did not produce their own food (Heng, 1988). By pushing for citizenship rights for Malayan Chinese under the new Malaysian constitution, the MCA significantly increased the political voice of food consumers, as all citizens were granted the vote.

Politics in Malaysia after independence in 1957 were dominated by relations between UMNO and MCA within the Alliance/BN. Major events such as the expulsion of Singapore from the Federation were examples of the sorts of elite power-sharing difficulties that were to plague the country until the early 1970s and that were finally resolved with – among other things – an interventionist agricultural policy that eased elite and mass Malay concerns about unequal development and the economic predominance of the Chinese population. Disputes among the Alliance member parties around communal issues such as citizenship for non-Malays and the language of school instruction had been simmering during the entire course of the transition from British rule to independence. They had been temporarily resolved through "the Bargain," or the basic deal struck around the new Malaysian constitution under which Malays were to retain political power in an Islamic state with Malay as the official language, in exchange for granting citizenship to non-Malays and the promise of unhindered economic activity in a laissez-faire policy environment (Mauzy, 1983, 20–22). In essence, this bargain formalized the status quo, reflecting the relatively equal balance of power between the UMNO and MCA until 1969. During this period, the MCA had a real voice in policy decisions and was able to effectively block UMNO proposals that ran counter to Chinese interests. For example, in 1949 the British set up the Communities Liason Committee to encourage local elites' cooperation with their postwar constitutional initiatives. Within this committee, MCA and UMNO representatives reached an agreement around Malay special rights and citizenship for non-Malays that was a relatively equal compromise. Malay politicians were "unaggressive and low-key" in asserting their interest in pro-Malay economic policies and happy to reach a limited bargain in which MCA assurances on Malays' special position as the original people of Malaya were traded for a liberalization of citizenship requirements for non-Malays (Heng, 1988, 147–156, 203). In the Alliance's 1955 election manifesto, responsibility for drafting economic and finance policy, as well as ethnically charged education policy, was delegated to MCA representatives, whose papers "contained clear-cut policies which were beneficial to Chinese interests."

Although the MCA was undoubtably the junior partner in the Alliance before 1969, it was able to block UMNO encroachments on what Chinese saw as their key interests, most importantly citizenship, Chinese-language education, and a commitment to noninterventionist economic policies. The reasons for the relatively equal balance of power between Malay and non-Malay politicians before 1969 did not lie directly in the demographic structure of Malaya. Excluding Singapore, Malays constituted around half the population of the country, and due to the restrictive citizenship regulations of the time, they made up a large majority of the electorate (Means, 1976, 12). However, the hand of the MCA was strengthened for several other reasons related to intra-elite politics. First, UMNO was determined to demonstrate to the British that an independent government would not involve the domination of other ethnic groups by Malays, and they used a collaboration with the MCA to this end. Second, the MCA was a wealthy and efficient party and able to contribute considerably to the Alliance electoral campaign in financial and organizational terms. Third, the generation of UMNO leaders of the day were primarily from aristocratic and bureaucratic backgrounds and were happy to defer to Chinese experts in the field of economic policy. Finally, the first generation of Malay and Chinese political elites had shared experiences such as English-language education, service in the British or Japanese civil service, and membership in the various committees set up by the British on the path to independence, which promoted a sense of common purpose and cooperation between the groups (Heng, 1988).

The Bargain maintained a relatively equal balance of power between urban Chinese and rural Malay interests until 1969, when the Malaysian regime was faced with "a crisis that ... threatened the survival of its principal political institutions and the maintenance of civil order within society" (Means, 1991, 1). The 1969 federal election was a defeat for the Alliance, though they maintained an absolute majority of seats in the House of Representatives, as is shown in Table 7.2. Their share of the popular vote collapsed by 15 percent as competitor Malay and Chinese parties, the PAS and DAP, respectively, made significant inroads into support for UMNO and the MCA. In the aftermath of the election, violence erupted in Kuala Lumpur as first Chinese opposition supporters, then Malay UMNO followers staged street demonstrations, which quickly escalated (Goh Cheng Teik, 1971). After the losses of the MCA in urban electorates in the state of Selangor, of which Kuala Lumpur is the capital, Malays were worried that opposition parties would take over the state government. At least partially provoked by processions on May 11 and 12, which celebrated the opposition successes, counterdemonstrations by Malays on May 13 careened out of control. Chinese residences and businesses in the city were looted and burned, and Chinese retaliated violently. Several hundred were killed, and around 6,000 people were made refugees from their destroyed homes (Means, 1991, 6–8).

Electorally, the rule of the Alliance was not threatened by their poor result in 1969. However, the political consequences of the election and the events of May 13 were significant. The migration of voters from the UMNO to the PAS, and the violence of Malay citizens in Kuala Lumpur against their Chinese and Indian countrymen, made Malay discontent with Alliance government patently clear. The inability of the MCA to appeal to Chinese voters, the intensity of the Malay response to DAP success, and the efficacy of the Malay-dominated security forces made the precarious political position of the Chinese in Malaya similarly clear (Heng, 1988, 261). The government declared a national state of emergency, suspended the constitution and parliament, and the 1969 elections for the Bornean states of Sabah and Sarawak were postponed indefinitely. Rule was delegated by cabinet to a small National Operations Council, headed by the Deputy Prime Minister, Tun Razak. During the period of emergency rule, a new political equilibrium emerged in Malaysia in which UMNO was the absolute political hegemon, and the MCA was relegated to a minor supporting role. As we will see, this development had implications for agricultural policy and regime stability.

7.4 SOCIOECONOMIC STRUCTURES, POLITICAL THREATS, AND THE 1969 PARLIAMENTARY ELECTION

In this section, I present an analysis of Alliance support at the 1969 parliamentary election in peninsular Malaysia. I examine an original dataset measuring the characteristics of Malaysian electorates and election results to explore where rural support for UMNO collapsed, causing the crisis within the party, which led to the adoption of the interventionist NEP. I find that the support of the rural sector was an important source of the UMNO vote at the election, even after controlling for the ethnic composition of a district. Both agricultural employment and landholding inequality are significantly correlated with a greater vote share for the Alliance. However, rural rice-growing areas deserted UMNO for the Islamic PAS opposition at the 1969 election. This shift in voting patterns among rural Malays occurred predominantly in the northern states of Kedah, Terengganu, and Kelantan and led to a change in the balance of power toward rural Malay elites in the aftermath of the election.

Malaysia in the 1960s and 1970s was only beginning the swift process of growth and structural transformation which by the 1990s would see it regarded as one of the world's most successful newly industrialized economies. Although economic growth rates averaged over 7 percent at this time, they occured from a moderately low base as GDP per capita in 1973 was only $3088, much lower than in Japan ($7133) but higher than in South Korea ($1782) (Drabble, 2000, 113, 183). The economy was still primarily agrarian, and urbanization was low. Agriculture made up more than half of total employment in peninsular Malaysia in 1970, while employment in the industrial and services sectors was relatively low at 5 percent and 15 percent of the total, respectively (Malaysia, 1970). Only 12 percent of the Malaysian population lived in Kuala Lumpur, the country's largest city (World Bank, 2012b). The consequences of the agrarian Malaysian economy in the 1960s and 1970s were a lack of a real threat of urban unrest on a scale that could *directly* threaten the regime and force it to implement consumer-friendly policies that would lower food prices. This was evident in the 1969 protests in Kuala Lumpur, which, though violent and shocking for the population and political leadership, never posed a significant threat to the regime, as they were effectively contained and did not spread to other urban centers (Goh Cheng Teik, 1971). Urban interests also had a relatively small voice in parliament, as only 6 seats of a total of 144 were allocated wholly to large urban centers, with a further 25 including both urban and rural areas (Rudner, 1970, 10–12).

The 1969 election forcefully illustrated the flagging support of the rural electorate for the Alliance. For the first – and until 2008, only – time in the history of Malaysia, the ruling coalition failed to secure a two-thirds super-majority in the Dewan Rakyat as it lost twenty-three seats, and its share of the popular vote fell from 59 percent to 45 percent (see Table 7.2). Contemporary analyses (Ratnam and Milne, 1970; Rudner, 1970) noted that the large losses experienced by the Alliance in 1969 came as a surprise. No single political issue, like independence in 1959 or the confrontation with Indonesia in 1964, dominated the campaign, and what Rudner (1970, 2) describes as "domestic tranquility" suggested that the Alliance government was well supported by the electorate at large. However, without an overriding drive for national unity or an external threat, voters deserted the interethnic governing coalition for opposition parties in droves. Appealing to solely Malay (rural) and Chinese (urban) voters, the PAS, DAP, and Gerakan made significant inroads into Alliance vote share.

I constructed an original dataset to model Alliance support in 1969. This is the first attempt to match election results to the socioeconomic characteristics of parliamentary districts during this time period, and I use data from both published and unpublished archival sources. I analyze only the districts of Peninsular Malaysia, excluding the states of Sabah and Sarawak in Borneo. These areas had only been recently included in the Federation, they have distinct politics from Peninsular Malaysia, and their elections were delayed due to the unrest after the election and are not easily comparable to the results on the Peninsula. I also excluded seats that were uncontested, leaving 94 parliamentary districts for analysis, of 144 total, which were matched to socioeconomic data from 62 administrative districts.

I estimate linear regressions of the Alliance vote share in each electoral district. I collected the dependent variable from official election results published by the Malaysian Election Commission (Election Commission, Malaysia, 1971, 52–69). Unfortunately, the results do not distinguish between the Alliance coalition parties but report only the total vote share for the ruling coalition, so I cannot analyze the vote shares of UMNO and the MCA separately. The average share of the vote won by the Alliance across all districts was 50 percent, the minimum was 18 percent in Ipoh, and the maximum was 80 percent in Johore Timor. A histogram of the Alliance vote is shown in the upper-left panel of Figure 7.1, and summary statistics of all variables included in the models are shown

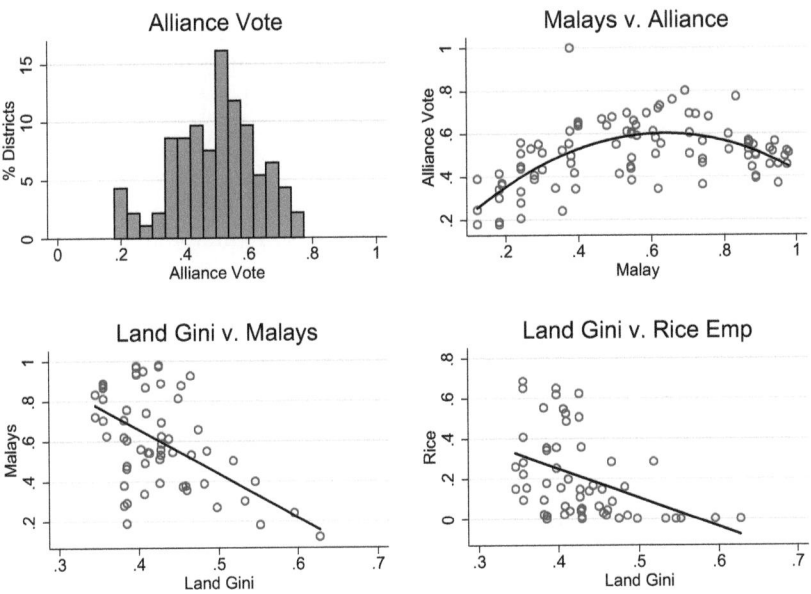

FIGURE 7.1 Party and Ethnicity Data, Malaysian 1969 Election

TABLE 7.3 *Independent Variables, Alliance Vote Models*

Variable	Mean	Std. Dev.	Min.	Max.
Alliance Vote	0.5	0.14	0.18	0.8
Malay	0.56	0.26	0.12	0.98
Indian	0.1	0.07	0	0.27
Chinese	0.33	0.21	0.02	0.68
Land Gini	0.45	0.08	0.35	0.63
Rice	0.19	0.21	0	0.69
Total Ag	0.48	0.24	0.03	0.91
Commerce	0.1	0.06	0.02	0.24
Rubber	0.21	0.17	0	0.63
N		94		

in Table 7.3. The election results were published in Malay and English and include an appendix of maps illustrating the boundaries of each electoral district. The maps allowed me to match the electoral districts to the subnational administrative districts used in the 1970 census.[3] I constructed the independent variables in my models from census data matched to electoral districts in this manner. The results of the 1970 population and housing census were not published by administrative district, so I collected these data at the library of the Department of Statistics in Kuala Lumpur (Malaysia, 1970). Reports available there give the number of people in the rural and urban sectors and by ten more detailed employment categories. Population is also given by ethnicity (Malay, Chinese, Indian, Other), from which I constructed measures of the ethnic composition of each district. I also constructed land inequality measures from the 1977 agricultural census (Khoo, 1981). Unfortunately, income and inequality data are not available, so I am not able to include these variables in my analysis.

I present six models of Alliance support at the 1969 election in Table 7.4. I begin by estimating a purely ethnic model of Alliance vote share, in Models 1 and 2, which includes indicators of the share of Malay, Chinese, and Indian population. Model 1 includes only a linear indicator of the share of Malays in an electoral district. However, this variable

[3] In most cases, administrative districts and electoral districts matched very closely: In many cases, the districts shared the same name and boundaries. Of ninety-five parliamentary districts included in the study, only nineteen shared an administrative district with another parliamentary district. The most parliamentary districts included within one administrative district were five, in the district of Kinta in Perak.

TABLE 7.4 *Alliance Vote Share Models, Malaysia*

	(1) Ethnic	(2) Ethnic	(3) Econ	(4) Comb	(5) Comb	(6) Comb
Malay	0.88	1.16**		0.90	1.44**	1.30**
	(0.63)	(0.53)		(0.59)	(0.66)	(0.60)
Malay Sq.		−1.05***		−0.85***	−0.96***	−0.90***
		(0.19)		(0.19)	(0.21)	(0.20)
Land Gini			0.40*	0.43*	0.77**	0.58**
			(0.23)	(0.23)	(0.34)	(0.24)
Total Ag			0.58*	0.21	0.75**	0.21**
			(0.30)	(0.32)	(0.30)	(0.09)
Ag*Land Gini					−1.24*	
					(0.66)	
Rice			−0.35	−0.16	−0.20***	0.95**
			(0.21)	(0.23)	(0.07)	(0.40)
Rice*Land Gini						−2.91***
						(1.08)
Rubber			−0.22	0.02		
			(0.22)	(0.23)		
Commerce			−0.34	−0.09		
			(0.68)	(0.68)		
Chinese	0.70	−0.16		−0.21	0.18	0.05
	(0.63)	(0.51)		(0.54)	(0.59)	(0.56)
Indian	0.59	−0.50		−0.53	−0.17	−0.23
	(0.64)	(0.52)		(0.58)	(0.60)	(0.59)
R^2	0.411	0.567	0.510	0.617	0.631	0.645
AIC	−147.12	−174.04	−160.36	−175.62	−180.98	−184.61
Observations	94	94	94	94	94	94

Standard errors in parentheses.
All models with robust standard errors.
All models control for number of voters.
* $p < 0.10$, ** $p < 0.05$, *** $p < 0.01$.

displays a nonlinear relationship with Alliance vote share, illustrated in the top-right panel of Figure 7.1, so in Model 2 I include its squared term also. These ethnic models show that the share of Malays in an electoral district is a significant predictor of Alliance vote share, when included alongside its squared term. In Model 1, the coefficients on the shares of all ethnicities are positive, but none are significant. Model 2 finds a significant nonlinear relationship between Malays and votes for the Alliance. The predicted Alliance vote share increases from 0.51 to 0.57 as Malay population share increases from 0.3 to 0.55. Above this level of Malay population, Model 2 predicts a decline in Alliance vote share to only 0.48 in districts with 85 percent Malay population. Because ethnic Malays were heavily concentrated in the countryside in 1969, these results provide the first evidence that these rural areas deserted the Alliance for the opposition PAS party at the election.

After considering a purely ethnic model of Alliance vote share in Models 1 and 2, Model 3 includes only economic variables measuring development, landholding inequality, the composition of the agricultural sector, and the size of the commercial sector. This model does not perform as well as Model 3 on measures of model fit, and only landholding inequality and the size of the agricultural sector are correlated with Alliance support. Districts that were characterized by higher levels of landholding inequality are associated with greater Alliance vote share in this model, pointing to the role rural elites played in mobilizing support for the ruling coalition. Agricultural areas, unsurprisingly, are also associated with greater Alliance support. However, distinctions in the composition of the agricultural sector in terms of rice and rubber production are not significantly associated with the Alliance vote, and neither is the size of the commercial sector.

I estimate four more models that combine ethnic and economic characteristics in Models 4–6. They all perform better on measures of model fit than either purely ethnic or economic models. Model 4 is simply the combination of the variables included in Models 2 and 3. Its results are broadly similar to those of previous models: There is a nonlinear relationship between Malay population share and Alliance support, with the Alliance vote share declining at levels of Malay population above 55 percent. Landholding inequality is positively associated with greater Alliance vote share, which increases from 0.46 to 0.55 with a two standard-deviation change in the land Gini from 0.35 to 0.55.

In two further models I use interactions to explore the rural basis of Alliance support further. In Model 5, I interact the land Gini variable with an indicator of total employment in the agricultural sector. Landholding inequality remains positively associated with Alliance support, but the magnitude of changes in predicted vote share associated with landholding inequality are only around half the size of those in Model 3. More agricultural areas are associated with greater levels of support for the Alliance, but only in areas with lower landholding inequality. Districts with both high agricultural employment and land Ginis saw significantly lower levels of support for the Alliance. In this model, greater levels of rice employment are also associated with lower vote share for

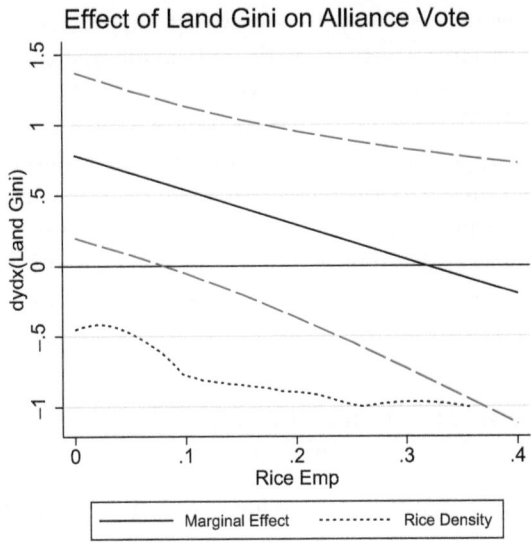

FIGURE 7.2 Landholding Inequality and Alliance Vote

the Alliance, an eight-percentage-point decrease across a two standard-deviation shift in the variable. In Model 7, I interact the land Gini with an indicator of the share of rice employment in a district. I graph key results of this model in Figure 7.2. This model still finds a significant nonlinear relationship between the proportion of Malay population in a district and Alliance vote share. The predicted Alliance vote increases from 39 percent to 61 percent as the Malay population varies from 30 percent to 80 percent of the total, decreasing very slightly at levels above 80 percent. The coefficient on the land Gini variable is positive and significant, but associated with only very small changes in Alliance vote share. This is because, as I illustrate in Figure 7.2, landholding inequality is only positively associated with greater Alliance vote share in areas that did not have a large proportion of employment in rice.

Several conclusions emerge from this analysis. First, support for the Alliance in the most Malay-dominated areas was no stronger than in areas with more ethnically mixed populations. Second, rural inequality and the composition of the agricultural sector had significant effects on the Alliance vote share. Districts with more unequal distributions of land were more likely to vote strongly for the ruling coalition, testament to the central role rural elites played within UMNO. However, the most impoverished rural ares, particularly those with a large share of peasant rice-growers, were less likely to see strong support for the Alliance. Inspection of electoral districts with high landholding inequality and rice employment reveals that they were concentrated in the northern states of Kedah, Terengganu, and Kelantan, where a combination of a strong Islamic opposition party and rural poverty reduced support for the government. In the following section, I will explore why rice-growing areas defected from the Alliance at the 1969 election, indirectly sparking a political crisis that destabilized the regime and caused it to implement the interventionist NEP, including significant support for the rural sector.

7.5 RURAL AND URBAN INTERESTS AND RICE POLICY BEFORE 1971

The political crisis sparked by the 1969 election in Malaysia was to set in motion events that would change the balance of power within the ruling coalition to the advantage of rural UMNO elites. To placate this ascendant group, the new government under Prime Minister Razak implemented agricultural policies in line with the interests of rural Malays, particularly politically powerful rice growers who, we have seen, deserted the Alliance at the 1969 election. In 1960s and 1970s Malaysia, the preferences of rice farmers and their UMNO patrons lay in an interventionist government policy that would increase the price they received for *padi*, as unmilled rice is called in the country. The exact means by which this policy goal was to be achieved by the government were not fully specified and could run through various measures, from a minimum price support, to input subsidies, or regulation of middlemen such as millers and buyers. However, Malay rice producers and their UMNO champions had, since independence, favored "drastic and direct government involvement" in the agricultural sector in order to increase the incomes of rural Malays (Heng, 1996, 5–7). Urban Chinese food consumers and processors were able to prevent such a policy from being implemented until the aftermath of the 1969 election and the introduction of the New Economic Policy in 1971.

Due to the relatively mountainous terrain in much of the peninsula, modern Malaysia has never been entirely self-sufficient in rice, even when the sector faced a very benign policy environment, and Malay rice producers were traditionally smallholders and relatively poor. Reluctant to commit government funds to supporting rice producers, the British colonial government had resisted using price supports to alleviate rural poverty and encourage higher yields, even in the face of shortages and widespread hunger in the post-war era (Tamin and Meyanathan, 1988). Colonial policies had also forbidden the sale of paddy land to non-Malays, and therefore rice growers were universally Malay (Shamsul, 2001). Due to their strong UMNO component, the first Alliance postindependence governments were already much more responsive to food producers' interests than the British administration. A guaranteed minimum price scheme was established, and the government rice stockpile was combined with some import restrictions in order to bolster domestic prices at the expense of consumers, who paid more for domestic rice and could not always access higher-quality foreign rice (Pletcher, 1989). This was significant, given that the average urban Malay resident's diet consisted of 40 percent rice in 1960, expenditure on which accounted for around 18 percent of consumers' total income (Brown, 1973, 164). Agencies such as the Federal Agricultural Marketing Authority (FAMA) and the Padi and Rice Marketing Board (PRMB) were established to implement government policies supporting rice farmers and to oversee rice milling and marketing (Tamin and Meyanathan, 1988, 103). However, producer support policies did not involve large market distortions during this period, as shown in Figure 7.3, moving mostly in tandem with world markets to stabilize farmers' incomes and not reaching levels of more than 25 percent of world market prices. Development schemes, especially irrigation projects, which allowed farmers to harvest a second annual rice crop, also went some way to enhancing rice farmers' welfare in 1960s Malaysia. The Muda river scheme in the northwestern states of Kedah and Perlis, for example, irrigated a full one-third of the country's padi land and allowed for double-cropping in this area (Brown, 1973, 165). The introduction of high-yield "green revolution" rice varieties, such as those developed and tested by the Rice Production Institute in Malaysia, also increased production on many rice farms, though these gains accrued disproportionately to larger rice farmers (Tamin and Meyanathan, 1988).

On the whole, however, agricultural policy in Malaysia before 1971 was largely laissez-faire, as significant government intervention in food markets ran directly against the interests of the urban population and the MCA. Urban food consumers, predominantly Chinese, naturally favored nonintervention in markets in the hope of benefiting from low average world food prices in the 1960s (Brown, 1973, 167). Chinese politicians also vehemently opposed a more interventionist policy turn in the agricultural sector due to their constituents' interests in rice trading and processing. The role of rice traders and millers, who often

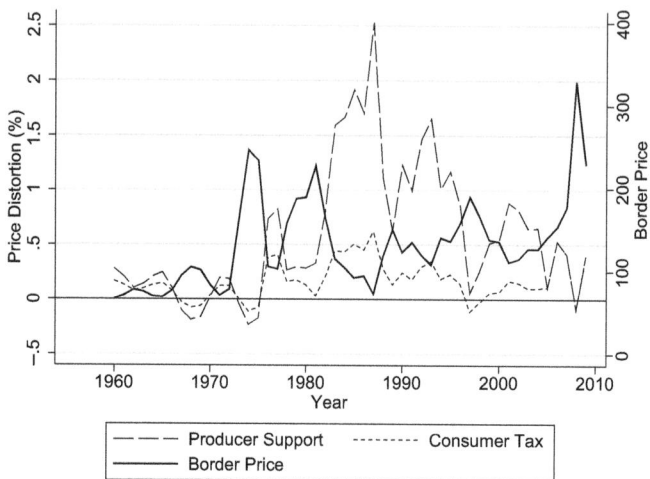

FIGURE 7.3 Rice Policy in Malaysia and International Price Fluctuations, 1960
to 2010
Source: Anderson and Nelgen (2012) and World Bank (2012a).

doubled as rural financiers, had commonly been regarded as harmful
to farmers who were seen as exploited by their lending practices and
monopsonistic positions in the countryside (Tamin and Meyanathan,
1988, 101–102). These middlemen had traditionally been Chinese, due
to colonial policies that restricted Malay movement out of the primary
sector. A popular policy proposal among Malay farmers and politicians
was the establishment of collective rice mills and state-run rice marketing
agencies. However, MCA opposition to such policies was able to minimize
such government intervention in rice markets until its position within the
ruling coalition was severely weakened after 1969. For example, in
1963 the MCA leader and Minister of Finance, Tan Siew Sin, persuaded
Prime Minister Rahman to remove the UMNO politician Abdul Aziz
Ishak from office after he proposed a policy that would have set up
state rice-milling cooperatives and cut Chinese millers out of the market
(Heng and Sieh, 2000, 128–131). Chinese politicians representing urban
interests were able to restrict the goal of policy at this point to "resolving
marketing problems of paddy smallholders by minimalist intervention ...
to ensure the orderly and efficient working of market forces" (Tamin and
Meyanathan, 1988, 101).

Apart from the specific matter of Chinese middlemen's positions within
the rice sector, the MCA elite consisted primarily of businessmen, whose
interest in lower food prices was combined with a strong aversion to
pro-Malay government intervention in the economy in general (Heng,

1988, 73–82). Because of British colonial policies that kept Malays predominantly tied to their traditional occupations in agriculture, before independence the Chinese had already occupied the central role in the construction, transportation, commercial, financial, and services sectors in the country. Therefore, the sorts of wide-ranging interventions to increase Malays' opportunities in these areas, which were often proposed by Malay politicians, met strong opposition by the MCA. Chinese political leaders ensured that a clause was included in the independence constitution that prevented parliament "restricting business or trade solely for the purpose of reservation for Malays." Following independence, free markets and open competition did indeed bring considerable economic rewards for Chinese businessmen, who by 1970 dominated the ownership of capital in the country alongside foreign investors, with Malay and Indian ownership of fixed assets amounting to only 1 percent of the total (Heng and Sieh, 2000, 128–131).

Rural development projects and a laissez-faire policy regime were not enough to remedy the relatively low incomes that predominated among Malaysian rice farmers, even a decade after independence. Poverty was endemic among rice-growers in the 1960s (Jomo, 1984) and seemed to be increasing with the integration of local producers into global markets (Scott, 1976; Shamsul, 1979). There was a continuing perception among the Malay population and politicians that the rural sector was being exploited by middlemen, and existing policies did not give rice farmers the support they needed in order to make a respectable living. These grievances were articulated by an increasingly vocal and well-organized Islamist opposition in the form of PAS, which was able to capitalize on them at the 1969 election (Noor, 2014, 67–75). The Alliance's losses in rural, rice-growing areas and the subsequent political turmoil in the country led to a shift in power from the MCA toward Malay hard-liners within UMNO. It also provided the political opportunity to implement policies that significantly increased the incomes of food producers in order to secure the support of the rural sector and maintain the stability of the regime.

7.6 MAKING POLICY: THE BREAKDOWN OF THE BARGAIN, UMNO HEGEMONY, AND AGRICULTURE

Before 1969, the MCA had been able to contain interventionist rural interests within UMNO and their pushes for policies that would favor Malay food producers. Ethnic-based intervention in markets was ruled out in the independence Constitution, and MCA leader and Finance Minister, Tan Siew Sin, had the final say on economic policy within the Alliance cabinet. However, the election of 1969 was a blow for the Alliance as a whole, including for UMNO, as it lost three northern seats to the Islamic PAS. The MCA fared particularly poorly, as both the opposition Gerakan and DAP parties emerged as serious contenders in urban Chinese seats. Their electoral success districts is illustrated by the fact they were able to win eight and thirteen seats in the Dewan Rakyat, respectively. The MCA was discredited within its core constituency; as Rudner (1970, 13) noted in the direct aftermath, "it is clear that the MCA can no longer claim custody over Chinese interest aggregation," and it is disputable whether it ever held a predominant position in this community in Malaysia again.

The MCA's 1969 losses in urban seats had both direct and indirect consequences. The direct consequence was that the party dramatically lost weight within the ruling coalition. Facing harsh criticism from Malay politicians in UMNO, MCA leader Tan Siew Sin decided after the election not to have his party take any seats in a new cabinet, a decision that called into question the Alliance's self-appointed role as guarantor of interethnic cooperation and political stability in the country (Means, 1991, 7). In the event, Tan's decision to remain outside the cabinet did not take immediate effect as a state of emergency was declared, and parliamentary government was suspended for twenty-one months in the wake of the unrest on May 13 (Lee and Heng, 2000, 207–208). The administration of the country in the interim was managed by a National Operations Council (NOC) under Deputy Prime Minister Abdul Razak. This body embodied a transfer of power from the multiethnic Alliance to a Malay coalition of UMNO politicians, the security forces and the bureaucracy. It included only one Chinese and Indian representative, with its remaining membership consisting of the (Malay) heads of the police, armed forces, public and foreign services, plus Razak (Means, 1991, 8–9). Within the NOC, and after 1971 in the enlarged Barisan Nasional government, urban interests' representation through the MCA was severely weakened.

The indirect effect of MCA losses was the outbreak of unrest in Kuala Lumpur, the outcome of which further undermined the position of the party within the ruling coalition. The exact course of events that led to the violent unrest on May 13 remains unclear, but most scholars agree that their initial impetus was in Gerakan and DAP supporters staging parades celebrating the Alliance's electoral losses in the May 10 elections (Goh Cheng Teik, 1971, 20). Racist language and provocations – from both opposition and government supporters – led the situation to escalate into violent clashes between ethnic mobs. The police and armed forces called in to restore order were predominantly Malay and were particularly harsh in their treatment of Chinese. Almost all of the 6,000 Kuala Lumpur residents who lost their homes to looting and fires were Chinese (Means, 1991, 6–8). The May riots revealed the "undisputable fact of Malay superior political power backed up by overwhelming Malay-controlled military force ... the Chinese became keenly aware that in a show-down they lacked the means to impose their will on any issue of fundamental concern to the Malays" (Heng, 1988, 261). In short, the threat of urban Chinese interests to the regime was revealed to be negligible, and the MCA was still more easily marginalized by UMNO in post-1969 politics.

While the election losses and mass unrest were considerably weakening the MCA within the Alliance, UMNO's relatively poor showing strengthened the hand of Malay hard-liners within the party, who called for economic policies that privileged their constituents at the expense of the urban non-Malay population. As shown earlier, UMNO candidates did not perform well in districts dominated by Malay rice-growers in 1969. Malay voters migrated to the PAS and its unequivocal advocacy of Malay interests, including policies granting assistance to Malay peasants, the implementation of more Islamic law, and special rights for *Bumiputera* (Means, 1991, 5). This shift did not go unnoticed by UMNO politicians. A vocal group emerged within the party – known as the "Ultras" – who criticized the government under Tunku Abdul Rahman for neglecting the Malay population and making too many policy concessions to non-Malays. The visibility and demands of these Malay chauvinists was further enhanced by the unrest of May 13, following which racial tensions ran extremely high. Led by Mahathir Mohamad, an UMNO politician who had lost his northern parliamentary seat to PAS and later went on to become the party's leader and Prime Minister, these ultras mobilized radical Malays in Kuala Lumpur, especially at the University of Malaya, in vocal opposition to the UMNO leadership (Means, 1991, 8–9). Mahathir penned an open and "deliberately offensive" letter calling on Prime Minister Rahman to resign, informing him that he was "the object of hatred of 'the Malays, whether they are UMNO or PMIP supporters'" (Khoo, 1995, 22).

Rahman was able to dismiss Mahathir and another Ultra, former UMNO Executive Secretary Musa Hitam, from the party, criticizing their "wild and fantastic theory of domination by one race over the other communities" (Means, 1991, 9-10). However the resonance of this demand within the party and the broader Malay community could not be ignored. Although the Ultras' calls for a one-party government under UMNO earned them temporary exile from the party, they decisively undermined the authority of Rahman and had a considerable effect on his successor Razak's strategy for recovering from the 1969 crisis (Khoo, 1995, 23–24). Rather than adopt a single-party dictatorship under UMNO, Razak did return the country to its former system of electoral authoritarianism after almost two years of emergency rule under the NOC in 1971. Alongside a policy called *Rukunegara*, which prohibited public discussion of many contentious political matters, Razak was committed to a program of deep economic reform that would benefit the impoverished and restive rural Malay population. As he put it in November 1969, "Democracy cannot work in Malaysia in terms of political equality alone. The democratic process must be spelt out also in terms of a more equitable distribution of wealth and opportunity" (Means, 1991, 11). The pre-1969 Bargain was thus destroyed. After the election and subsequent unrest in Kuala Lumpur, the balance of power within the Malaysian regime had shifted decisively away from the MCA and the more moderate wing of UMNO. Under pressure from the Ultras and the broader Malay population, Razak abandoned the central economic plank of the Bargain enshrined in the independence Constitution: the premise that the Malaysian government should not intervene in the economy for the benefit of Malays.

The New Economic Policy and Agriculture

Following the May 1969 crisis, Razak was the director of the interim governing body, the National Operations Council (NOC) and in September 1970 became Malaysia's second Prime Minister. Alongside a reputation as an efficient administrator and manager, Razak was widely perceived as a more pro-Malay politician than his predecessor, and he was determined to make UMNO the mass base of political support for the government. His vision of a Malay-dominated political system found its first realization in the NOC, which he used to determine the government's response to the crisis without gathering significant input from rival political groups. This primarily Malay body decided on policies, most notably the *Rukunegara* and the broad outlines of the NEP, and had them symbolically ratified by a National Consultative Council (NCC), a body including representatives from all ethnic groups and political parties in the country. This process took place behind closed doors, without formal voting, and the NCC consisted primarily of government officials and Malays. This interim government was able to restore order to the country and formulate coherent policy responses to the crisis, but it was a decisive step away from democratic accountability in Malaysia and raised the very real danger that parliamentary rule might never be restored (Means, 1991, 10–11).

Facing no formal opposition and without the need for agreement with the MCA, the NOC under Razak had a free hand in economic policymaking. However, in formulating and implementing the NEP, Razak's administration faced one significant problem, in that the bureaucracy was strongly opposed to his plans for an interventionist shift in economic policy. The country's main economic policymaking entities, the Economic Planning Unit (EPU), Treasury, the *Bank Negara* (Central Bank), the Statistics Department, and Federal Industrial Development Agency all disagreed with Razak's plans. Pointing to the country's successful development record under a laissez-faire policy environment coupled with strict fiscal discipline and a favorable environment for foreign direct investment, the EPU and its allies were alarmed at the government's plans for a radical, interventionist shift (Faaland, Parkinson, and Saniman, 1990, 27–29). Therefore, Razak was compelled to create a new economic planning agency reporting directly to the Prime Minister's department, the Department of National Unity (DNU), which identified with his new priorities in policymaking (Heng, 1997, 265). The DNU argued that the 1969 riots were evidence of fundamental structural deficits in Malaysia, through which the Malay population was destined to languish in poverty and pose a risk to national political stability. For the DNU, economic growth was only desirable to the extent that it was coupled with decreasing interethnic inequality in incomes, as well as in other development outcomes such as sectoral employment, health, and education (Faaland, Parkinson, and Saniman, 1990, 31–34). The DNU approach, rather than the preferences of the EPU and its allied ministries, was reflected in the formulation of the NEP, which embodied a radical shift away from previous economic policymaking in its seven main goals (Faaland, Parkinson, and Saniman, 1990, 69–72). These were: A reduction in urban and rural poverty, regardless of race, but due to the relatively low incomes of the Malay populations this goal came to focus on rural Malays; A reduction in racial economic imbalances in terms of income, employment, and wealth, which, due to the initial position of the Malay population, in practice involved decreasing barriers to Malay participation in the economy; A target growth rate of 6.4 percent per annum until 1985; Full employment; An active role for federal and state governments in ensuring that Malays achieved more equal levels of participation in the economy; Supplemental policies for ameliorating ethnic conflict in the country; and A comprehensive apparatus for implementing policies directed at the preceding goals, and monitoring progress toward them.

The New Economic Policy, as laid out in the Second Malaysia Plan, had important consequences for the rural sector, and for rice policy in particular. Indeed, increased support for rural Malay farmers was the primary element of the new development strategy laid out in the DNU's policy recommendations (Faaland, Parkinson, and Saniman, 1990, 49–52). The most important institutional innovation of the new era in rice producer supports was the creation of the National Padi and Rice Authority (LPN) in 1971.[4] The Authority had four basic roles: to ensure fair and stable prices for rice farmers; to ensure fair and stable prices for consumers; to ensure sufficient rice supplies, including imports; and to make policy recommendations for the development of the rice industry. It became the sole importer of rice to Malaysia and the sole authority able to grant licenses to millers, wholesalers, and traders. The LPN became responsible for administering the government guaranteed minimum price and price subsidy schemes for rice, which dictated prices for unmilled rice and also granted farmers a lump-sum payment for each ton of unmilled rice delivered to mills (Tamin and Meyanathan, 1988, 99–125). In addition, the LPN became directly involved in rice markets, as a miller and wholesaler, gradually driving private middlemen out of the market by accepting lower-quality produce from farmers at higher prices than private enterprises, and granting them large lump-sum "discount" payments for deliveries. The creation of the LPN therefore ran directly against the interests of Chinese rice millers and traders, as staunchly defended by the MCA until their exile from government in 1969. As a result, the proportion of unmilled rice purchased by the private sector declined from 88 percent to 54 percent between 1974 and 1985, a trend that continued despite the government agency's rising deficits (Tamin and Meyanathan, 1988, 114, 125).

Through the guaranteed minimum price scheme and its control of rice imports, LPN moved to significantly increase the price of rice in Malaysia after the implementation of the NEP, as shown in Figure 7.3. The minimum price paid to farmers increased from M$264 to M$463 in 1975. As international food market prices declined after the first oil shock in 1973,

---

[4] In 1994, LPN was corporatized and renamed National Rice Corporation (*Padiberas Nasional Bhd*/BERNAS).

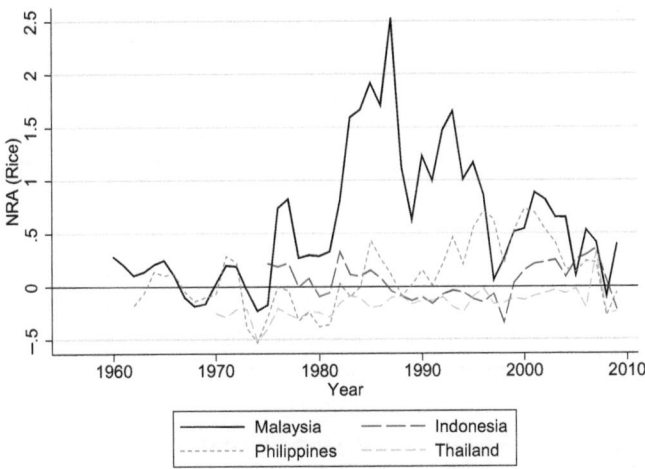

FIGURE 7.4 Rice Policy in Malaysia and Selected ASEAN Countries, 1960 to 2010
Source: Anderson and Valenzuela (2008) and Anderson and Nelgen (2012).

domestic producer prices in Malaysia soared, averaging 25 percent above world market prices for the 1970s as a whole and reaching levels double or triple world market prices in the 1980s. In the 1980s, consumer rice prices in Malaysia reached levels 20 percent to 40 percent above those on world markets. These rural-biased policies were significantly more advantageous to rice farmers than those of neighboring governments in South-East Asia, as shown in Figure 7.4. Malaysia's levels of price supports for rice farmers were above those of Indonesia, Thailand, and the Philippines from the mid-1970s until the late 1990s, and in the 1980s they were over 100 percentage points higher than those in these other countries, which provided at best a neutral price policy compared to world markets.

Apart from these measures affecting the price received by rice farmers, the government also implemented a number of input subsidies under the NEP. Farmers were sold urea fertilizer at heavily subsidized rates and given seed, chemicals, and insecticides free or at low prices. Access to credit for rural farmers was also enhanced under the government-owned *Bank Pertanian Malaysia* (Malaysian Agricultural Bank), which gave short-term loans at zero interest or below-market interest rates (Tamin and Meyanathan, 1988, 107–109). This institution further impeded the activities of private rice traders in the countryside, who had traditionally also provided much of the rural lending in these areas.

The effects of the interventionist policy on rice farmers' incomes were significant. Jomo (1984) found that government price supports and input subsidies were crucial for increasing the incomes of rice smallholders and reducing poverty among this group. The poverty incidence rate among rice smallholders declined from 88 percent in 1970 to 77 percent in 1975 and 55 percent in 1980, and this cannot be accounted for by productivity gains but only through the increases in rice prices dictated by the government under the NEP. Larger farmers, who tended to be well connected to UMNO, gained even more than smaller farmers because the absolute value of government support varied either directly or indirectly with the size of holdings. Fertilizer subsidies, for example, were based on a per hectare application rate. Price supports are, of course, based on output volumes and therefore even under constant returns to scale tend to benefit larger farmers. In 1981–1982, for example, the largest 25 percent of farmers received 75 percent of the rice coupon subsidy in Malaysia (Tamin and Meyanathan, 1988, 135–137).

The political crisis of 1969 led to the decline of urban interests' power within the ruling coalition, as the MCA withdrew from cabinet, and UMNO ultras had a growing influence on government policy. In order to address this shifting support coalition and placate ascendent rural Malay interests, the new Prime Minister Razak implemented the interventionist New Economic Policy. By increasing consumer food prices and decreasing the share of rice processed and traded by private companies, the NEP ran directly counter to the interests of urban food consumers and Chinese businessmen. However, it simultaneously benefited the Malay interests that had become significantly more powerful within the ruling coalition since the election and unrest of May 1969. By using a more interventionist agricultural policy to address these interests, Razak was able to shore up flagging support for the Alliance and maintain regime stability in the country.

7.7 THE EFFECTS OF THE NEP AND AGRICULTURAL SUPPORT ON REGIME DURABILITY

In the short term, the introduction of the NEP served to placate hardline Malay politicians within UMNO and prevent a shift toward one-party dictatorship. In the wake of the 1969 political crisis, the Malysian regime was in danger of collapsing into single-party rule under UMNO. This was primarily due to the challenge of chauvinist Malay Ultras within UMNO and their demands for Malay political hegemony in the country.

Politicians such as Mahathir Mohamad had become a powerful and vocal group in the ruling party and the Malay community after the events of May 1969, calling for the resignation of Prime Minister Rahman, who they portrayed as an apologist for urban Chinese interests and demanding radical measures be taken that would increase economic opportunities for Malays, at the expense of other ethnic groups (Khoo, 1995, 19–30).

This group advocated for the continuation of the autocratic government in place under the Malay-dominated National Operations Council, the interim governing body installed in the wake of the May unrest. In opposition was the first generation of Malaysian leaders around Tunku Abdul Rahman, who were convinced of the need for a parliamentary, electoral regime to ensure the popular support and legitimacy of the government. The new Prime Minister Razak, in Means' (1991, 10–12) account, was convinced that government could not return to business as usual and agreed to a return to parliamentary government only on the condition that drastic measures be taken to restructure society and "overcome the inferior economic position of the Malays" (Means, 1991, 11). The new generation of Malay elites within UMNO were only prepared to accept a reprise of the pre-1969 regime, which included electoral institutions in Malaysia, in conjunction with the New Economic Policy and the interventionist, pro-farmer agricultural policies that it entailed.

Razak's advocacy of the NEP, and the creation of the Department of National Unity with which to formulate and implement it, therefore placated the demands of the Malay Ultras within UMNO and allowed the Malaysian regime to restore parliamentary government, avoiding the instability of a true regime change to single-party authoritarian rule. However, the Malaysian regime after 1971 was not the same as its precrisis predecessor. In Razak's first Cabinet, all ministerial positions were filled by Malays from UMNO except for the MCA leader Tan Siew Sin, who continued as Minister of Finance until 1974. First-generation leaders from the Rahman administration were removed from Cabinet and replaced with pro-Malay hard-liners who had been elevated to powerful positions within UMNO in party elections. These hard-liners included Ultras such as Mahathir and Musa Hitam, who had been ejected from the party by Rahman (Means, 1991, 21).

In order to minimize opposition to the government's new economic policies, and to avoid political mobilization over extremely sensitive ethnic issues, Razak also moved to create a larger institutional structure to replace the Alliance and co-opt a larger group of parliamentary parties into the UMNO regime. The result was the *Barisan Nasional*

(BN/National Front), a new organization that was to field candidates in the first post-1969 elections in 1974. Decisions on the number of seats to be contested by each party were henceforth to be decided by the UMNO leader, and BN formulated policies in a Supreme Council headed by the UMNO leader. BN incorporated the main parties from the Bornean states of Sabah and Sarawak, plus Gerakan, the People's Progressive Party and the Pan-Malaysian Islamic Party (PAS) (Milne, 1975). It therefore massively impeded the size and capabilities of the opposition, as well as the power of the MCA within the government, as it was no longer the sole representative of Chinese interests within the ruling coalition. The position of UMNO, as the arbiter of disputes within BN and with its ability to disburse political patronage in order to induce cooperation from coalition members, was even stronger than under the Alliance (Means, 1991, 27–32). In 1974, BN handily defeated the opposition in parliamentary elections, winning 88 percent of the seats and 61 percent of the popular vote (see Table 7.2).

After the 1974 elections, the Malaysian regime under UMNO had emerged from the shadow of a severe political crisis in 1969. Although the country had avoided slipping into a true one-party dictatorship, because junior partners have always been included in the ruling coalition, it had definitely become less competitive: Case (1996b) describes the post-1969 era as one of "UMNO Paramountcy." The introduction of the NEP and its support for rural Malays played a key part in easing intra-elite conflicts and directing the regime away from total collapse, and the new orthodoxy of pro-Malay policies continued, leading to new requirements for Malay ownership and employment in private businesses, for example (Heng, 1988, 263–264). However, it is more difficult to assess the impact of the NEP's agricultural support programs on mass politics, that is, support for UMNO and BN in the rural Malay areas, which had abandoned the ruling coalition in 1969 and sparked the crisis. Jomo (1989) argues that the main economic benefits from the NEP ended up accruing to the elite political class who were able to benefit from widespread corruption and access to government rents under the new interventionist regime. UMNO and MCA had no interest in broad distribution of the benefits of development, but instead directed state support and protection to particularly powerful interests within their ranks. Combined with the authoritarian shift in Malaysian politics after 1971 and the increasing irrelevance of electoral politics to the regime, it seems that on balance, the agricultural protection regime's political purpose was more to ease intra-elite power struggles than to shore up mass support for the regime.

7.8 CONCLUSION

Malaysia is one of the most puzzling cases of stable authoritarianism in the world, given its remarkably high level of development and the political transitions experienced by its South-East Asian neighbors. In this chapter, I have shown that at one of the most critical periods of political instability in Malaysia's history, after the ruling coalition's surprise election losses in 1969, an interventionist, pro-rural agricultural policy was a key element of the regime's strategy for easing intra-elite discord and restoring political stability. I have therefore introduced a novel element to the dominant explanations for continued authoritarianism in Malaysia, which focus on intra-elite cooperation facilitated by party structures and electoral institutions. Cooperation between competing factions within the ruling coalition displayed extreme volatility in the late 1960s, which threatened to bring the regime as a whole to its knees; only through his pro-Malay and rural-biased New Economic Policy was Razak able to persuade restive UMNO hard-liners to support the restoration of parliamentary government.

Politics in Malaysia after 1971 was characterized by stable BN government at the federal level, with both the participants in the political system and the scope of policy changes severely constrained. Real participation in Malaysian politics was effectively limited to the leaders of the BN constituent parties, while non-BN party leaders and most of the voting public were reduced to to roles of permanent opposition and political observers, respectively. Policies such as the NEP and the *Rukunegara* were deemed too contentious for debate, and decisions in other areas were made in nonpublic inter-communal bargains within BN. Due to the predominant position of UMNO in the new ruling bloc, the most important political divisions within the country became those within UMNO. For example, the competition between Mahathir Mohamad and Tengku Razaleigh for the UMNO Presidency in 1987 was probably the most important political conflict in the country's post-1971 history, leading as it did to a concentration and personalization of power in Prime Minister Mahathir (Means, 1991; Slater, 2003).

The interventionist economic policy shift begun in 1971 under the NEP can be said to have contained at least some of the seeds of the Malaysian regime's current difficulties, however. Because the MCA could no longer attain UMNO support for its constituents' most important interests (a laissez-faire economic policy environment), the party continued to struggle to garner support from urban non-Malay voters. The "general feeling of being used for political support of the government while being largely ignored in policy matters" in turn led to intraparty strife and a further problems for the MCA (Means, 1991, 57). Although opposition parties found it difficult to make any progress against BN electorally for several decades after its formation in 1974, the last three general elections in 2008, 2013, and 2018 have seen dramatically reduced support for the ruling coalition under UMNO, especially among non-Malay and urban voters (Pepinsky, 2009b; Welsh, 2013, 2018). There are, of course, many reasons for this decrease in BN support. However, one contributing factor is the effect of the NEP. Because the reputation of the non-Malay BN parties has been so discredited since the introduction of the NEP, they now struggle to win support from their core constituencies, which in turn has become a major problem for the BN government. Therefore, although the interventionist, pro-rural shift which the NEP embodied was essential for restoring short-term intra-elite stability in the country after the events of 1969, the long-term effects of this policy, which essentially aimed to fundamentally change the socioeconomic structures of the country, could not have been foreseen and may not have been as effectively managed by UMNO.

8

Conclusion

Freedoms are not only the primary ends of development, they are among
its principal means.
  (Amartya Sen, Development as Freedom, *p. 10.)*

This book is about the link between economic development and political
regime type. I find that growth is by no means an apolitical, exogenous
force pushing states toward democracy. Instead, it is profoundly shaped
by interventions in agricultural markets by self-interested governments
seeking to secure their grip on power. Authoritarian regimes, in particular,
make agricultural policy by responding to political threats, implementing
urban-biased policies to appease powerful urban interests and taking a
rural-biased stance when the rural sector is threatening. Because urban
interests are often, but not always, powerful, authoritarian governments
tend to follow policies that significantly decrease the prices of agricultural
commodities and food. Intervening in these markets in this way helps to
stabilize undemocratic governments, but has significant negative consequences for the welfare of powerless farmers or food consumers, who
are at the mercy of an unelected and unaccountable regime. Agricultural
policies also have consequences for long-run growth and structural transformation, as they shape patterns of production and investment in the
economy and the broader process of development.

The economic consequences of urban-biased policies are relatively
clear. Poverty is more prevalent in the rural areas of urban-biased regimes,
and decreasing the incomes of farmers leads to disproportionately large
increases in poverty among the poorest rural residents (Senauer, 2002).

By stunting growth in the agricultural sector, urban-biased policies also depress national output growth overall (Timmer, 1988). In addition, urban-biased policies are a push factor behind rural–urban migration, as they increase the income differential between cities and the countryside (Williamson, 1988). Higher rates of productivity and wage growth in the industrial sector compared to agriculture, combined with urban-biased policies that increase rural poverty and encourage migration to the cities, lead to increased economic inequality in a polity (Yang, 1999). The political consequences of urban-biased policies are also relatively clear. Countries where the population is concentrated in a few large cities are prone to political instability (Smith, 2004; Wallace, 2013), and these same countries will eventually have small domestic agricultural sectors, making them dependent on international food markets and susceptible to unrest driven by price shocks on world markets such as those witnessed during the Arab Spring (Bellemare, 2015). In the long run, government policies that tax the agricultural sector lead to rural poverty, urbanization, and political instability.

Consider, however, the rural-biased regimes explored in this book: those which face significant political threats from rural interests and that implement pro-farmer policies increasing agricultural prices. These regimes are more likely to lock their countries into a long-run development trajectory that significantly decreases the risk of political instability and authoritarian regime collapse. By bolstering the incomes of rural farmers, they mitigate poverty, slow rural–urban migration, promote economic growth, and decrease inequality. This list of outcomes accurately describes the main contours of the development process in Malaysia after the implementation of the pro-rural New Economic Policy in 1971 (Kuhonta, 2011). Directing resources toward the agricultural sector strengthens the positions of rural elites, who go on to demand and receive continuing government support for their interests and thus lock the country into a pro-rural development trajectory. This is, essentially, the path taken by Germany from the passage of the protectionist tariff studied in this book, which a whole generation of historians such as Gerschenkron (1943) and Rosenberg (1967) saw as so vitally important for explaining the stability of the authoritarian monarchy in their country until the First World War.

Democratization leads to moderation in agricultural policy. Their dependence on the votes of rural interests makes elected governments less likely to impose punitive policies on the sector and more likely to stabilize the incomes of farmers in the face of international commodity

TABLE 8.1 *Agricultural Policy and Political Stability*

	Interests			Political Outcome	
	Rural	Urban	Policy	Failure	Urban Unrest
Authoritarianism		↑	Urban-Biased		↓
	↑		Rural-Biased	↓	
	↑	↑		Instability	
Democracy		↑	Urban-Biased		
	↑		Rural-Biased	Stability	
	↑	↑	Moderate		

price fluctuations. Democracies, being inherently more stable political systems than authoritarian regimes, are less beholden to the interests of urban food consumers and do not fear unrest in the face of higher food prices. It is this benign shift in political incentives and freedoms under democracy that Sen (1999) sees as so important for preventing famines and contributing to the broader development process. Famines do not occur in democracies, because they are far more likely to take measures which increase the incomes of the poor and grant them access to food markets. Its tendency to prevent such major crises, driven by the greater accountability of democratic governments to their citizens, makes democracy a crucial precondition for sustainable and equitable economic development.

The analysis presented in this book informs our understanding of the link between democratization and economic development. However, it also holds lessons for scholars of authoritarian politics. As I lay out in Table 8.1, the rural-urban cleavage is the dominant distributional conflict facing developing dictatorships. However, agricultural policy has the inconvenient characteristic for authoritarian regimes of creating both winners and losers. Rulers confronted with significant threats from both large concentrations of urban food consumers *and* landed elites cannot effectively use the policies explored in this book to address this conflict, because measures that are in the interests of the rural sector run invariably counter to those of the urban sector. These leaders are thus faced with unique challenges to their rule and a high likelihood of political instability.

One likely outcome of a situation in which both rural and urban interests are powerful is a military dictatorship, which maintains a greater degree

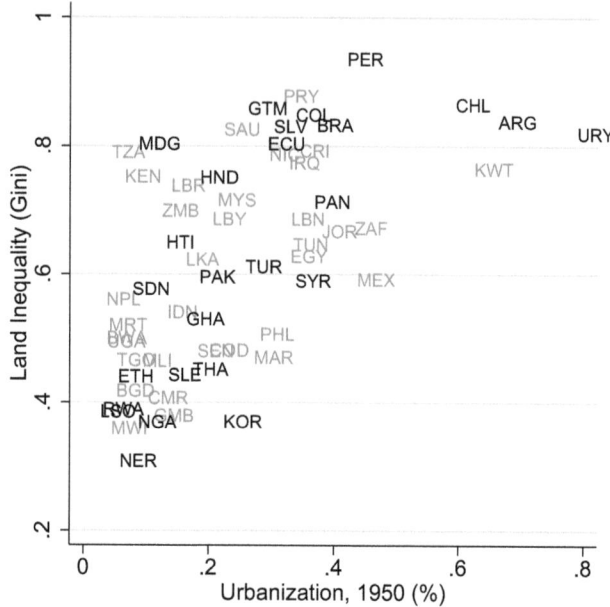

FIGURE 8.1 Initial Conditions and Regime Outcomes

of autonomy from societal cleavages, particularly due to its propensity to use repression. Military rule is more likely to emerge and endure in societies characterized by both high landholding inequality and high urbanization. I illustrate this point empirically in Figure 8.1, where I plot these initial conditions and their association with military dictatorship. I show urbanization in 1950 on the *x*-axis and the earliest land inequality data available on the *y*-axis for a sample of 52 countries in Africa, Asia, and Latin America. I use abbreviated country names as markers, shading countries that experienced a period of military rule between 1946 and 1989 in black, and other countries in gray.[1] At low levels of initial urbanization and landholding inequality, only a small proportion of countries experienced military rule during the Cold War. However, moving toward the upper-right quadrant of the graph, a large proportion of countries experienced military rule, most notably Latin American nations with very high levels of urbanization and landholding inequality

[1] Only countries that experienced some authoritarian rule during this period are included in the sample. Urbanization data are from United Nations (2014), landholding inequality data are from Thomson (2016), and regime type data are from Geddes, Wright, and Frantz (2014).

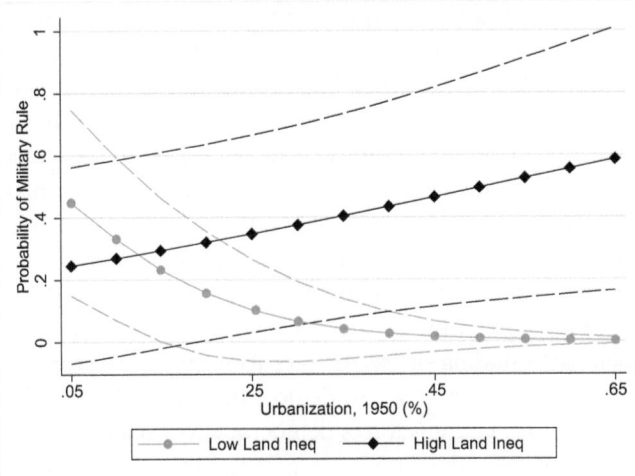

FIGURE 8.2 Probability of Military Rule by Initial Conditions

such as Argentina, Uruguay, and Chile.[2] A simple statistical test of this relationship reveals that the initial balance of power between rural and urban interests after World War Two had a significant effect on the likelihood of subsequent military rule, even when controlling for colonial legacies. As I illustrate in Figure 8.2, countries that were highly urbanized in 1950 were very unlikely to experience military dictatorship between 1946 and 1989, when landholding inequality was low. However, countries with both high levels of urbanization and high landholding inequality directly following World War Two were much more likely to experience military rule.[3] In this way, the structure of the rural–urban cleavage and the distributional challenges that it presents have significant effects not only on short-term regime durability, but also on the type of authoritarian regime that is likely to emerge during the course of development (O'Donnell, 1978).

[2] Note also that several countries that shared these inauspicious structural conditions but did not become military regimes were themselves outliers in terms of regime type: the authoritarian monarchies of the Middle East and the apartheid regime in South Africa, for example.
[3] Figure 8.2 graphs the predicted probabilities from a logistic regression, with a dependent variable that takes a 1 if a country experienced any period of military rule between 1946 and 1990. The number of observations in the model is fifty-two, of which twenty-one experienced military rule. Low land inequality indicates a Land Gini of 0.40 and high corresponds to a Gini of 0.85. Thin solid lines are 90 percent confidence intervals. The model also controls for previous colonial power using data by Hensel (2014).

In this book, I argue that agricultural policy under authoritarianism is driven by short-term political expediency and has significant effects on regime stability. However, I would like to conclude my study by reemphasizing that the political importance of agricultural policy runs far deeper than its effects on regime durability or urban unrest in the short run. As we have seen, the management of the rural–urban cleavage plays a role in broader regime outcomes, and where this problem is very challenging the likelihood of a repressive military dictatorship emerging is high. Moreover, the structural transformation of an economy in the course of development is by definition a process centered on agriculture. The policy environment surrounding the sector is crucial for its transformation process and the chances for long-run democratization. My model does not predict under which circumstances democracy will emerge: A democratic transition is possible under conditions of instability and unrest, promoted by urban-biased development; democracy can also result from a longer, more stable growth process promoted by rural-biased agricultural policies. What does emerge from my findings, however, is the idea that once democracy does emerge, it will have positive effects on the growth process through the benign policy environment it creates for the agricultural sector. For this reason, development and democratization will be self-reinforcing.

My findings on the determinants of agricultural policy under authoritarianism raise new and provocative questions on the nature of the development process under authoritarianism and its consequences for political change. In scholars' ongoing explorations of the link between development and democracy, we should direct our attention to the feedback mechanisms between regime type, policy, and development. The story of agriculture and democratization here tells us a great deal about the trajectory of economic and political change followed by societies in the early stages of development. This is a stage that is complete in large parts of the world, including in many countries still ruled by authoritarian regimes. However, unelected governments do not intervene in their economies and shape the development process only in the agricultural sector. Through state- or military-owned corporations and the civil service, tariffs and subventions for manufacturing industries, and national oil companies, the role of authoritarian regimes in their economies is large. To understand the nature of contemporary authoritarian regimes and the chances for democratization, it would be fruitful to further explore the ways in which unelected governments intervene in the economy and how these interventions shape the nature of political threats to their rule.

Bibliography

Abdih, Yassir, Ralph Chami, and Jihad Dagher. 2012. "Remittances and Institutions: Are Remittances a Curse?" *World Development* 40 (4):657–666.

Acemoglu, Daron and James Robinson. 2006. *Economic Origins of Democracy and Dictatorship*. New York: Cambridge University Press.

Ahmed, Faisal Z. 2012. "The Perils of Unearned Income Foreign Income: Aid, Remittances and Government Survival." *American Political Science Review* 106 (1):146–165.

Albertus, Michael. 2015a. *Autocracy and Redistribution: The Politics of Land Reform*. New York: Cambridge University Press.

2015b. "The Role of Subnational Politicians in Distributive Politics: Political Bias in Venezuela's Land Reform Under Chávez." *Comparative Political Studies* 48 (13):1667–1710.

2017. "Landowners and Democracy: The Social Origins of Democracy Reconsidered." *World Politics* 69 (2):233–276.

Albertus, Michael, Thomas Brambor, and Ricardo Ceneviva. 2016. "Land Inequality and Rural Unrest: Theory and Evidence from Brazil." *Journal of Conflict Resolution* 62 (3):557–596.

Andersen, Jorgen J. and Michael L. Ross. 2014. "The Big Oil Change: A Closer Look at the Haber-Menaldo Analysis." *Comparative Political Studies* 47 (7):993–1021.

Anderson, Kym. 1998. Agriculture, WTO, and the Next Round of Multilateral Trade Negotiations. WTO Trade and Development Center, Adelaide, Australia. http://citeseerx.ist.psu.edu/viewdoc/download?doi=10.1.1.188.243&rep=rep1&type=pdf.

2009. *Distortions to Agricultural Incentives: A Global Perspective 1955–2007*. New York: Palgrave Macmillan.

Anderson, Kym, editor. 2010. *The Political Economy of Agricultural Price Distortions*. New York: Cambridge University Press.

Anderson, Kym and Alberto Valdes, editors. 2008. *Distortions to Agricultural Incentives in Latin America*. Washington, DC: The World Bank.

Anderson, Kym, Betina Dimaranan, Joe Francois, Tom Hertel, Bernard Hoekman, and Will Martin. 2001. "The Cost of Rich (and Poor) Countries' Protection to Developing Countries." *Journal of African Economies* 10 (3):227–257.

Anderson, Kym, Marianne Kurzweil, Will Martin, Damiandro Sandri, and Ernesto Valenzuela. 2008. "Measuring Distortions to Agricultural Incentives, Revisited." *World Trade Review* 7 (4):675–704.

2010. *Methodology for Measuring Distortions to Agricultural Incentives.* In Anderson (2010), 565–582.

Anderson, Kym and Signe Nelgen. 2012. "Updated National and Global Estimates of Distortions to Agricultural Incentives, 1955 to 2010." www .worldbank.org/agdistortions.

Anderson, Kym and Will Martin. 2009. *Distortions to Agricultual Incentives in Asia.* Washington, DC: The World Bank.

Anderson, Kym and William A. Masters, editors. 2009. *Distortions to Agricultural Incentives in Africa.* Washington, DC: The World Bank.

Anderson, Kym and E. Valenzuela. 2008. "Global Estimates of Distortions to Agricultural Incentives, 1955 to 2007." www.worldbank.org/agdistortions.

Anderson, Kym and Yujiro Hayami. 1986. *The Political Economy of Agricultural Protection: East Asia in International Perspective.* Sydney: Allen & Unwin.

Anderson, Margaret Lavina. 2000. *Practicing Democracy: Elections and Political Culture in Imperial Germany.* Princeton, NJ: Princeton University Press.

Angrist, Joshua D. and Jörn-Steffen Pischke. 2009. *Mostly Harmless Econometrics.* Princeton, NJ: Princeton University Press.

Ansell, Ben W. 2008. "Traders, Teachers, and Tyrants: Democracy, Globalization and Public Investment in Education." *International Organization* 62 (2):289–322.

Ansell, Ben W. and David J. Samuels. 2014. *Inequality and Democratization: An Elite-Competition Approach.* New York: Cambridge University Press.

Arezki, Rabah and Markus Brückner. 2011. "Food Prices and Political Instability." IMF Working Paper.

Arias, Enrique Desmond. 2013. "The Impacts of Differential Armed Dominance of Politics in Rio de Janeiro, Brazil." *Studies in Comparative International Development* 48 (3):263–284.

Athukorala, Prema-Chandra and Wai-Heng Loke. 2009. *Malaysia.* In Anderson and Martin (2009), 197–221.

Auvinen, Juha Y. 1996. "IMF Intervention and Political Protest in the Third World: A Conventional Wisdom Refined." *Third World Quarterly* 17 (3):377–400.

Baland, Jean-Marie, Pranab K. Bardhan, and Samuel Bowles, editors. 2007. *Inequality, Cooperation and Environmental Sustainability.* Princeton, NJ: Princeton University Press.

Baland, Jean-Marie and Jean-Philippe Platteau. 1997. "Wealth Inequality and Efficiency in the Commons. Part I: The Unregulated Case." *Oxford Economic Papers* 49 (4):451–482.

2007. *Collective Action on the Commons: The Role of Inequality.* In Baland, Bardhan, and Bowles (2007), 10–35.

Baland, Jean-Marie and James Robinson. 2012. "The Political Value of Land: Political Reform and Land Prices in Chile." *American Journal of Political Science* 56 (3):601–619.

Bates, Robert H. 1981. *Markets and States in Tropical Africa: The Political Basis of Agricultural Policies.* Berkeley: University of California Press.

  1983. *Essays on the Political Economy of Rural Africa.* Cambridge, UK: Cambridge University Press.

  1993. "'Urban Bias': A Fresh Loook." *Journal of Development Studies* 29 (4):219–228.

Bates, Robert H. and Steven A. Block. 2011. "Political Institutions and Agricultural Trade Interventions in Africa." *American Journal of Agricultural Economics* 93 (2):317–323.

  2013. "Revisiting African Agriculture: Institutional Change and Productivity Growth." *American Journal of Political Science* 75 (2):372–384.

Beall, Jo, Tom Goodfellow, and Dennis Rodgers. 2013. "Cities and Conflict in Fragile States in the Developing World." *Urban Studies* 50 (15):3065–3083.

Beck, Nathaniel, Jonathan N. Katz, and Richard Tucker. 1998. "Taking Time Seriously: Time-Series-Cross-Section Analysis with a Binary Dependent Variable." *American Journal of Political Science* 42 (4):1260–1288.

Beghin, John C. and Mylene Kherallah. 1994. "Political Institutions and International Patterns of Agricultural Protection." *The Review of Economics and Statistics* 76 (3):482–489.

Bellemare, Marc F. 2015. "Rising Food Prices, Food Price Volatility, and Political Unrest." *American Journal of Agricultural Economics* 97 (1):1–21.

Bellemare, Marc F., Takaaki Masaki, and Thomas B. Pepinsky. 2015. "Lagged Explanatory Variables and the Estimation of Causal Effects." Working paper.

Bellin, Eva. 2012. "Reconsidering the Robustness of Authoritarianism in the Middle East: Lessons from the Arab Spring." *Comparative Politics* 44 (2):127–149.

Berger, Helge and Mark Spoerer. 2001. "Economic Crises and the European Revolutions of 1848." *The Journal of Economic History* 61 (2):293–326.

Berman, Sheri E. 2001. "Modernization in Historical Perspective: The Case of Imperial Germany." *World Politics* 53 (3):431–462.

Bernstein, Thomas P. and Xiaobo Lü. 2003. *Taxation without Representation in Contemporary China.* Cambridge, UK: Cambridge University Press.

Bezemer, Dirk and Derek Headey. 2008. "Agriculture, Development and Urban Bias." *World Development* 36 (8):1342–1364.

Bidder, Benjamin. 2016. "Agrarboom in Russland." *Spiegel Online*: www.spiegel .de/wirtschaft/unternehmen/russland-landwirtschaft-boomt-a-1109524.html.

Bienen, Henry S. and Mark Gersovitz. 1986. "Consumer Subsidy Cuts, Violence, and Political Stability." *Comparative Politics* 19 (1):25–44.

Birner, Regina and Danielle Resnick. 2010. "The Political Economy of Policies for Smallholder Agriculture." *World Development* 38 (10):1442–1452.

Blaydes, Lisa. 2011. *Elections and Distributive Politics in Mubarak's Egypt.* New York: Cambridge University Press.

Blaydes, Lisa and Mark Andreas Kayser. 2011. "Counting Calories: Democracy and Distribution in the Developing World." *International Studies Quarterly* 55 (4):887–908.

Boix, Carles. 2003. *Democracy and Redistribution*. New York: Cambridge University Press.

Boix, Carles, Michael Miller, and Sebastian Rosato. 2012. "A Complete Dataset of Political Regimes, 1800–2007." *Comparative Political Studies* 46 (12).

Boix, Carles and Susan Stokes. 2003. "Endogenous Democratization." *World Politics* 55 (4):517–549.

Boix, Carles and Milan W. Svolik. 2013. "The Foundations of Limited Authoritarian Government: Institutions, Commitment and Power-Sharing in Dictatorships." *Journal of Politics* 75 (2):300–316.

Boone, Catherine and Michael Wahman. 2015. "Rural Bias in African Electoral Systems: Legacies of Unequal Representation in African Democracies." *Electoral Studies* 40:335–346.

Born, Karl Erich. 1959. *Eulenburg, Botho Wend August Graf zu*, vol. 4. 680. www.deutsche-biographie.de/pnd116603887.html.

Bräutigam, Deborah A. and Steven Knack. 2004. "Foreign Aid, Institutions and Governance in Sub-Saharan Africa." *Economic Development and Cultural Change* 52 (2):255–285.

Brawley, Mark R. 1997. "Factoral or Sectoral Conflict? Partially Mobile Factors and the Politics of Trade in Imperial Germany." *International Studies Quarterly* 41 (4):633–653.

Brentano, Lujo. 1911. *Die Deutschen Getreidezölle: Eine Denkschrift*. Berlin: J. D. Cotta'sche Buchhandlung.

Brown, C. P. 1973. "Rice Price Stabilization and Support in Malaysia." *The Developing Economies* 11 (2):164–183.

Brownlee, Jason. 2007. *Authoritarianism in an Age of Democratization*. New York: Cambridge University Press.

Brunt, P. A. 1966. "The Roman Mob." *Past & Present* 35:3–27.

Buccola, Steven T. and James E. McCandlish. 1999. "Rent Seeking and Rent Dissipation in State Enterprises." *Review of Agricultural Economics* 21 (2):358–373.

Bueno de Mesquita, Ethan, Bruce, Alastair Smith, Randolph M. Siverson, and James D. Morrow. 2003. *The Logic of Political Survival*. Cambridge, MA: MIT Press.

Bueno de Mesquita, Ethan. 2010. "Regime Change and Revolutionary Entrepreneurs." *American Political Science Review* 104 (3):446–466.

Buhaug, Halvard and Henrik Urdal. 2013. "An Urbanization Bomb? Population Growth and Social Disorder in Cities." *Global Environmental Change* 23 (1):1–10.

Busch, Marc L. and Eric Reinhardt. 2005. "Industrial Location and Voter Participation in Europe." *British Journal of Political Science* 35:713–730.

Cambanis, Thanassis. 2015. "The Arab Spring was a Revolution of the Hungry: The Arab World Can't Feed Itself, and That's How the Region's Dictators Like It." *The Boston Globe*. www.bostonglobe.com/ideas/2015/08/22

/the-arab-spring-was-revolution-hungry/K15S1kGeO5Y6gsJwAYHejI/ story.html.

Cameron, A. Colin and Pravin K. Trivedi. 2013. *Regression Analysis of Count Data*, 2nd ed. New York: Cambridge University Press.

Canis, Konrad, Lothar Gall, Klaus Hildebrand, and Eberhard Kolb, editors. 2008. *Otto von Bismarck: Gesammelte Werke. Schriften 1877–1878*, vol. 3. Paderborn: Ferdinand Schöningh.

Case, William. 1996a. *Elites and Regimes in Malaysia: Revisiting a Consociational Democracy*. Clayton, Victoria: Monash Asia Institute.

1996b. "UMNO Paramountcy: A Report on Single-Party Dominance in Malaysia." *Party Politics* 2 (1):115–127.

2004. "New Uncertainties for an Old Pseudo-Democracy: The Case of Malaysia." *Comparative Politics* 37 (1):83–104.

Cassing, James, Saad Nassar, Gamal Siam, and Hoda Moussa. 2009. *Arab Republic of Egypt*. In Anderson and Masters (2009), 71–98.

Chang, Eric C. C., Mark Andreas Kayser, Drew A. Linzer, and Ronald Rogowski. 2011. *Electoral Systems and the Balance of Consumer-Producer Power*. New York: Cambridge University Press.

Cheibub, Jose Antonio, Jennifer Gandhi, and James Raymond Vreeland. 2010. "Democracy and Dictatorship Revisited." *Public Choice* 143 (1–2):67–101.

Chenery, Hollis and T. N. Srinivasan, editors. 1988. *Handbook of Development Economics*, vol. 1. Amsterdam: North-Holland.

Chestnut-Greitens, Sheena. 2016. *Dictators and Their Secret Police: Coercive Institutions and State Violence*. New York: Cambridge University Press.

Chomchuen, Warangkana and Isabella Steger. 2014. "Thai Rice Released Amid High Demand." *The Wall Street Journal*.

Collier, Paul and Anke Hoeffler. 2004. "Greed and Grievance in Civil War." *Oxford Economic Papers* 56 (4):563–595.

Cooksey, Brian. 2011. "Marketing Reform? The Rise and Fall of Agricultural Liberalisation in Tanzania." *Development Policy Review* 29 (S1):S57–S81.

Coppedge, Michael, John Gerring, David Altman, Michael Bernhard, Steve Fish, Allen Hicken, Matthew Kroenig, Staffan I. Lindberg, Kelly McMann, Pamela Paxton, Holli A. Smetko, Svend-Erik Skaaning, Jeffrey Staton, and Jan Teorell. 2011. "Conceptualizing and Measuring Democracy: A New Approach." *Perspectives on Politics* 9 (2):247–267.

Corrales, Javier and Franz von Bergen. 2016. "Coup Nouvelle: Did We Just Witness a New Type of Coup in Venezuela?" *Latin America Goes Global*. latinamericagoesglobal.org/2016/07/coup-nouvelle-just-witness-coup-venezuela/.

Dahl, Robert A. 1971. *Polyarchy: Participation and Opposition*. New Haven, CT: Yale University Press.

Davenport, Christian. 2007a. "State Repression and Political Order." *Annual Review of Political Science* 10:1–23.

2007b. "State Repression and the Tyrannical Peace." *Journal of Peace Research* 44 (4):485–504.

De Boef, Suzanna and Luke Keele. 2008. "Taking Time Seriously." *American Journal of Political Science* 52 (1):184–200.

De Gorter, Harry and Johan F. M. Swinnen. 2002. *Political Economy of Agricultural Policy*, chap. 36. In Gardner and Rausser (2002), 1893–1932.

Della Porta, Donnatella. 2014. *Mobilizing for Democracy: Comparing 1989 and 2011*. Oxford, UK: Oxford University Press.

Deutscher Reichstag. 1879. "Deutscher Reichstag: 80. Sitzung am 12. Juni 1879." *Stenographische Berichte über die Verhandlungen des Deutschen Reichstags* 1, 4. Legislaturperiode:2362–2364. 1st Tariff Law Vote.

Diamond, Larry J. 2002. "Thinking about Hybrid Regimes." *Journal of Democracy* 13 (2):21–35.

2015. "Facing Up to the Democratic Recession." *Journal of Democracy* 26 (1):141–155.

Dietrich, Simone and Joseph Wright. 2015. "Foreign Aid Allocation Tactics and Democratic Change in Africa." *Journal of Politics* 77 (1):216–234.

Drabble, John H. 2000. *An Economic History of Malaysia, c. 1800–1900: The Transition to Modern Economic Growth*. London: MacMillan.

Dunning, Thad. 2004. "Conditioning the Effects of Aid: Cold War Politics, Donor Credibility, and Democracy in Africa." *International Organization* 58 (2):409–423.

2008. *Crude Democracy: Natural Resource Wealth and Political Regimes*. New York: Cambridge University Press.

Easterly, William. 1993. "How Much Do Distortions Affect Growth?" *Journal of Monetary Economics* 32 (2):187–212.

2005. "What Did Structural Adjustment Adjust? The Association of Policies and Growth with Repeated IMF and World Bank Adjustment Loans." *Journal of Development Economics* 76 (1):1–22.

Eberhardt, Markus and Dietrich Vollrath. 2017. "The Effect of Agricultural Technology on the Speed of Development." *World Development* 109:483–496

Economic Research Service, USDA. 2011. "Food, CPI, Prices and Expenditures: Expenditure Tables." www.ers.usda.gov/Briefing/CPIFoodAndExpenditures/Data. Published online. Accessed May 2, 2013.

Economist. 2012. "Let Them Eat Baklava: Food Prices and the Arab Spring." *The Economist*.

2013. "The Rice Mountain." *The Economist*.

2016. "Russia's Dairy Embargo: War and Cheese." *The Economist*. www.economist.com/europe/2016/04/07/war-and-cheese.

Eddie, Scott M. 2008. *Landownership in Eastern Germany Before the Great War: A Quantitative Analysis*. New York: Oxford University Press.

Egorov, Georgy, Sergei Guriev, and Konstantin Sonin. 2009. "Why Resource-Poor Dictators Allow Freer Media: A Theory and Evidence from Panel Data." *American Political Science Review* 103 (4):645–668.

Election Commission, Malaysia. 1971. *Report on the Parliamentary (Dewan Ra'ayat) and State Legislative Assembly General Elections 1969 of the States of Malaya, Sabah and Sarawak*. Kuala Lumpur, Malaysia: Election Commission.

Erickson, Lennart and Dietrich Vollrath. 2004. "Dimensions of Land Inequality and Economic Development." IMF Working Paper. Number WP/04/158.

Escribá-Folch, Abel. 2013. "Accountable for What? Regime Types, Performance and the Fate of Outgoing Dictators, 1946–2004." *Democratization* 20 (1):160–185.

Escribá-Folch, Abel, Covandonga Meseguer, and Joseph Wright. 2015. "Remittances and Democratization." *International Studies Quarterly* 59 (3):571–586.

Evans, Peter B. 1989. "Predatory, Developmental and Other Apparatus: A Comparative Political Economy Perspective on the Third World State." *Sociological Forum* 4 (4):561–587.

Faaland, Just, J. R. Parkinson, and Rais Saniman. 1990. *Growth and Ethnic Inequality: Malaysia's New Economic Policy*. London: Hurst.

Fairfield, Tasha. 2011. "Business Power and Protest: Argentina's Agricultural Producers Protest in Comparative Perspective." *Studies in Comparative International Development* 46 (4):424–453.

2015. "Structural Power in Comparative Political Economy: Perspectives from Policy Formulation in Latin America." *Business and Politics* 17 (3):411–441.

Fane, George and Peter Warr. 2009. *Indonesia*. In Anderson and Martin (2009), 165–195.

Fearon, James. 2011. "Self-Enforcing Democracy." *Quarterly Journal of Economics* 126 (4):1661–1708.

Fearon, James D. and David D. Laitin. 2003. "Ethnicity, Insurgency and Civil War." *American Political Science Review* 97 (1):75–90.

Fjelde, Hanne and Nina von Uexkuell. 2012. "Climate Triggers: Rainfall Anomalies, Vulnerability and Communal Conflict in Sub-Saharan Africa." *Political Geography* 31 (7):444–453.

Földes, Béla. 1905. "Die Getreidepreise im 19. Jahrhundert." *Jahrbücher für Nationalökonomie und Statistik* 3 (29):467–518.

Food and Agriculture Organization of the United Nations. 1997. *Additional International Comparison Tables*. Rome: FAO. www.fao.org/economic/the-statistics-division-ess/world-census-of-agriculture/additional-international-comparison-tables-including-gini-coefficients/.en. Table 2: Number and Area of Holdings, and Gini's Index of Concentration.

Foros, Carolina L., Timothy J. Power, and James C. Garand. 2004. "Explaining Voter Turnout in Latin America, 1980 to 2000." *Comparative Political Studies* 37 (8):909–940.

Frankema, Ewout. 2010. "The Colonial Roots of Land Inequality: Geography, Factor Endowments, or Institutions?" *The Economic History Review* 63 (2):418–451.

Freedom House. 2017. *Freedom in the World 2017*. Washington, DC: Freedom House.

Freeman, John R. and Dennis P. Quinn. 2012. "The Economic Origins of Democracy Reconsidered." *American Political Science Review* 106 (1):58–80.

Galbraith, James K. and Hyunsub Kum. 2005. "Estimating the Inequality of Household Incomes: A Statistical Approach to the Creation of a Dense and Consistent Global Data Set." *Review of Income and Wealth* 51 (1):115–143.

Galor, Oded, Omer Moav, and Dietrich Vollrath. 2009. "Inequality in Landownership, the Emergence of Human-Capital Promoting Institutions, and the Great Divergence." *Review of Economic Studies* 76 (1):143–179.

Gandhi, Jennifer and Adam Przeworski. 2006. "Cooperation, Cooptation, and Rebellion under Dictatorships." *Economics & Politics* 18 (1):1–26.

2007. "Authoritarian Institutions and the Survival of Autocrats." *Comparative Political Studies* 40 (11):1279–1301.

Gardner, Bruce L. and Gordon C. Rausser, editors. 2002. *Handbook of Agricultural Economics*. Amsterdam: North-Holland.

Gates, Scott, Havard Hegre, Mark P. Jones, and Havard Strand. 2006. "Institutional Inconsistency and Political Instability: Polity Duration, 1800–2000." *American Journal of Political Science* 50 (4):893–908.

Geddes, Barbara. 1999. "What Do We Know about Democratization after Twenty Years?" *Annual Review of Political Science* 2:115–144.

Geddes, Barbara, Joseph Wright, and Erica Frantz. 2014. "Autocratic Breakdown and Regime Transitions: A New Dataset." *Perspectives on Politics* 12 (2):313–331.

Gerring, John, Strom C. Thacker, and Rodrigo Alfaro. 2012. "Democracy and Human Development." *The Journal of Politics* 74 (1):1–17.

Gerschenkron, Alexander. 1943. *Bread and Democracy in Germany*. Berkeley: University of California Press.

Gleditsch, Kristian Skrede. 2002. "Expanded Trade and GDP Data." *Journal of Conflict Resolution* 46 (5):712–724.

Gleditsch, Nils Petter, Peter Wallensteen, Mikael Eriksson, Margareta Sollenberg, and Havard Strand. 2002. "Armed Conflict 2001–1946: A New Dataset." *Journal of Peace Research* 39 (5):615–637.

Goemans, Henk E., Kristian Skrede Gleditsch, and Giacomo Chiozza. 2009. "Introducing Archigos: A Dataset of Political Leaders." *Journal of Peace Research* 46 (2):269–283.

Goh Cheng Teik. 1971. *The May Thirteenth Incident and Democracy in Malaysia*. Kuala Lumpur, Malaysia: Oxford University Press.

Goldstone, Jack A. 2010. "The New Population Bomb: The Four Megatrends That Will Change the World." *Foreign Affairs* 89 (1):31–43.

Gomez, Edmund Terence and Kwame Sundaram Jomo. 1999. *Malaysia's Political Economy: Politics, Patronage and Profits*, 2nd ed. Cambridge, UK: Cambridge University Press.

Gottwald, Herbert. 1986. *Vereinigung der Steuer- und Wirtschaftsreformer (VSW) 1876–1928*, vol. IV. Köln, Germany: Pahl-Rugenstein Verlag, 358–367.

Gourevitch, Peter Alexis. 1977. "International Trade, Domestic Coalitions, and Liberty: Comparative Responses to the Crisis of 1873–96." *The Journal of Interdisciplinary History* 8 (2):281–313.

1978. "The Second Image Reversed: International Sources of Domestic Politics." *International Organization* 32 (4):881–912.

Grant, Oliver. 2002. "Does Industrialisation Push Up Inequality? New Evidence on the Kuznets Curve from Nineteenth Century Prussian Tax Statistics." Working paper.

   2005. *Migration and Inequality in Germany, 1870–1913*. Oxford, UK: Oxford University Press.

Grossman, Gene M. and Elhanan Helpman. 1994. "Protection for Sale." *American Economic Review* 84 (4):833–850.

Gutner, Tamar. 2002. "The Political Economy of Food Subsidy Reform: The Case of Egypt." *Food Policy* 27 (5–6):455–476.

Haber, Stephen and Victor Menaldo. 2011. "Do Natural Resources Fuel Authoritarianism? A Reappraisal of the Resource Curse." *American Political Science Review* 105 (1):1–26.

Hankla, Charles R. and Daniel Kuthy. 2013. "Economic Liberalism in Illiberal Regimes: Authoritarian Variation and the Political Economy of Trade." *International Studies Quarterly* 57 (3):492–504.

Haunfelder, Bernd. 1999. *Reichstagsabgeordnete der Deutschen Zentrumspartei 1871–1933*. Düsseldorf: Droste.

   2004. *Die liberalen Abgeordneten des Deutschen Reichstags 1871–1918*. Münster: Aschendorff.

   2010. *Die konservativen Abgeordneten des Deutschen Reichstags*. Münster: Aschendorff.

Hendrix, Cullen S. and Henk-Jan Brinkman. 2013. "Food Insecurity and Conflict Dynamics: Causal Linkages and Complex Feedbacks." *Stability: International Journal of Security & Development* 2 (2):1–18.

Hendrix, Cullen S. and Stephan Haggard. 2015. "Global Food Prices, Regime Type, and Urban Unrest in the Developing World." *Journal of Peace Research* 52 (2):143–157.

Heng, Pek Koon. 1988. *Chinese Politics in Malaysia: A History of the Malaysian Chinese Association*. Singapore: Oxford University Press.

   1996. "Chinese Responses to Malay Hegemony in Peninsular Malaysia 1957–96." *Southeast Asian Studies* 34 (3):500–523.

   1997. "The New Economic Policy and the Chinese Community in Malaysia." *The Developing Economies* 35 (3):262–292.

Heng, Pek Koon and Lee Mei Ling Sieh. 2000. *The Chinese Business Community in Peninsular Malaysia, 1957–1999*, chap. 5. In Lee (2000), 123–168.

Hensel, Paul R. 2014. "Issue Correlates of War Colonial History Data Set, Version 1.0." Published online. www.paulhensel.org/icow.html.

Herbst, Jeffrey. 1988. "Societal Demands and Government Choices: Agricultural Producer Price Policy in Zimbabwe." *Comparative Politics* 20 (3):265–288.

   1990. "The Structural Adjustment of Politics in Africa." *World Development* 18 (7):949–958.

Hirth, Georg, editor. 1878. *Deutscher Parlaments-Almanach*, vol. 13. Leipzig: G. Hirth. www.reichstagsprotokolle.de/Blatt4_h1_bsb00003561_00000.html.

Hoffmann, Walther G. 1965. *Das Wachstum der deutschen Wirtschaft seit der Mitte des 19. Jahrhunderts*. Berlin: Springer.

Hollyer, James R., B. Peter Rosendorff, and James Raymond Vreeland. 2015. "Transparency, Protest and Autocratic Instability." *American Political Science Review* 109 (4):764–784.

Hunt, James. 1974. "Peasants, Grain Tariffs and Meat Quotas: Imperial German Protectionism Reexamined." *Central European History* 7 (4):311–331.

Hyde, Susan D. and Nikolay Marinov. 2012. "Which Elections Can Be Lost?" *Political Analysis* 20 (2):191–210.

IFAD. 2016. *Rural Development Report 2016: Fostering Inclusive Rural Transformation*. Rome: International Fund for Agricultural Development.

Jacks, David S. 2006. "What Drove 19th Century Commodity Market Integration?" *Explorations in Economic History* 43 (3):383–412.

Jacobs, Eduard. 1908. "Stolberg-Wernigerode, Otto." *Allgemeine Deutsche Biographie* 54:551–564. www.deutsche-biographie.de/pnd118618555 .html?anchor=adb.

Javeline, Debra. 2002. "The Role of Blame in Collective Action: Evidence from Russia." *American Political Science Review* 97 (1):107–121.

Jenkins, Glenn P. and Andrew Kwok Kong Lai. 1989. *Trade, Exchange Rate, and Agricultural Policies in Malaysia*. World Bank Comparative Studies: The Political Economy of Agricultural Pricing Policy. Washington, DC: World Bank.

Johnson, J. Keith, editor. 1988. *Evaluating Rice Market Intervention Policies: Some Asian Examples*. Manila: Asian Development Bank.

Jomo, Kwame Sundaram. 1984. "Productivity, Prices and Poverty: A Brief Survey of Some Recent Trends in Malaysia." *Kajian Ekonomi Malaysia* XXI (2).

1989. "Malaysia's New Economic Policy and National Unity." *Third World Quarterly* 11 (4):36–53.

Josling, Tim. 2009. *Western Europe*. In Anderson (2009), 115–176.

Kaiserliches Statistisches Amt. 1881. "Durchschnittspreise wichtiger Waaren im Grosshandel. Jahr 1881." *Monatshefte zur Statistik des Deutschen Reichs* 48 (12):57–59.

1884a. "Durchschnittspreise wichtiger Waren im Grosshandel. Jahr 1884." *Monatshefte zur Statistik des Deutschen Reichs* 65 (12):77.

1884b. "Ergebnisse der Viehzählung vom 10. Januar 1883 im Deutschen Reich." *Monatshefte zur Statistik des Deutschen Reichs* 1:20–24.

Kalyvas, Stathis N. 2004. "The Urban Bias in Research on Civil Wars." *Security Studies* 13 (3):160–190.

Kayser, Mark Andreas and Michael Peress. 2012. "Benchmarking across Borders: Electoral Accountability and the Necessity of Comparison." *American Political Science Review* 106 (3):661–684.

Keefer, Philip and Stephen Knack. 2007. "Boondoggles, Rent-Seeking, and Political Checks and Balances: Public Investment under Unaccountable Governments." *Review of Economics and Statistics* 89 (3):566–572.

Keesing's. Various. *Keesing's World News Archive*. Keesings Worldwide. www .keesings.com/.

Kherallah, Mylene, Christopher Delgado, Eleni Gabre-Madhin, Nicholas Minot, and Michael Johnson. 2000. "The Road Half Traveled: Agricultural Market

Reform in Sub-Saharan Africa." International Food Policy Research Institute Food Policy Report.

Khoo, Boo Teil. 1995. *Paradoxes of Mahathirism: An Intellectual Biography of Mahathir Mohamad*. Kuala Lumpur, Malaysia: Oxford University Press.

Khoo, Teik Huat. 1981. *1977 Census of Agriculture, Malaysia: Main Report*. Kuala Lumpur, Malaysia: Department of Statistics.

Kindleberger, C. P. 1975. "The Rise of Free Trade in Western Europe, 1820–1875." *Journal of Economic History* 35 (1):20–55.

Kirsten, Johann, Johan van Zyl, and Nick Vink, editors. 1998. *The Agricultural Democratisation of South Africa*. Cape Town, South Africa: Africa Institute for Policy Analysis and Economic Integration.

Kirsten, Johann, Lawrence Edwards, and Nick Vink. 2009. *South Africa*. In Anderson and Masters (2009), 147–174.

Klug, Adam. 2001. "Why Chamberlain Failed and Bismarck Succeeded: The Political Economy of Tariffs in British and German Elections." *European Review of Economic History* 5 (2):219–250.

Knickmeyer, Ellen. 2008. "In Egypt, Upper Crust Gets the Bread." *The Washington Post*. www.washingtonpost.com/wp-dyn/content/article/2008/04/04/AR2008040403937_pf.html.

Kondalamahanty, Aditya. 2015. "Thailand Farmer Subsidies: Thai Junta Announces Subsidies to Avert Protests." *International Business Times*. www.ibtimes.com/thailand-farmer-subsidies-thai-junta-announces-subsidies-avert-protests-2168526.

Konings, Piet. 1986. *The State and Rural Class Formation in Ghana: A Comparative Analysis*. London: KPI.

Kostadinova, Tatiana and Timothy J. Power. 2007. "Does Democratization Depress Participation? Voter Turnout in the Latin American and Eastern European Transitional Democracies." *Political Research Quarterly* 60 (3):363–377.

Krueger, Anne O. 1974. "The Political Economy of the Rent-Seeking Society." *American Economic Review* 64 (3):291–303.

1989. "Asymmetries in Policy between Exportables and Import-Competing Goods." NBER Working Paper Series No. 2904.

1990. "Government Failures in Development." NBER Working Paper Series No. 3340.

1992. *The Political Economy of Agricultural Pricing Policy*. Baltimore, MD: Johns Hopkins University Press.

Krueger, Anne O., Maurice Schiff, and Alberto Valdes. 1988. "Agricultural Incentives in Developing Countries: Measuring the Effect of Sectoral and Economy-Wide Policies." *World Bank Economic Review* 2 (3):255–271.

Kuhonta, Erik Martinez. 2011. *The Institutional Imperative: The Politics of Equitable Development in Southeast Asia*. Stanford, CA: Stanford University Press.

Kuran, Timur. 1989. "Sparks and Prairie Fires: A Theory of Unanticipated Political Revolution." *Public Choice* 61 (1):41–74.

Lambi, Ivo Nikolai. 1963. *Free Trade and Protection in Germany 1868–1879.* Vierteljahrschrift für Sozial- und Wirtschaftgeschichte. Wiesbaden: Franz Steiner.

Lapper, Richard and Andy Webb-Vidal. 2004. "Will Oil Keep Chavez in Power?" *Financial Times.* www.ft.com/content/9d0b3920-ec8c-11d8-b35c-00000e2511c8.

LeBas, Adrienne. 2013. "Violence and Urban Order in Nairobi, Kenya and Lagos, Nigeria." *Studies in Comparative International Development* 48 (3):240–262.

Lee, Kam Hing and Pek Koon Heng. 2000. *The Chinese in the Malaysian Political System*, chap. 7. In Lee (2000), 194–227.

Lee, Kam Hing; Tan Chee-Beng, editor. 2000. *The Chinese in Malaysia.* Selangor Darul Ehsan, Malaysia: Oxford University Press.

Levi, Margaret. 1981. "The Predatory Theory of Rule." *Politics and Society* 10 (4):431–465.

1989. *Of Rule and Revenue.* Berkeley: University of California Press.

Levitsky, Steven and Lucan A. Way. 2010. *Competitive Authoritarianism: Hybrid Regimes After the Cold War.* New York: Cambridge University Press.

Lindberg, Staffan I., Michael Coppedge, John Gerring, and Jan Teorell. 2014. "V-Dem: A New Way to Measure Democracy." *Journal of Democracy* 25 (3):159–169.

Lipset, Seymour Martin. [1959] 1963. *Political Man: The Social Bases of Politics.* New York: Doubleday.

Lipton, Michael. 1975. "Urban Bias and Food Policy in Developing Countries." *Food Policy* 1 (1):41–53.

1977. *Why Poor People Stay Poor: A Study of Urban Bias in World Development.* Cambridge, MA: Harvard University Press.

1984. "Urban Bias Revisited." *Journal of Development Studies* 20 (3):139–166.

1993. "Urban Bias: Of Consequences, Classes and Causality." *Journal of Development Studies* 29 (4):229–258.

Lohmann, Susanna. 1994. "The Dynamics of Informational Cascades: The Monday Demonstrations in Leipzig, East Germany, 1989–91." *World Politics* 47 (1):42–101.

Magaloni, Beatriz. 2006. *Voting for Autocracy: Hegemonic Party Survival and Its Demise in Mexico.* New York: Cambridge University Press.

Magaloni, Beatriz and Ruth Kricheli. 2010. "Political Order and One-Party Rule." *Annual Review of Political Science* 13:123–143.

Malaysia. 1970. *Schedules: Population Schedules, Population and Housing Census 1970 [Jadual–Jadual Banci Penduduk 1970].* Kuala Lumpur, Malaysia: Library, Department of Statistics, Malaysia. Various volumes.

Malesky, Edmund J. and Paul Schuler. 2011. "The Single-Party Dictator's Dilemma: Information in Elections without Opposition." *Legislative Studies Quarterly* 36 (4):491–530.

Mander, Benedict. 2009a. "Chávez Blamed for Coffee Industry Plight." *Financial Times.* www.ft.com/content/fa1bef56-97d6-11de-8d3d-00144feabdc0.

2009b. "Venezuelan Troops Ordered into Rice Mills." *Financial Times*. www
.ft.com/content/e44e3e1a-068e-11de-abof-000077b07658.

2011. "Venezuela: Rotting Away?" *Financial Times*. blogs.ft.com/beyond-brics/
2011/08/25/venezuela-rotting-away/.

Mares, Isabela. 2015. *From Open Secrets to Secret Voting: Democratic Electoral Reforms and Voter Autonomy*. New York: Cambridge University Press.

Marshall, Monty G. and Benjamin R. Cole. 2011. *Global Report 2011: Conflict, Governance and State Fragility*. Vienna, VA: Center for Systemic Peace. www.systemicpeace.org.

Mauzy, Diane K. 1983. *Barisan Nasional: Coalition Government in Malaysia*. Kuala Lumpur, Malaysia: Marican & Sons.

McCorriston, Steve and Donald MacLaren. 2016. "Parastatals as Instruments of Government Policy: The Food Corporation of India." *Food Policy* 65:53–62.

Means, Gordon P. 1976. *Malaysian Politics*, 2nd ed. London: Hodder and Stoughton.

1991. *Malaysian Politics: The Second Generation*. Singapore: Oxford University Press.

Meltzer, Allan and Scott Richard. 1981. "A Rational Theory of the Size of Government." *Journal of Political Economy* 89 (5):914–927.

Miller, Harry. 1959. *Prince and Premier: A Biography of Tunku Abdul Rahman Putra Al-Haj, First Prime Minister of Federation of Malaya*. London: George G. Harrap.

Miller, Michael K. 2015. "Elections, Information and Policy Responsiveness in Autocratic Regimes." *Comparative Political Studies* 48 (6):691–727.

Milne, R. S. 1975. "Malaysia and Singapore in 1974." *Asian Survey* 15 (2):166–173.

Moncada, Eduardo. 2013. "The Politics of Urban Violence: Challenges for Development in the Global South." *Studies in Comparative International Development* 48 (3):217–239.

Moore, Barrington. 1966. *Social Origins of Dictatorship and Democracy: Lord and Peasant in the Making of the Modern World*. Boston: Beacon Press.

Morrison, Kevin M. 2009. "Oil, Nontax Revenue and the Redistributional Foundations of Regime Stability." *International Organization* 63 (1):107–138.

Munck, Gerardo L. and Jay Verkuilen. 2002. "Conceptualizing and Measuring Democracy: Evaluating Alternative Indices." *Comparative Political Studies* 35 (1):5–34.

Noor, Farish A. 2014. *The Malaysian Islamic Party PAS, 1951–2013: Islam in a Mottled Nation*. Amsterdam: Amersterdam University Press.

North, Douglass C. and Barry R. Weingast. 1989. "Constitutions and Commitment: The Evolution of Institutional Governing Public Choice in Seventeenth-Century England." *Journal of Economic History* 49 (4):803–832.

NSTP Research and Information Services. 1999. *Elections in Malaysia: A Handbook of Facts and Figures on the Elections, 1955–1995*. Kuala Lumpur, Malaysia: New Straits Times Press.

O'Donnell, Guillermo. 1978. "States and Alliances in Argentina, 1956–1976." *Journal of Development Studies* 15 (1):3–33.

Oi, Jean C. 1993. "Reform and Urban Bias in China." *Journal of Development Studies* 29 (4):129–148.

Olper, Alessandro. 2001. "Determinants of Agricultural Protection: The Role of Democracy and Instituitional Setting." *Journal of Agricultural Economics* 52 (2):75–92.

2007. "Land Inequality, Government Ideology and Agricultural Protection." *Food Policy* 32 (1):67–83.

Olper, Alessandro and Valentina Raimondi. 2011. "Constitutional Reforms and Food Policy." *American Journal of Agricultural Economics* 93 (2):324–331.

2013. "Electoral Rules, Forms of Government and Redistributive Policy: Evidence from Agriculture and Food Policies." *Journal of Comparative Economics* 41 (1):141–158.

Olson, Mancur. 1965. *The Logic of Collective Action: Public Goods and the Theory of Groups*. Cambridge, MA: Harvard University Press.

1982. *The Rise and Decline of Nations: Economic Growth, Stagflation and Social Rigidities*. New Haven, CT: Yale University Press.

1993. "Dictatorship, Democracy and Development." *American Political Science Review* 87 (3):567–576.

O'Rourke, Kevin H. 1997. "The European Grain Invasion, 1870–1913." *The Journal of Economic History* 57 (4):775–801.

Pack, Wolfgang. 1961. *Das parlamentarische Ringen um das Sozialistengesetz Bismarcks, 1878–1890*. Düsseldorf: Droste.

Paige, Jeffrey M. 1975. *Agrarian Revolution: Social Movements and Export Agriculture in the Underdeveloped World*. New York: Free Press.

Park, Jong Hee and Nathan Jensen. 2007. "Electoral Competition and Agricultural Support in OECD Countries." *American Journal of Political Science* 51 (2):314–329.

Peel, Michael. 2014a. "Army Battles to Maintain Role as Guardian of 'Thainess'." *Financial Times*. www.ft.com/content/607c76b2-e0ed-11e3-a934-00144feabdc0.

2014b. "Thailand Rushes to Sell Rice Stockpile to Appease Farmers." *Financial Times*. www.ft.com/content/0055c5e6-94a2-11e3-af71-00144feab7de.

2015. "Thailand's Yingluck Due in Court on Negligence Charges." *Financial Times*. www.ft.com/content/34365fc8-fd2a-11e4-9e96-00144feabdc0.

Peltzman, Sam. 1976. "Toward a More General Theory of Regulation." *Journal of Law and Economics* 19 (2):211–240.

Pepinsky, Thomas B. 2009a. *Economic Crises and the Breakdown of Authoritarian Regimes: Indonesia and Malaysia in Comparative Perspective*. New York: Cambridge University Press.

2009b. "The 2008 Malaysian Elections: An End to Ethnic Politics?" *Journal of East Asian Studies* 9:87–120.

2014. "The Institutional Turn in Comparative Authoritarianism." *British Journal of Political Science* 44 (3):631–653.

Pflanze, Otto. 1990. *Bismarck and the Development of Germany*, vol. III. Princeton, NJ: Princeton University Press.

Pierskalla, Jan H. 2016. "The Politics of Urban Bias: Rural Threats and the Dual Dilemma of Political Survival." *Studies in Comparative International Development* 51 (3):286–307.

Pletcher, James. 1989. "Rice and Padi Market Management in West Malaysia, 1957–1986." *The Journal of Developing Areas* 23 (3):363–384.

Ploss, Sidney I. 1965. *Conflict and Decision-Making in Soviet Russia: A Case Study of Agricultural Policy, 1953–1963*. Princeton, NJ: Princeton University Press.

Przeworski, Adam. 1991. *Democracy and the Market: Political and Economic Reforms in Eastern Europe and Latin America*. New York: Cambridge University Press.

Przeworski, Adam, Michael E. Alvarez, Jose Antonio Cheibub, and Fernando Limongi. 2000. *Democracy and Development: Political Institutions and Well-Being in the World, 1950–1990*. New York: Cambridge University Press.

Rama, Martin. 1993. "Rent-Seeking and Economic Growth: A Theoretical Model and Some Evidence." *Journal of Development Economics* 42 (1):35–50.

Rashid, Shahidur and Ralph Cummings. 2007. "Grain Marketing Parastatals in Asia: Results from Six Case Studies." *World Development* 35 (11):1872–1888.

Rathbone, John Paul. 2016. "Nicás Maduro, Venezuela's Lord of Misrule." *Financial Times*. www.ft.com/content/f7ae1936-1ddc-11e6-a7bc-ee846770ec15.

Ratnam, K. J. and R. S. Milne. 1970. "The 1969 Parliamentary Election in West Malaysia." *Pacific Affairs* 43 (2):203–226.

Richardson, Neal P. 2009. "Export-Oriented Populism: Commodities and Coalitions in Argentina." *Studies in Comparative International Development* 44 (3):228–255.

Rogowski, Ronald. 1989. *Commerce and Coalitions: How Trade Affects Domestic Political Alignments*. Princeton, NJ: Princeton University Press.

Rosenberg, Hans. 1967. *Grosse Depression und Bismarckzeit: Wirtschaftsablauf, Gesellschaft und Politik in Mitteleuropa*. Veröffentlichungen der Historischen Kommission zu Berlin. Berlin: Walter de Gruyter & Co.

Ross, Michael L. 2001. "Does Oil Hinder Democracy?" *World Politics* 53 (1):325–361.

  2006. "Is Democracy Good for the Poor?" *American Journal of Political Science* 50 (4):860–874.

  2012. *The Oil Curse: How Petroleum Wealth Shapes the Development of Nations*. Princeton, NJ: Princeton University Press.

Rudner, Martin. 1970. "The Malaysian General Election of 1969: A Political Analysis." *Modern Asian Studies* 4 (1):1–21.

Ruel, Marie T., Lawrence Haddad, and James L. Garratt. 1999. "Some Urban Facts of Life: Implications for Research and Policy." *World Development* 27 (11):1917–1938.

Rueschmeyer, Dietrich, Evelyne Huber Stephens, and John D. Stephens. 1992. *Capitalist Development and Democracy*. Cambridge, UK: Polity Press.

Samuels, David and Richard Snyder. 2001. "The Value of a Vote: Malapportionment in Comparative Perspective." *British Journal of Political Science* 31 (4):651–671.

Sayamwala, Amma and Suthad Setboonsarn. 1989. *Trade, Exchange Rate, and Agricultural Policies in Thailand*. Washington, DC: World Bank.

Schedler, Andreas, editor. 2006. *Electoral Authoritarianism: The Dynamics of Unfree Competition*. Boulder, CO: Lynne Rienner.

Schipani, Andres. 2016a. "Venezuelans Resort to Looting as Food Shortages Hit Crisis Point." *Financial Times*. www.ft.com/content/oc2bodb8-21a4-11e6-9d4d-c11776a5124d.

2016b. "Venezuelans Turn Out in Mass Protest against Maduro." *Financial Times*. www.ft.com/content/2aed562e-707e-11e6-9ac1-1055824ca907.

2016c. "Venezuela's Armed Forces Tighten Grip as Food Crisis Grows." *Financial Times*. www.ft.com/content/6a84236e-50f1-11e6-9664-eobdc13c3bef.

2016d. "Venezuela's Latest Ruse to Tackle Shortages: Fingerprint Scanners in Supermarkets." *Financial Times*. www.ft.com/content/1e9815a0-2aeb-3b88-a669-680e4f179566.

Schissler, Hanna. 1980. "Die Junker. Zur Sozialgeschichte und historischen Bedeutung der agrarischen Elite in Preußen." *Geschichte und Gesellschaft* 60:89–122.

Schmidt-Bückeburg, Rudolf. 1933. *Das Militärkabinett der preußischen Könige und deutschen Kaiser*. Berlin: E. S. Mittler & Sohn.

Schmitter, Philippe C. and Terry Lynn Karl. 1991. "What Democracy Is... and Is Not." *Journal of Democracy* 2 (3):75–88.

Schöne, Jens. 2005. *Frühling auf dem Lande? Die Kollektivierung der DDR-Landwirtschaft*. Berlin: Ch. Links Verlag.

Schonhardt-Bailey, Cheryl. 1998. "Parties and Interests in the 'Marriage of Iron and Rye'." *British Journal of Political Science* 28:291–332.

2006. *From the Corn Laws to Free Trade: Interests, Ideas, and Institutions in Historical Perspective*. Cambridge, MA: MIT Press.

Schröder, Wilhelm Heinz. 1995. *Sozialdemokratische Parlamentarier in den Deutschen Reichs- und Landtagen 1867–1933: Biographien, Chronik, Wahldokumentation: ein Handbuch*. Düsseldorf, Germany: Droste.

Schumpeter, Joseph R. 1942. *Capitalism, Socialism and Democracy*. New York: Harper & Row.

Scott, James C. 1976. *The Moral Economy of the Peasant: Rebellion and Subsistence in Southeast Asia*. New Haven, CT: Yale University Press.

1985. *Weapons of the Weak: Everyday Forms of Peasant Resistance*. New Haven, CT: Yale University Press.

Sen, Amartya. 1999. *Development as Freedom*. New York: Alfred A. Knopf.

Senauer, Ben. 2002. "A Pro-Poor Growth Strategy to End Hunger." *American Journal of Agricultural Economics* 84 (3):826–831.

Shamsul, Amri Baharuddin. 1979. "The Development of the Underdevelopment of the Malaysian Peasantry." *Journal of Contemporary Asia* 9 (4):434–454.

1986. *From British to Bumiputera Rule: Local Politics and Rural Development in Peninsular Malaysia*. Singapore: Institute of Southeast Asian Studies.

2001. "A History of Identity, an Identity of a History: The Idea and Practice of 'Malayness' in Malaysia Reconsidered." *Journal of Southeast Asian Studies* 32 (3):355–366.

Shaw, William. 1976. *Tun Razak: His Life and Times*. London: Longman.

Shifa, Abdulaziz B. 2013. "The Dual Policy in the Dual Economy: The Political Economy of Urban Bias in Dictatorial Regimes." *Journal of Development Economics* 105:77–85.

Silva, Eduardo. 1993. "Capitalist Coalitions, The State and Neoliberal Economic Restructuring: Chile, 1973–88." *World Politics* 45 (4):526–559.

Skocpol, Theda. 1979. *States and Social Revolutions: A Comparative Analysis of France, Russia and China*. New York: Cambridge University Press.

1982. "What Makes Peasants Revolutionary?" *Comparative Politics* 14 (3):351–375.

Slater, Dan. 2003. "Iron Cage in an Iron Fist: Authoritarian Institutions and the Personalization of Power in Malaysia." *Comparative Politics* 36 (1):81–101.

2010. *Ordering Power: Contentious Politics and Authoritarian Leviathans in Southeast Asia*. New York: Cambridge University Press.

Smith, Ben. 2004. "Oil Wealth and Regime Survival in the Developing World, 1960–1999." *American Journal of Political Science* 48 (2):232–246.

Smith, Todd Graham. 2014. "Feeding Unrest: Disentangling the Causal Relationship Between Food Price Shocks and Sociopolitical Conflict in Africa." *Journal of Peace Research* 51 (6):679–695.

Snyder, Richard and David Samuels. 2004. *Legislative Malapportionment in Latin America: Historical and Comparative Perspectives*, chap. 4. Baltimore, MD: Johns Hopkins University Press, 131–172.

Statistisches Bundesamt. 2013. "Household consumption expenditure on food." www.destatis.de/EN/FactsFigures/CountriesRegions/InternationalStatistics/Topic/Definitions/HouseholdExpFood.html. Published online. Accessed May 2, 2013. Statistics gathered from national statistical services.

Statistisches Reichsamt. 1879. "Ergebnisse der Reichstagswahlen 1878." *Statistik des Deutschen Reichs* 37, Juni-Heft.

1880. "Erntestatistik 1879/80." *Statistik des Deutschen Reichs* 43 (2):X.9–X.25.

1883. "Ergebnisse der Volkszählung von 1880 im Deutschen Reich." *Statistik des Deutschen Reichs* 57.

1884. "Berufsstatistik der grösseren Verwaltungsbezirke." *Statistik des Deutschen Reichs* 2, N.F.

1885. "Ergebnisse der Landwirtschaftlichen Betriebszählung von 1882 im Deutschen Reich." *Statistik des Deutschen Reichs* 5. N.F.:1–107.

Steinberg, David A. and Krishan Malhotra. 2014. "The Effect of Authoritarian Regime Type on Exchange Rate Policy." *World Politics* 66 (3):491–529.

Steinberg, David A. and Victor C. Shih. 2012. "Interest Group Influence in Authoritarian States: The Political Determinants of Chinese Exchange Rate Policy." *Comparative Political Studies* 45 (11):1405–1434.

Steinberg, Jonathan. 2011. *Bismarck: A Life*. New York: Oxford University Press.

Stigler, George J. 1971. "The Theory of Economic Regulation." *The Bell Journal of Economics and Management Science* 2 (1):3–21.

Stolper, Wolfgang Friedrich and Paul A. Samuelson. 1941. "Protection and Real Wages." *Review of Economic Studies* 9 (1):58–73.

Sturzenegger, Adolfo C. and Mariana Salazni. 2008. *Argentina*. In Anderson and Valdes (2008), 59–86.

Svolik, Milan W. 2009. "Power Sharing and Leadership Dynamics in Authoritarian Regimes." *American Journal of Political Science* 53 (2):477–494.

  2012. *The Politics of Authoritarian Rule*. New York: Cambridge University Press.

Swinnen, Johan F. M. 2009. "The Growth of Agricultural Protection in Europe in the 19th and 20th Centuries." *The World Economy* 32 (11):1499–1537.

  2010a. *Agricultural Protection Growth in Europe, 1870–1969*, chap. 6. In Anderson (2010), 141–161.

  2010b. *Political Economy of Agricultural Distortions: The Literature to Date*. In Anderson (2010), 81–104.

Tamin, Mokhtar and Sahathavan Meyanathan. 1988. *Malaysia*, chap. III. In Johnson (1988), 91–150.

Teichmann, Ulrich. 1955. *Die Politik der Agrarpreisstützung: Marktbeeinflussung als Teil des Agrarinterventionismus in Deutschland*. Köln-Deutz, Germany: Bund-Verlag.

Thies, Cameron G. 2015. "The Declining Exceptionalism of Agriculture: Identifying the Domestic Politics and Foreign Policy of Agricultural Trade Protection." *Review of International Political Economy* 22 (2):339–359.

Thies, Cameron G. and Schuyler Porche. 2007. "The Political Economy of Agricultural Protection." *Journal of Politics* 69 (1):116–127.

Thomson, Henry. 2015. "Landholding Inequality, Political Strategy and Authoritarian Repression: Structure and Agency in Bismarck's 'Second Founding' of the German Empire." *Studies in Comparative International Development* 50 (1):73–97.

  2016. "Rural Grievances, Landholding Inequality and Civil Conflict." *International Studies Quarterly* 60 (3):511–519.

Thomson, Henry, Halvard Buhaug, Elisabeth Rosvold, and Henrik Urdal. 2017. "Democratization, Elections and Urban Social Disorder in the Developing World." APSA Annual Meeting Paper. https://papers.ssrn.com/sol3/papers.cfm?abstract_id=3054750.

Tilly, Charles. 1978. *From Mobilization to Revolution*. New York: McGraw-Hill.

Timmer, C. Peter. 1988. *The Agricultural Transformation*. Vol. 1 of Chenery and Srinivasan (1988), 275–331.

  1989. "Food Price Policy: The Rationale for Government Intervention." *Food Policy* 14 (1):17–27.

  1993. "Rural Bias in the East and South-East Asian Rice Economy: Indonesia in Comparative Perspective." *The Journal of Development Studies* 29 (4):149–176.

  2009. *A World Without Africulture: The Historical Paradox of Agricultural Development*. Washington, DC: AEI Press.

Tipton, Frank B. 2001. *A History of Modern Germany Since 1815*. Berkeley: University of California Press.

Torp, Cornelius. 2005. *Die Herausforderung der Globalisierung: Wirtschaft und Politik in Deutschland 1860–1914*. Göttingen: Vandenhoeck & Ruprecht.

Tullock, Gordon. 1967. "The Welfare Costs of Tariffs, Monopolies and Theft." *Economic Inquiry* 5 (3):224–232.

United Nations. 2014. *World Urbanization Prospects: 2014 Revision*. New York: United Nations.

Annual. *Demographic Yearbook*. New York: United Nations Department of Economic and Social Development, Statistical Division.

Urdal, Henrik. 2008. "Urban Social Disturbance in Africa and Asia: Report on a New Dataset." www.prio.org/Data/Armed-Conflict/Urban-Social-Disorder/v1/.

Urdal, Henrik and Kristian Hoelscher. 2012. "Explaining Urban Social Disorder and Violence: An Empirical Study of Event Data from Asian and Sub-Saharan African Cities." *International Interactions* 38:512–528.

Varshney, Ashutosh. 1993. "Self-Limited Empowerment: Democracy, Economic Development and Rural India." *Journal of Development Studies* 29 (4):177–215.

1995. *Democracy, Development and the Countryside: Urban-Rural Struggles in India*. Cambridge, UK: Cambridge University Press.

von Uexkuell, Nina, Mihai Croicu, Hanne Fjelde, and Halvard Buhaug. 2016. "Civil Conflict Sensitivity to Growing-Season Dought." *Proceedings of the National Academy of Sciences* 113 (44):12391–12396.

Wain, Barry. 2009. *Malaysian Maverick: Mahathir Mohamad in Turbulent Times*. London: Palgrave Macmillan.

Wallace, Jeremy. 2013. "Cities, Redistribution, and Authoritarian Regime Survival." *The Journal of Politics* 75 (3):632–645.

2014. *Cities and Stability: Urbanization, Redistribution & Regime Survival in China*. New York: Oxford University Press.

Walton, John and David Seddon. 1994. *Free Markets and Food Riots: The Politics of Global Adjustment*. Oxford: Blackwell.

Warr, Peter and Archanun Kohpaiboon. 2009. *Thailand*. In Anderson and Martin (2009), 255–280.

Webb, Simon and Pairat Temphairojana. 2015. "Thaksin Tells Thailand's Red-Shirt Opposition: 'Play Dead' ... For Now." *Reuters*. www.reuters.com/article/us-thailand-politics-idUSKCN0RK02F20150920.

Webb-Vidal, Andy. 2006. "Venezuelan Price Controls Lead to Food Shortages." *Financial Times*. www.ft.com/content/e0d7320e-7e39-11da-8ef9-0000779e2340.

Wehler, Hans Ulrich. 1969. *Bismarck und der Imperialismus*. Berlin: Kiepenheuer & Witsch.

Weinberg, Joe. 2012. "Do Majoritarian Electoral Systems Favor Consumers: Identifying Cross-National Consumer Bias." *International Studies Quarterly* 56 (4):820–826.

Weingast, Barry R. 1997. "The Political Foundations of Democracy and the Rule of Law." *American Political Science Review* 91 (2):245–263.

Welsh, Bridget. 2013. "Malaysia's Elections: A Step Backwards." *Journal of Democracy* 24 (4):136–150.

2018. "Malaysia's Political Transformation(s): Preliminary Reflections." *New Mandala*. www.newmandala.org/malaysias-political-transformations-preliminary-reflections-bridget-welsh/.

Wengle, Susanne A. 2017. "Understanding the New Land Rush: How Capital Inflows Transformed Russia's Rural Economy." *Governance*. https://doi.org/10.1111/gove.12287.

Widner, Jennifer A. 1993. "The Origins of Agricultural Policy in Ivory Coast 1960–86." *Journal of Development Studies* 29 (4):25–59.

Williamson, Jeffrey G. 1988. *Migration and Urbanization*, chap. 11. Vol. 1 of Chenery and Srinivasan (1988), 425–465.

Windmeijer, F. A. G. and J. M. C. Santos Silva. 1997. "Endogeneity in Count Data Models: An Application to Demand for Health Care." *Journal of Applied Econometrics* 12 (3):281–294.

Wintrobe, Ronald. 1990. "The Tinpot and the Totalitarian: An Economic Theory of Dictatorship." *American Political Science Review* 84 (3):849–872.

1998. *The Political Economy of Dictatorship*. Cambridge, UK: Cambridge University Press.

Wood, Elisabeth Jean. 2003. *Insurgent Collective Action and Civil War in El Salvador*. New York: Cambridge University Press.

World Bank. 2008. *World Development Report 2008: Agriculture for Development*. Washington, DC: World Bank.

2012a. "World Bank Commodity Price Data (Pink Sheet)." http://data.worldbank.org/data-catalog/commodity-price-data. Online dataset, this version from July 5, 2012.

2012b. "World Development Indicators 1960–2011." http://data.worldbank.org/data-catalog/world-development-indicators.

Wright, Joseph. 2008. "Do Authoritarian Institutions Constrain? How Legislatures Affect Economic Growth and Investment." *American Journal of Political Science* 52 (2):322–343.

2009. "How Foreign Aid Can Foster Democratization in Authoritarian Regimes." *American Journal of Political Science* 53 (3):552–571.

Wright, Joseph, Erica Frantz, and Barbara Geddes. 2015. "Oil and Autocratic Regime Survival." *British Journal of Political Science* 45 (2):287–306.

Yang, Dennis Tao. 1999. "Urban-Biased Policies and Rising Income Inequality in China." *American Economic Review* 89 (2):306–310.

Ziblatt, Daniel. 2007. "Electoral District Boundaries, Germany 1871–1918." Computer file. http://hgl.harvard.edu.

2008a. "Does Landholding Inequality Block Democratization?" *World Politics* 60 (4):610–641.

2008b. "Landholding Inequality in Germany, at the Reichstag Constituency Level, and Prussian Chamber of Deputies Constituency Level, 1895." Computer file. http://scholar.harvard.edu/dziblatt/data.

2009. "Shaping Democratic Practice and the Causes of Electoral Fraud: The Case of Nineteenth-Century Germany." *American Political Science Review* 103 (1):1–21.

Zurayk, Rami. 2011. "Use Your Loaf: Why Food Prices Were Crucial in the Arab Spring." *The Observer*. www.theguardian.com/lifeandstyle/2011/jul/17/bread-food-arab-spring.

Index

For EU product safety concerns, contact us at Calle de José Abascal, 56–1°, 28003 Madrid, Spain or eugpsr@cambridge.org.

www.ingramcontent.com/pod-product-compliance
Ingram Content Group UK Ltd.
Pitfield, Milton Keynes, MK11 3LW, UK
UKHW040620240426
470322UK00011B/235